D1457339

Alejandro García-Rivera

The Community of the Beautiful

A Theological Aesthetics

A Michael Glazier Book
THE LITURGICAL PRESS
Collegeville, Minnesota

A Michael Glazier Book published by The Liturgical Press

Cover art: "Light from Light" by Arthur Poulin, Franciscan. Used with permission. Cover design by Ann Blattner.

Excerpts are taken from the New American Bible, © 1991, 1986, 1970 by the Confraternity of Christian Doctrine, 3211 Fourth Street N.E., Washington, DC 20017-1194 and are used by permission of the copyright holder. All rights reserved.

1   2   3   4   5   6   7   8

Library of Congress Cataloging-in-Publication Data

García-Rivera, Alex.
    The community of the beautiful : a theological aesthetics /
Alejandro García-Rivera.
        p.   cm.
    "A Michael Glazier book."
    Includes bibliographical references (p.   ) and index.
    ISBN 0-8146-5923-3 (alk. paper)
    1. Aesthetics—Religious aspects—Christianity.   2. Hispanic
American theology.   I. Title.
BR115.A8G37   1999
230'.089'68—dc21   98-34347
                                                              CIP

Contents

Acknowledgments   vi

Introduction   vii

Preface   1

1. Pied Beauty   7

Introduction   7
What Is Theological Aesthetics?   9
Glory and Praise   12
Nature and Plow   16
Dawn's Dappling Light   20
Fresh-Firecoal Chestnut Falls   26
Skies of Couple-Colour   34
Wrapping Up   37

2. A Different Beauty   39

"Difference"   41
A New Faith Seeking Understanding   44
An Unfortunate Rpression   49
Medellín   50
Popular Catholicism   52
Hispanic Theology and Aesthetics   54

3. Seeing the Form   63

From a Philosophical to a Theological Aesthetics   65
Albertus and Sophia: A Dialogue   65
The Two Poles of Philosophical Aesthetics   69
The Decisive Difference: The Incarnation   73

The *Capax Dei*   74

> The First Dimension of the *Capax Dei*:
> Intrinsic Grace   77
> The Second Dimension of the *Capax Dei*:
> The Analogy of Being   78
> The Third Dimension of the *Capax Dei*:
> The Word Became Flesh   82
> The Fourth Dimension of the *Capax Dei*:
> "Seeing the Form"   86

From Form to Sign   90

4. The Community of the True   91

Charles Sanders Peirce   96
A Different Razor   97
The Logic of Signs   103
Peirce's Aesthetics   113
Aesthetics: A Normative Science   114

5. The Community of the Good   119

From the True to the Good   122
Between Fact and Idea   124

> The First Conception of Being   126
> The Second Conception of Being   127
> The Third Conception of Being   128
> The Key to Truth   129
> The Fourth Conception of Being   130

A New Direction   132
The Community of Interpretation   133

> Interpreting Signs in the Garden of Good and Evil   134
> The Knowledge of Good and Evil   135

Crossing the Boundary   136
Loyalty   138
The Community of the Good   142
Royce's Hidden Aesthetics   143
A Living Logic   146

> The Aesthetics of Negation   150

6. The Community of the Beautiful   155

An Aesthetic Conception of Being   158

　　The Poetry of Being   164
　　Semiotic Aesthetics   165
　　Being as Foregrounding   168

A Third Type of Knowing   170

　　The Spiritual Senses   171

What Moves the Heart?   174

　　The Yetzer   175
　　From the Old to the New Testament   178
　　Mary's Song   181

The Anagogical Imagination   182

7. Lifting Up the Lowly   187

　　Mary of Guadalupe and the Mary of Faith   192
　　Sophia and Beatrice   192

Bibliography   197

Index   208

Acknowledgments

Anyone who has tried writing a book soon realizes that it is no solitary effort. The writing of this book has entailed advise and counsel from a multitude of people. I am in great debt to Don Gelpi, S.J., for his support and inspiration not only in this particular project but as a colleague and as a friend. I would like to thank Dean Margaret Miles for her comments on Augustine and Professor Ted Peters for his critical reading of the first chapter. I would also like to thank the John Courtney Murray group, and especially Frank Oppenheim, S.J., who reviewed chapter 5 and gave excellent suggestions for improving it. The Murray group has truly been a Community of Interpretation for me. The lion's share of my gratitude, however, goes to my graduate students, Sue Ashbourne, Nancy Pineda, Rob Marsh, Lynn Bridgers, and Michelle Gonzalez. They have tirelessly pored over the dreadful first drafts of this book with kindness and compassion. I think of them less as students but as my colleagues and friends. This book owes a great deal of its existence to their wonderful enthusiasm and love of theology.

I am also quite grateful for the unselfish comments from members of the Academy of Hispanic Theologians in the United States, especially Peter Casarella, Orlando Espín, Jean-Pierre Ruiz, Allan Figueroa-Deck, and Virgilio Elizondo. The beautiful cover art from this book is the creation of Fr. Arthur Poulin, a member of the Camaldolese monastic community of which I am an oblate. I am in great debt to him for his generosity and great talent. Finally, I am fortunate to have a wonderful wife who has generously given her time to edit the final draft. If it were not for Kathryn and the kind support from my two lovely daughters, Elisabet and Sophia, this book could not have been written. Indeed, this book was not a solitary effort but the product of a part of the Community of the Beautiful.

Introduction

Books on theology appear every year; but only once in a blue moon does one have the opportunity to read a watershed book, one which opens up a whole new way of doing theology. In my judgment, Alejandro Garcia-Rivera's *The Community of the Beautiful* creates a new watershed in Hispanic theology in the United States. It does so by putting the Hispanic experience into serious dialogue with American pragmatism. Cornel West has made an analogous move in African-American liberation theology; but, whereas West has to date contented himself with writing prophetic essays of topical interest, Professor Garcia-Rivera engages the systematic implications of pragmatic philosophy in order to develop a theological aesthetic with profound speculative implications not only for theology but for metaphysics and semiotics as well.

Among Hispanic theologians, Virgilio Elizondo created and popularized the notion of *mestizaje* as an important key to Hispanic experience in the United States. *Mestizaje* connotes a unique kind of ethnic and cultural blending; and, to date, Hispanic theological reflection, following Elizondo's lead, has tended to focus on the rich Hispanic experience of unique cultural diversity in a thoroughly pluralistic society. Professor Garcia-Rivera takes the notion of *mestizaje* very seriously; but, by putting Hispanic experience into conscious dialogue with the American pragmatic tradition, he endows it with a new kind of intellectual bite and challenge.

Professor Garcia-Rivera senses, quite correctly in my estimation, the fundamental unity of pragmatic thought. By that I mean that Charles Sanders Peirce, the founder of pragmatism and a philosophical genius of the stature of Plato or Aristotle, in developing what he eventually called his pragmaticism, created a logical and metaphysical frame of reference which other pragmatists subsequently developed in consistent and organic ways. In this work, Professor Garcia-Rivera puts the pragmatic philosophy and theology of the mature Josiah Royce into very fruitful dialogue with Peirce's five insights in order to develop his own original theological aesthetic.

If Professor Garcia-Rivera's book did nothing more than that, it would rank as a major theological achievement. In fact, it does much more. Among contemporary theologians, Hans Urs von Balthasar has done the most to develop a systematic theological aesthetic. Professor Garcia-Rivera argues, correctly and persuasively, that the logic and metaphysics of relations developed by both Peirce and Royce offers sounder philosophical underpinnings for a theological aesthetic than those provided by von Balthasar. Peirce understood the intimate and dynamic relationship between the philosophical normative sciences of aesthetics, ethics, and logic. As a result, Peirce, as Professor Garcia-Rivera shows, in demonstrating the dynamic relationship between the beautiful, the good, and the true, invited an anagogic reading of aesthetics which endows it with both ethical and metaphysical implications.

Professor Garcia-Rivera's theological aesthetic deals, however, not with abstractions but with living human experience and with the experience of Hispanic Americans in particular. He shows that his theological aesthetics makes sense of fundamental Hispanic perceptions of the relational continuity between the orders of creation and of redemption and of the beauty of otherness. Invoking the insights of Jan Mukarovsky, founder of the Prague school of philosophical and linguistic aesthetics, this theological aesthetics also gives a much-needed speculative grounding to Latin liberation theology's call for a preferential option for the poor. Using Mukarovsky's notion of "foregrounding," Professor Garcia-Rivera shows how in its own shared perception of ultimate beauty the Christian community of the Beautiful with aesthetic and moral inevitability joins with Mary's Magnificat in "lifting up the lowly."

Professor Garcia-Rivera has written a profound and moving work and has done so with the aesthetic sensitivity which he celebrates. He addresses the heart at the same time that he challenges the mind. He invites readers to probe the depths of that most fundamental of all human experiences: the perception of created and divine excellence. With the publication of *The Community of the Beautiful*, Professor Garcia-Rivera joins the ranks of major theologians in the United States; and in the true spirit of *mestizaje*, his work not only endows Hispanic-American theology with new depth of insight, but it also enriches theologically the entire Church. It simultaneously advances both Hispanic-

American and Euro-American theology by setting those two cultural and theological traditions into a remarkably creative and fruitful speculative dialogue. One senses instinctively that this work lays important foundations for Professor Garcia-Rivera's future theological studies, which, I predict, will equal and even outstrip the creativity and originality of this one.

Donald L. Gelpi, S.J.
The Jesuit School of Theology at Berkeley

Preface

The impetus for a theological aesthetics emerges, for me, out of my own personal experience of the Latin church of the Americas.[1] In my tumultuous youth, I separated myself from the ecclesial experience of my Cuban boyhood for what I thought was a more certain, more satisfying experience, the life of a professional physicist. A love for the logic of Nature promised me certain answers to the deep questions that had arisen in the tragic experience of exile that was the bitter lot of my family. That promise proved illusory when my professional career as a physicist took a tragic turn. I had been assigned as an employee of Boeing Company to be a supportive member of the team designing the Air Launch Cruise Missile. As I looked at the equations of fuel flow and trajectory, I suddenly realized that these abstract forms on a computer screen corresponded to the very concrete reality of an atomic explosion aimed at a large community of people. At that point, something died

[1] By "Latin Church of the Americas," I mean the entire Latin American ecclesial tradition which began with the evangelizing efforts of the Dominican, Augustinian, Franciscan, and Jesuit missionaries of Europe and ended in a unique blend of Indigenous, African, and fifteenth-century European Catholicism. The Latin Church of the Americas includes the ecclesial tradition that continues in the former Spanish-speaking territories of the United States but is now expanded to include the entire United States through continual immigration. Thus, the Latin Church of the Americas denotes not only what is ordinarily understood as Latin America but also what is known in the United States as the Hispanic or Latino communities of the United States. The use of the terms "Hispanic" and "Latino" reflect the complexity of the political, historical, and cultural realities of Latin ecclesial tradition in the eve of the twenty-first century. Indeed, the term "Hispanic" or "Latino" denotes more a political reality than a cultural entity. Nonetheless, the terms "Hispanic" and "Latino" do refer to a communal reality that continues the Latin Church of the Americas' ecclesial tradition and is rapidly producing penetrating insights into its nature and theology.

inside me and I knew that I could no longer pursue the beguiling call that the logic of Nature had been for me.

By this time, I had married an attractive and charming Lutheran woman from Ohio. Though I had strayed far away from any religious commitment, she introduced me into the very Lutheran custom of Bible study. As I read and studied with her and her church group the captivating story of the Creator God, who sent his Son to be born of a humble woman even while the cosmos sang and kings paid homage, only to be crucified unjustly in order to rise again, I heard the call that I thought I had lost at Boeing. Like a siren song, it beckoned me to follow. And I did, or, at least, I thought I did. I became a Lutheran pastor with a first assignment to start a Hispanic ministry in the Pennsylvania Dutch town of Allentown, Pennsylvania. My ministry grew quickly. Soon I had a respectable number of Hispanics worshipping at the small auditorium of a host church. By then the inevitable conflict of two very different cultural traditions began to surface.

The difference between the two groups worshipping at St. Paul's Lutheran Church in Allentown, Pennsylvania, became most pronounced in the celebration of the feast of the Incarnation, i.e., Christmas. The English-speaking community that worshipped "downstairs" in the church proper had the custom of putting up a fifteen to eighteen foot natural fir next to the sanctuary. This beautiful tree would be decorated with simple white lights and "Chrismons," white, traditional Christian symbols such as a "chi-rho" and the cross. In contrast, the (very poor) largely Puerto Rican community that worshipped "upstairs" in the small auditorium, had purchased a four foot artificial tree decorated with flashing colored lights, its limbs bending over by the weight of the tinsel that hung from every inch of available surface. At the very top of the tree, someone had graciously donated a rotating light that swept the worship space in dizzying circles. Around the tree, the community had also cut out life-size plywood representations of a Nativity scene with a large star hanging over the crib borrowed from the Moravian community of nearby Bethlehem.

When the community "downstairs" saw the Christmas decorations of the community "upstairs," they, recoiling in horror, would inevitably exclaim, "How gaudy!" When the community "upstairs" saw the Christmas decorations of the community "downstairs," they, also recoiling in horror, would inevitably exclaim, "How lifeless!" Such differences would be repeated over and over again in all the details that make up a parish's life. It was inevitable, then, that the host church decided that the Hispanic community might be happier somewhere else. Thus, the bishop suggested that the Hispanics of St. Paul's ought to form their own independent church. "What do you wish to call it?," he asked. "Let me ask the folks," I replied. It did not take much deliberation for the Hispanic "church council" to decide on a name. "Alex, tell the bishop we want to be known as St. Martin de Porres Lutheran Church." St. Martin de Porres, for those unfamiliar with American hagiography, was a black, Dominican mulatto of Peru who was one of the first saints offered by the Americas for canonization (1675) yet had to wait until 1962 for that honor. Devotion to St. Martin de Porres by Hispanics is estimated to be second only to the devotion to Our Lady of Guadalupe. As such, the proposal by my church council put me in an awkward spot.

How was I to tell my Lutheran bishop we wanted a Lutheran church named after a Latin American saint? Lutheran churches are named after saints but only saints in the Bible. Moreover, I had the unpleasant difficulty of explaining to the bishop why a Dominican, former pursuers against Lutheranism, ought to name a Lutheran church. Even more problematic, it was a mulatto Dominican from the Latin America of the seventeenth century! When my bishop heard the proposal, he apparently misunderstood. "You mean they want to name the church after Luther?" "No, no, bishop," I replied, "not Martin Luther, but Martin de Porres." The bishop looked at me with perplexed, perhaps worried, eyes and said, "OK, who is he?" After I explained to the bishop the historical, even natural, devotion many Hispanics have towards St. Martin de Porres, he graciously agreed to propose the name at the national council of the Lutheran Church. He warned me, however, that he didn't think it would be approved. Much to his surprise which was no less than mine, the name was approved and now there exists in the Pennsylvania Dutch town of Allentown, Pennsylvania, a St. Martin de Porres Lutheran Church.

It was here that I first experienced what I call the Community of the Beautiful. The call I had heard as a young man, and then at Boeing had been the call of Beauty. It was Beauty at her most beautiful. Subversive, yet gracious, ever hoping and fresh, Beauty crossed barriers and created community. Beauty's call made possible the impossible and made visible the invisible. Beauty could cross differences made long ago. Indeed, Beauty loved difference. Beauty reveled in the contrast between the "upstairs" and the "downstairs" Christmas decorations. Beauty loved the Moravian star hanging in the midst of a Catholic Nativity scene. Beauty loved a Lutheran church named after a Dominican saint. Thus, I heard Beauty's call once again and I knew then when and where I had first heard it, namely, in the Roman Catholic Church of my boyhood, in the ecclesial tradition of the Latin Church of the Americas. Having heard Beauty's call so clearly, I knew I had to return once again to the original place of my pilgrimage and try to learn how to speak about it.

After the experience of St. Martin de Porres Lutheran Church, I found myself entranced by the power and vitality of Beauty's call incarnated in the Community of the Beautiful. What was the nature and origin of that power? How could I describe the experience? These questions were pressing upon me when I took the thirty-day Ignatian retreat at Wernerville's Institute of Spirituality. Ignatius' Spiritual Exercises revealed to me the fountains of Beauty's call. It also revealed to me that I needed to finish my doctorate not in physics, the love of the logic of Nature, but in theology, the love of the logic of a loving Wisdom, and return to the Church where I had first heard Beauty's call.

This long story serves to provide the context by which the reader may understand the impetus for this attempt towards a theological aesthetics. It rises out of a personal struggle to articulate an experience of what I call the Community of the Beautiful. This personal struggle, however, I believe is also the wider struggle of the ecclesial tradition known as the Latin Church of the Americas. Like my personal struggle, this ecclesial tradition began with struggle. The early evangelization of indigenous Mexico and Peru, done in the context of good people trying to preach the gospel of salvation and bad people trying to exploit both the land and the people of the land, raised from the very beginning prophetic voices and innovative inculturation.[2] Indeed, these twin elements of prophetic calls against justice and faithful calls to inculturating the Gospel were, I believe, the same voice. Beauty's call as manifested in these voices and practices, however, began to be suppressed as early as 1550 by an anxious Rome trying to prevent the popularity of the Reformation to cross the Atlantic. More than four hundred years later, the anxiety over the Reformation officially ended with the convocation of Vatican II. The Latin American bishops responded with a council of their own in Medellín, Colombia. For the first time in four hundred years, the nature of the Latin American Church was officially explored. The Medellín documents had the effect of raising anew the twin problematics of the early Latin American Church: the call for prophetic voices and the need for innovative inculturation. These twin problematics found contemporary incarnation in the call for a theology of liberation and for serious study on the product of the early inculturation, popular religion.

[2]This will be explained in chapter 2.

The history of the development of liberation theology is well known. Lesser known is the development of the serious study of signs and symbols in the popular Catholicism of the Latin American Church. That study has taken place by the devoted, if at times ignored, work of Hispanic and Latino theologians in the United States. Emerging from this work is a new attention to theological aesthetics as a way of understanding the signs and symbols of popular Hispanic Catholicism. Such an approach is driven by the necessity of the pastoral realities of the United States Catholic Church (over half its members claim Hispanic heritage) and by the excitement of discovering a new interpretation and synthesis of two ancient theological traditions, semiotics (the science of signs and symbols) and aesthetics. Indeed, the experience of the ecclesial tradition of the Latin church of the Americas is the experience of a Community of the Beautiful. It is the experience of Beauty in the furnace of a violent history. As such, the theological aesthetics explored within the pages of this book is not so much a theology *of* the Latin Church of the Americas but a theology *from* the Latin Church of the Americas. Thus, it is my hope that in the struggle to articulate this experience *from* the particular ecclesial tradition of the Latin church of the Americas, I shall be articulating as well an experience common *of* all the ecclesial traditions which shape and form the one Church.

1

"Pied Beauty"

Glory be to God for dappled things—
    For skies of couple-colour as a brinded cow;
        For rose-moles all in stipple upon trout that swim;
Fresh-firecoal chestnut-falls; finches' wings;
        Landscape plotted and pieced—fold, fallow, and plough;
        And áll trádes, their gear and tackle and trim.
All things counter, original, spare, strange;
        Whatever is fickle, freckled, (who knows how?)
        With swift, slow; sweet, sour; adazzle, dim;
He fathers-forth whose Beauty is past change:
        Praise Him.

Gerard Manley Hopkins, "Pied Beauty"

INTRODUCTION

How is a poem read? The question ought to raise a suspicion in the reader that the following material might require a different style of reading than one ordinarily expects. A poem, for example, is not read for content. Indeed, the literal reading of a poem kills its meaning. Neither does a poem begin with a thesis sentence from which each point in the sentence is discussed in minute detail. Such a beginning would suggest the writer has a point to communicate thereby reducing the poem to a mere message. Neither information nor communication is the aim of a poem. Rather, a poem must be read line by line. Each line, however, though read as a unique entity must also be read in the faith that it manifests a greater whole.

It is as if each line were branches of a tree and, we, who read its lines, begin near treetop level. We see each branch graced with its unique twists and turns, a stem, only to branch out again. In the sensual contradiction of each branch, the unique stem and the proliferating branching, we begin to sense that these branches themselves are but parts of another sensual contradiction, the branching out of a larger yet unique stem, a trunk. A poem as it is read delights us with its details of rhythm and diction while at the same time letting us sense a "higher" and a "lower," revealing the gravitational pull of its beauty. It is only then we realize. We are high above the ground defying the gravity of the literal text.

This book, of course, is not a poem. It is, however, an attempt to think poem-like which, again, is not to say that it is poetry. I am referring to that process of thinking which Charles Sanders Peirce, the great American philosopher, called interpretive musement—thinking at "treetop" level. It is not purely conceptual thinking having its home in the heavens. It is neither purely perceptual having its home on the ground. It is a "third" type of knowing that finds its home in the "in-between" of heaven and earth, "treetop" level thinking, which allows one a vision of the whole. If most theological writing begins with the "trunk" and then proceeds to the "branches," then interpretative musement may be said to begin with the "branches" in order to reveal the "trunk." In other words, it is poem-like or, stated another way, it is inductive-like rather than deductive-like. It coaxes vision rather than develops form. It attempts, in a sense, what von Balthasar called "seeing the form."

Each chapter will consist of various "branches," each interesting in itself yet suggestive of even more branchings, which, through interpretive musement, "coax" a vision of the whole—leaves, stems, branches, and trunk. Each chapter, in turn, may also be seen as a "branch," an interpretive musement towards that whole, that sense of a higher and a lower, the felt gravitational pull of that which is the subject and object of this book, a theological aesthetics. Thus, the reader ought to be prepared for what I hope will be a process of interpretive musement which attends to a delightful variety of "branches"—Hispanic theology, semiotics, logic, truth, goodness, Beauty, Charles Sanders Peirce, Hans Urs von Balthasar, Josiah Royce, etc.—towards a vision of the whole from "treetop" level, i.e., a theological aesthetics of "lifting up the lowly." It is my hope to entice the reader to enter the interpretative musement process with me, to examine each branch and discover a common stem. Perhaps by the end of the book the reader has also come to feel the gravitational pull such "treetop" thinking affords and has joined me in the vision these particular heights allow: the dazzling vision of the Community of the Beautiful.

WHAT IS THEOLOGICAL AESTHETICS?

It may surprise that the term "aesthetics" did not appear in its contemporary meaning, i.e., the philosophy and science of the beautiful, until the eighteenth century. Alexander G. Baumgarten coined the term in 1735 to describe what he called the new "science of sensory cognition."[1] Let me propose, however, that aesthetics may be recast as the science which asks a more profound question: *what moves the human heart?* Put in this way, aesthetics has existed since the first human heart was moved by the influence of the beautiful. The cave paintings of Lascaux or Altamira, for example, still manage to affect the modern heart after thousands and thousands of years. As Jean Clottes, France's foremost expert on prehistoric rock art, confessed: "I remember standing in front of the paintings of the horses facing the rhinos and being profoundly moved by the artistry. Tears were running down my cheeks. I was witnessing one of the world's great masterpieces."[2] Asking the question, *what moves the human heart?*, I believe, brings us closer to the mysterious experience of the truly beautiful, an experience that transcends geological space and prehistoric time, an experience that holds the most persuasive claim to being what has become an *aporia* in our day, the real universal. Moreover, the tears of Msr. Clottes, like the tears shed by St. Ignatius in his mystical trances, speak as well of a religious experience. Indeed, recasting the question of aesthetics as the question of what moves the human heart is nothing more than following St. Augustine's approach in his *Confessions.* As such, it allows aesthetics a philosophical approach while leaving open the possibility of a theological contribution, i.e., a theological aesthetics.

Theological aesthetics recognizes in the experience of the truly beautiful a religious dimension.[3] This religious dimension is evident in the Lascaux and Altamira paintings. Most anthropologists, for ex-

[1]The term is found in Alexander G. Baumgarten, *Meditationes Philosophicae de Nonnullis Ad Poema Pertinentibus* (1735). Today, the meaning is expanded to include questions about art and its nature, conditions, and consequences. This meaning makes aesthetics equivalent to the philosophy and psychology of art.

[2]Bruce Crumley, "Archaeology: Cave Art in France," *Time Magazine* 145, no. 5 (1995).

[3]As von Balthasar said: "All great art is religious, an act of homage before the glory of what exists." Hans Urs von Balthasar, *The Realm of Metaphysics in Antiquity,* vol. 4 of

ample, believe the paintings to be religious in nature. Somehow Beauty and religious sentiment go hand in hand. As Jean Anouilh (1910–1987), the French playwright, asserts in his play on Thomas à Becket, "Beauty is one of the rare things that do not lead to doubt of God." Beauty's trace reveals a divine starting point. Indeed, Beauty's religious dimension is found in its origins. It is little wonder then that throughout the history of theology, Beauty has played a major role, both implicit and explicit, in theological reflection. Why, then, not simply speak of a theology of Beauty rather than a "theological aesthetics"?

It is true that until very recently, i.e., the eighteenth century, the long history of theological reflection emphasized Beauty rather than its experience. A theology of Beauty alone clearly does justice to the absolute origins of God's Beauty. God is not simply beautiful. Beauty originates in God's Own Self. There is, however, another dimension of divine Beauty that must be considered. What is Beauty if it is not received? A theology of Beauty alone leaves open the question of the inner dynamism of the human spirit.[4] How can the finite human creature name the nameless, perceive the imperceptible, make visible the invisible? For Pseudo-Dionysius, however, it was not so much a matter of "can" but of "how." Denys never questioned whether the human creature can experience the divine. His question simply was: *how?* Dionysius' "how" is also the question of theological aesthetics. Its answer must account both for Beauty's divine origins as well as its reception by the finite human heart. If the grand tradition of the theology of Beauty never spoke of an "aesthetics," it is because it never questioned the human creature's capacity to receive divine Beauty.

The assumption of receptivity, however, began to be questioned in the eighteenth century. Alexander Baumgarten asked the question not about Beauty but about the beautiful. How, exactly, is the beautiful experienced? In asking the question, Baumgarten reversed the assumptions of the theology of Beauty. If the pre-modern reflection of the beautiful had assumed the human capacity to receive Beauty, Baumgarten's aesthetics begins with such capacity as problematic. And if the classical and medieval tradition speculated on Beauty's divine origins, Baumgarten's

---

The Glory of the Lord: A Theological Aesthetics, English trans. of *Herrlichkeit: Eine Theologie Ästhetik*, Band III, I:*Im Raum der Metaphysik*, Teil I: *Alterium* (Verlag, Einsiedeln) John Riches, ed., trans. by Oliver Davies, Andrew Louth, Brian McNeil, C.R.V., and John Saward, Williams, reprint, 1967 (San Francisco: Ignatius Press, 1989) 22.

[4]Matthew A. Daigler, "Heidegger and von Balthasar: A Lovers' Quarrel Over Beauty and Divinity," *American Catholic Philosophical Quarterly* 69, no. 2 (1995) 387.

aesthetics essentially assumed them by methodically ignoring the issue. In disengaging Beauty from the beautiful, Baumgarten revealed a trend that has reached its apex in our day. We have lost confidence, perhaps belief, in the human capacity to know and love God as Beauty. Thus, while some may still believe that God is the source of Beauty, and many that the beautiful can be experienced, few would be willing to say that these two are connected in a profound and organic way.

The theological stakes are enormous. Do we believe in a God who wishes to be known and loved by his human creation? Does the human creature, in turn, have the capacity to know and love this God? At the heart of these questions, this brewing theological hurricane, is the doctrine of the Incarnation. Indeed, Beauty's transcendental nature, which nevertheless emerges into the human heart's experience of the beautiful, is a parallel of the Incarnation. Divine and human merge mysteriously in an act of divine initiation and human response, an act which is both knowledge and love. Irenaeus, the great theologian of the second century, exquisitely phrased it: "the Glory of the Lord is living human being and human being lives for the vision of God."[5]

Theological aesthetics addresses this modern theological crisis by doing justice to these twin aspects of Beauty: its absolute origins in the transcendent God who nonetheless wishes to be known and loved by his human creation.[6] Theological aesthetics attempts to make clear once again the connection between Beauty and the beautiful, between Beauty's divine origins and its appropriation by the human heart. In doing so, theological aesthetics discloses the importance of restoring the connection between Beauty and the beautiful which, in our day, has been severed. Human life has a worth and a dignity which only Beauty can reveal through the beautiful. Without the language and experience of Beauty and the beautiful, the Church will find difficult the expression of her faith, much less her conviction of the dignity of the human person, and, even less, be a sacrament to the world. There is, however, a more personal and concrete reason for a reconsideration of the organic connection between Beauty and the beautiful. It is the experience of a particular living ecclesial tradition, the Latin Church of the Americas, whose voice may add a guiding light in the present darkness

[5]"Gloria enim Dei vivens homo, vita autem hominis visio Dei" found in Irenaeus, *Adversus Haereses*, IV.20.7. See also the excellent exposition in Mary Ann Donovan, "Alive to the Glory of God: A Key Insight in St. Irenaeus," *Theological Studies* 49, no. 2 (1988) 283–98.

[6]So begins the *Catechism of the Catholic Church* (Washington: United States Catholic Conference, 1992) 1.1.

of the Church's pilgrimage. As the Church faces the dissolution of Modernity, Beauty's call as experienced by the Latin Church of the Americas may serve as guiding buoy in the tempest ahead.

Towards this end, I would like to offer the reader a "preview" of the major themes covered in the book. In order to do so, I now ask the reader to consider each of the "branches" of Hopkins' poem above. I am using the poem as a device to "interpretively muse" the whole of the book. In other words, I aim to introduce through an interpretive muse- ment of Hopkins' poem the various themes present in the book. Each "branch," of course, is meant only to introduce not develop each theme. As such, the reader is bound to feel some frustration. If I've done my job right, interpretative musement, as I mentioned before, in- troduces a certain "pull" which the uninitiated might find, at first, un- comfortable. On the one hand, each "branch" examined suggests numerous "branchings" aiming skywards even as an underlying "stem" or "trunk" pulls us downwards. Such is the "pull" of gravity of a third type of knowing which is unfamiliar to us today. I ask the reader to bear with me and enjoy each "branch" even if, at times, one feels there is no ground beneath the feet. If that is all I leave the reader, then I rightly should be excoriated. My hope, however, is that the reader will, by the end of the book, discover the sensation of no ground beneath the feet to be, rather, the sensation of vision given at "treetop" level. In this par- ticular chapter, all I ask the reader is to relax, enjoy each "branch" and let the process of interpretative musement give a poetic-like vision of the themes to be discussed.

GLORY AND PRAISE

"Glory be to God for dappled things . . . Praise Him." Hopkins' poem begins with an echo of the Jesuit axiom *Ad Majorem Dei Gloriam* and ends in poetic eucharist. Glory and praise frame Hopkins' celebra- tion of God's Beauty denoting two intrinsic dimensions of a theologi- cal aesthetics. Indeed, it is these two dimensions which distinguish theology's aesthetics from its companion science, philosophical aes- thetics. Ernst Cassirer summarizes centuries of philosophical aesthetics in terms of an inherent antagonism: "language and art are constantly oscillating between two opposite poles, an objective and a subjective pole.[7] Before the eighteenth century, the objective pole dominated and

---

[7]Ernst Cassirer, "Art," in *Critical Theory Since Plato*, Hazard Adams, ed. (New York: Harcourt Brace Jovanovich College Publishers, 1992) 326.

art was seen as mimesis, or imitative. In other words, Beauty was thoroughly objective. By copying Beauty, the artist produced a beautiful work of art. Such objective Beauty, however, could only be found in Nature. Thus, classical aesthetics simply sought the elements of natural Beauty which, if successfully copied onto a sensuous medium, would reproduce its Beauty. The principle, *ars simiae naturae,* i.e., "art imitates nature," characterized this aesthetics.

An underlying tension, however, could not be ignored. Bosanquet, the great historian of aesthetics, put it:

> Even the idea of imitation, indeed, contains the germ of a fuller aesthetic truth than was ever attained by Hellenic thought; for the translation of an object into a plastic medium involves a double and not merely a single element,—not merely a consideration of the object to be represented, but a consideration of the art of imaginative production by which it is born again under the new conditions imposed by another medium.[8]

In other words, a work of art is, essentially, an incarnation involving a triadic relation of object, medium, and the human imagination. Indeed, the translation of object to its incarnation reveals the essential role of the artist's imagination. To the extent that modern philosophical aesthetics saw such imagination as subjective, then classical aesthetics was chastized for having ignored the role of the subject. The emphasis on the subject appeared as a much needed correction to the classical discussion on Beauty. When Kant appeared on the scene relatively soon after Baumgarten's proposal, philosophical aesthetics decidedly shifted from an emphasis on the objectivity of Beauty to its subjective reception (and creation) as the beautiful. In terms of philosophical categories this meant a shift in emphasis from an objective metaphysics of Beauty to the transcendental analysis of the subjective or intersubjective process which accounts for Beauty's reception within human experience.[9]

The effect of such a shift has the ultimate effect of disengaging Beauty from the beautiful. One is forced to choose between the mistaken, primitive discussion that had Beauty as purely objective (from the modern perspective) over the irrational, modern overemphasis on

---

[8]Bernard Bosanquet, *A History of Aesthetic* (Cleveland: World Publishing, Meridian, 1957) 12.

[9]Richard Dien Winfield, "The Dilemmas of Metaphysical and Transcendental Aesthetics," in *Systematic Aesthetics* (Gainesville, Fla.: University Press of Florida, 1995) 1–58.

the subjectivity of the beautiful (from the classicist perspective). These two perspectives coexist in contemporary philosophical aesthetics but only as irreconcilable differences. They are, in a sense, symptoms of Modernity. Modernity can be characterized by its dichotomies of either-or, i.e., object or subject, nature or culture, matter or spirit, and, more relevant, Beauty or the beautiful. Theological aesthetics, on the other hand, may not abandon centuries of classicist thought found in the metaphysics of Beauty. Neither may it reject the great insights of Modernity into the dynamism of the human spirit which is, after all, the receptor of Beauty. Hopkins' poem suggests two fundamental theological aesthetic categories, Glory and Praise, which might allow the theologian to address contemporary philosophical aesthetics yet distinguish him or herself from it.

The theological categories of Glory and Praise both affirm and transcend the twin philosophical aesthetic insights, the objective and subjective poles of Beauty. Glory asserts the objective pole of Beauty. Beauty's glory "fathers-forth." It is radiant, original light rather than mere reflection. Glory, then, affirms the insight of a metaphysics of Beauty. Beauty is objective. Yet Glory goes further. Beauty's light does not merely fall upon material objects. It shines forth. Glory's objectivity lies not in the concreteness of beautiful objects. Such objectivity is verified only through light's reflection. Glory's objectivity is not verified in the reflection of light, but rather in the embodiment of Glory's radiance itself. Like classical notions of Beauty, Hopkins saw it "shine" throughout the natural world, even in the "rose moles . . . upon trout that swim."

For Hopkins, Beauty's objectivity is not so much verified in the fact that the natural world is beautiful but that Beauty is embodied in the natural world. Beauty's "shine," then, attests to more than simple objectivity. Glory's radiance affirms its originality. In other words Beauty shines forth from an origin. This origin, however, is not natural. The natural world only embodies Beauty's radiance. Beauty's origin, theological aesthetics asserts, is divine. Beauty's origin is God himself. This theological insight, however, reveals a chasm. An abyss, as deep as the one between the divine and the finite, separates Creator and creature. A theology of Beauty alone would take the creature to this abyss and be content to leave him and her there to ponder the infinite distance between him/herself and his/her Creator. The category of Glory, however, reveals a theological aesthetics. Beauty's Glory crosses the divine chasm between Creator and creature and shines forth in the creature's side of the abyss. Conceiving this crossing is both at the heart of theological aesthetics and its greatest problematic. Nonetheless, it is the most fecund of theological reflections. Such was von Balthasar's insight.

Hans Urs von Balthasar first brought theological aesthetics to the attention of the Church with his magnum opus *Herrlichkeit* or *The Glory of the Lord*. The abyss that would separate us from our Creator turns out not to be an abyss at all but the form of revelation. By revelation, von Balthasar did not mean some incredible text to be studied for understanding, nor as Tillich once said of Barth's theology of Word, a "rock" thrown into the well of human experience. He meant revelation as divine self-revelation, at once intimate yet ungraspable, meant to move the human heart into union with divine self even as it reveals that this cannot be done by the human heart alone. Indeed, the infinite distance between Creator and creature attests not so much to "God's self-alienation" from the creature but rather to the "appearance . . . of the God who in himself is incomprehensible in his love for the world."[10] Balthasar transformed the abyss between Creator and creature into the theological aesthetics of "seeing the form."

Von Balthasar justifies the theological transformation of divine abyss to human vision in the doctrine of the incarnation. For Balthasar, Jesus is form to the Father's content.[11] Thus, "whoever sees me sees the Father" (John 14:9).[12] Jesus as glorious form becomes both vision of and identical with the Father and, thus, "the aesthetic model of all Beauty"[13] This incarnational aesthetics has an important corollary. Jesus' incarnation was meant both to give form to and to glorify the Father. Jesus giving form results in glorifying the Father as the "act that ascribes to the Father his true worth and honours (timan) him as exalted Lord—in the same way that figure and splendour, form and light are one in the beautiful."[14] In other words, Balthasar, like Hopkins, ends his reflection on the form of Glory with its "just and necessary" return in the form of Praise.

The theological category of Praise affirms philosophical aesthetics' insight into the subjectivity of Beauty. Yet praise's abrupt irruption as end

---

[10]Hans Urs von Balthasar, *Seeing the Form*, vol. 1 of *The Glory of the Lord: A Theological Aesthetics*, trans. of *Herrlichkeit: Eine theologische Ästhetik, I: Schau der Gestalt*, Joseph Fessio and John Riches, eds., trans. Erasmo Leiva-Merikakis (New York: Crossroads, 1983) 462.

[11]". . . the relationship between Father and Son is indeed revealed through the Son. The Father is ground; the Son is manifestation. The Father is content, the Son form—in the unique way shown in revelation." Von Balthasar, *Glory, Vol 1*, 611.

[12]von Balthasar, *Glory, Vol 1*, 611.

[13]Ibid., 609.

[14]Ibid., 612.

to "Pied Beauty" signals the transcending of the philosophical category. It is as if the radiance Hopkins has been describing cannot be contained within the sheet of paper and breaks out of its pulpy prison. Beauty reaches across the supposedly objective chasm between author and work so that Hopkins, apparently moved by a power beyond his own subjectivity, ends the poem praising. The theological category of praise suggests another dimension of the connection between Beauty and the beautiful. Beauty and the beautiful participate in a type of liturgy.

NATURE AND PLOW

Glory and praise also frame in Hopkins' poem two very different types of work. "Whatever is fickle, freckled," "finches' wing's," and "rose moles all in a stipple upon trout that swim" describe one type of work, the *ars divina,* i.e., the works of God.[15] "Landscape plotted and pieced-fold, fallow and plough," "all trades," "their gear and tackle, their trim," describe another type of work, the *ars humana,* the work of the human creature. That Hopkins would include the *ars divina,* i.e., Nature, within Beauty's glory and praise comes as no surprise. Natural Beauty is self-evident and needs little justification. That *ars humana,* the artifacts of human culture, is included does, on the other hand, surprise. Indeed, human works as contrasted with the natural, in our day, offend. The natural and the artificial have become for us as antonyms of value rather than synonyms of Beauty. Yet Hopkins would depict Nature and Plow as children of Beauty. Both types of work Beauty "fathers-forth." Hopkins' inclusion of Nature and Plow in Pied Beauty could easily be attributed to his Jesuit outlook. Jesuits, after all, have been formed to "see God in all things." I believe, however, Hopkins is after much more.

Art, in its most general sense, refers to the basic activities by which the human creature installs him or herself in the world.[16] These basic

---

[15]Nature, as an "external, present, intelligible, and active reality" that could be confronted, was "discovered," according to M.D. Chenu in the twelfth century. M. D. Chenu, "The Symbolist Mentality," in *Nature, Man and Society in the Twelfth Century: Essays on New Theological Perspectives in the Latin West,* trans. of *La théologie au douzième siècle,* original work published: 1957, preface by Etienne Gilson, trans. Jerome Taylor and Lester K. Little (Chicago: University of Chicago Press, 1968) 4–5. See also Clarence J. Glacken, *Traces on the Rhodian Shore: Nature and Culture in Western Thought from Ancient Times to the End of the Eighteenth Century* (Berkeley: University of California Press, 1967). According to Glacken, fecundity is the earliest attribute given to Nature.

[16]"Art," in *New Catholic Encyclopedia,* William J. McDonald, ed. (New York: McGraw Hill Co., 1967).

human activities include *poiesis* (the making of things), *theoria* (the knowledgeable envisioning and seeking of scientific truth), and *praxis* (the moral action for good). Additionally, *poiesis* differentiates itself from *techne* (productive or useful work).[17] The ancients distinguished between the crafting of the beautiful and the crafting of the useful. The distinction appears obvious. A plow's primary value is utilitarian. A beautiful statue, on the other hand, has no useful purpose. Its value is intrinsic. Yet, Hopkins would include the utilitarian plow as part of the beautiful. This, I believe, is more than poetic license on the part of Hopkins. A basic presupposition of Modernity is being challenged. Hopkins, I believe, is asking a question which goes to the very heart of the meaning of human art. What is the relation between human thought and human action upon the sensuous medium that is the natural world?

This, in a sense, is the question that Charles Sanders Peirce, the great American philosopher, answered with what he called pragmatism. Peirce realized that Modernity had made arbitratry dichotomies in what is, essentially, a continuum. Peirce saw a great continuity in all of reality. Nowhere was this continuity most challenged by Modernity than in the continuity between human thought and Nature's acts. Peirce realized that act and thought were continuous with one another. Peirce, a great logician, explored this continuous role of act and thought in his famous semiotics, the logic of signs. Peirce's logic of signs will be a key component of this proposal for a theological aesthetics and will be explored in great detail in the following chapters. One of Peirce's greatest contributions to this project, nonetheless, may be described as clarifying the fundamental relationship between our acts and our thoughts. It becomes a way by which the theologian may describe the aesthetic underpinnings of human work, i.e., human art.

As such, the ultimate aesthetics of human work may be described as liturgy. Liturgy, i.e., *Leit-ourgos,* the work of the people, may be seen as the human art which receives Glory and returns Praise.[18] As such, liturgy

---

[17]The perceptive reader may see these triadic distinction of human activity as corresponding to what is known as the three transcendentals of Being, the True *(theoria)*, the Good *(praxis)*, and the Beautiful *(poiesis)*.

[18]Thus Augustine confesses "Great are you, O Lord, and exceedingly worthy of praise; your power is immense, and your wisdom beyond reckoning. And so we humans, who are **a due part of your creation**, long to praise you. . . ." (emphasis mine). Aurelius Augustine, *The Confessions*, vol. 1 of *The Works of Saint Augustine: A Translation for the 21st Century*, A project of the Augustinian Heritage Institute, ed., John E. Rotelle, O.S.A., Maria Boulding, O.S.B., trans. (Hyde Park, N.Y.: New City Press, 1997) I.1. The emphasis demonstrates another dimension of the relation between Nature and Plow.

is an act whose boundaries go far beyond church walls. Indeed, liturgy takes on the form of Chardin's *Mass for the Earth,*

> Since once again, Lord—though this time not in the forests of the Aisne but in the steppes of Asia-I have neither bread nor wine, nor altar, I will raise myself beyond these symbols, up to the pure majesty of the real itself; I, your priest, will make the whole earth my altar and on it will offer you all the labours and sufferings of the world.[19]

Liturgy, in its most general sense, may be seen as the theological aesthetic category of human art. It suggests that at the heart of human art is the unity between *poiesis* and *techne,* which, ultimately, becomes a liturgical act of receiving Glory and returning praise.

Hopkins inclusion of Nature and Plow challenges Modernity's split between natural object and cultural artifact. It also points to an understanding of liturgy beyond stony walls. Liturgy encompasses more than the assembly of the faithful, but the entire cosmos itself. This is more than poetical hyperbole. Hopkins offers a more substantial vision. Hopkins' vision of Beauty leads him to praise. If Hopkins' praise had simply been a response to the Beauty of Nature, then his praise would be a response to an experience of awe or admiration. Praise, however, given in the context of the plow suggests another type of experience. Praise, in the context of plow, gear, tackle, and trim suggests, above all, a giving thanks. These items are, after all, the means by which we receive our daily bread. If there is a giving thanks, however, then there must be gift. Nature and plow not only exist in Hopkins poem as a challenge to Modernity's assumptions, but also to give context to praise. Nature and plow correspond to a liturgical *exitus* and *reditus,* of Gift and giving thanks, of Gift and eucharist. The liturgical and eucharistic nature of Hopkins' poem ought not to surprise us.

At the very heart of Hopkins' "Pied Beauty" is the incarnation, i.e., the logical consequence of Beauty's "fathering-forth," God's very Son. As commentator James Cotter put it:

> Hopkins placed Christ the Savior at the source of creation. These two orders of reality are not located side by side in history or on two separate planes; the order of redemption exists within that of creation but penetrates it, colors it and transfuses it with Christ's victorious love. The world is incorporated in all its naturality into mysterium Christi.[20]

---

[19]Pierre Teilhard de Chardin, *The Divine Milieu,* translation of: *Le Milieu Divin,* original work published: Paris: Éditions du Seuil, 1957 (New York: Harper and Row, Harper Torchbooks/Library, 1960) 19.

[20]James Finn Cotter, *Inscape: The Christology and Poetry of Gerard Manley Hopkins* (Pittsburg: University of Pennsylvania Press, 1965) 134.

It is another way of saying that Jesus had an earthly body but with pro-found implications. Redemption is not so much a "rescue mission" for a lost humanity but, rather, the fulfillment of Glory's demand, i.e., the entire creation participating in a liturgy of praise.

It is in this way, then, that one can speak of Hopkins' praise as eu-charist. If "Pied Beauty" is actually a vision of Jesus as cosmic incarna-tion, then, truly, Hopkins' celebration of Beauty becomes a celebration of Jesus' body, i.e., a cosmic eucharist. For Hopkins, however, more must be said. Jesus' incarnation implicates the body-giving role of his mother. Indeed, Mary played an essential part in Hopkins' theology and poetry,[21] The "couple-colour" of the skies, blue and white, are also the colors associated with Mary.[22] If Jesus is placed at the source of all creation, then Mary's role takes on cosmic implications. For Hopkins, Mother Mary now encompasses Mother Earth. Mary's fiat, her saying "yes" in human freedom, was also a saying "yes" to the Glory in all crea-tion. Mary's appropriation of Glory reveals both the natural and human capacity for Original Gift. Mary's Magnificat, in turn, reveals the human role in and for all creation, i.e., the human capacity for praise.

Mary's fiat and Magnificat discloses the incarnation's implications concerning human praise. The mystery of the incarnation depends on the mystery of human freedom. Like Glory, praise is also original. It is original thanks for it rises forth out of the context of human freedom and so it is given fresh and new from the depths of the original freedom of the human heart. A confidence in human freedom, as Von Balthasar so well described, became shattered under the influence of the severity of the Reformation's *sola's; sola fides, sola Scriptura, sola gratia.*[23] Mary, in the Roman Catholic tradition, articulates the conviction that *fides* is as well a *fiat,* not simply reception but reception appropriated and re-turned as response.

---

[21]Ibid.

[22]The colors, blue and white, are actually the colors prescribed for any representa-tion of Mary as the Immaculate Conception. Representations of the Immaculate Conception flourished in the Spain of the seventeenth century. Blue and white were eventually canonized by the influence of Francisco Pacheco, painter and father-in-law of the great painter Velasquez. In his very popular book of 1649, *El arte de la pintura,* Pacheco made dogma that the Immaculate Conception "be painted wearing a white tunic and a blue mantle." Peter and Linda Murray, "The Immaculate Conception," *The Oxford Companion to Christian Art and Architecture* (Oxford: Oxford University Press 1996).

[23]von Balthasar, *Glory, Vol 1,* 45–57.

This is the mystery theological aesthetics seeks to address. God's Beauty has the human heart as aim in all its freedom and response. God's Beauty may issue forth as Glory throughout all creation but does not find completion until it ends as creation's praise. A theology of Beauty alone would leave us at the edge of a divine abyss. Beauty means to be received but not as passive object. Beauty's reception involves the dynamism of the human spirit in original freedom. Yet as the caves of Lascaux and Altamira demonstrate, the original freedom of the human heart is not arbitrary freedom. It has an orientation. As Augustine insightfully observed: "our hearts are restless until they rest in Thee."[24] Beauty's reception moves the human heart not simply in pointless agitation but towards that vision upon which the heart may rest. Theological aesthetics asserts the human creature is created *eis epainon dokses,* i.e., "to the praise of God" (Eph 1:6). Theological aesthetics recognizes both that the divine abyss is meant to be crossed and that the pure Gift is meant to be appropriated by the human heart. Thus the two fundamental dimensions to Beauty are Beauty's issuing forth and the movement of the human heart giving thanks for Beauty on behalf of all creation.[25] Glory and Praise frame theological aesthetics which reveal, in turn, the human capacity for a cosmic liturgy which receives Gift and returns Eucharist.

DAWN'S DAPPLING LIGHT

Glory and praise, these two irreducible dimensions of theological aesthetics have their linguistic counterpart. When it comes to Beauty, there is need for two grammatical forms, noun and adjective. The Greeks, for example, had two words for Beauty, *kallos* (a noun whose root meaning is "to call") and *to kalon* (an adjective whose equivalent meaning may be proposed as "the called").[26] The Romans, likewise, used *pulchrum* (noun) and *pulchritudo* (adjective). In fact, most languages exhibit this twin reference of Beauty and the beautiful. Indeed,

---

[24]Augustine, op. cit., I.i.

[25]"It is only when there is an analogy (be it only distant) between the human sense of the divine and divine revelation that the height, the difference, and the distance of that which the revelation discloses may be measured in God's grace." Hans Urs von Balthasar, *The Realm of Metaphysics in Antiquity,* vol. 4, *The Glory of the Lord* (New York: Crossroads, 1984) 14.

[26]Tracing the linguistic origins of Beauty and the beautiful as "call" and "the called" reveals its dynamic in the theological categories of Glory and Praise. Glory is indeed the call of the lover, and praise the response of the loved, i.e., the "called."

Beauty cannot be spoken about in most languages without these two forms.[27] The nominal form or noun, refers to the abstract quality of Beauty. The other form, the adjectival, i.e., the beautiful, refers to the sensual quality of Beauty. Abstract Beauty and the sensually beautiful correspond in an interesting way to the ancient quarrel regarding the abstract intellect and the concrete senses.

The great physicist, Erwin Schrödinger, resurrects this ancient argument in his marvelous little book *What is Life?*:

> Galenus has preserved us a fragment (Diels, fr. 125), in which Democritus introduces the intellect (dianoia) having an argument with the senses (aisthesis) about what is "real." The former says: 'Ostensibly there is colour, ostensibly sweetness, ostensibly bitterness, actually only atoms and the void', to which the senses retort: "Poor intellect, do you hope to defeat us while from us you borrow your evidence? Your victory is your defeat."[28]

Color, sweetness, and bitterness speak concretely, i.e., positively, of the world. The intellect, on the other hand, suspects such sensuality. The felt quality of the world amounts to mere adjectives. On the other hand, "atoms" can be named by the intellect, i.e., their atomic singularity can be conceived intellectually in terms of nouns. Such capacity to be named, however, is bought at a price. The intellect must conceive the atoms as existing in a "void." Atomic singularity, paradoxically enough, can only be conceived negatively. Nevertheless, the quarrel refers to an actual tension in reality itself. Nouns and adjectives both play an essential part of our description of the world because the world itself must be described through nouns and adjectives. There is, apparently, a negative and a positive dimension to reality that is reflected in our language describing reality.

The argument between the senses and the intellect finds fresh life in the distinction between Beauty and the beautiful. The beautiful must be sensed or felt but Beauty, like atoms, must be "seen," but "seen" against the background of the "void." As such, the quarrel may be understood not as originating in two different unrelated realities but as originating in a difference between two types of perception. The senses "perceive" with the warm light of the sensually concrete. They perceive "positively," or as it is known in the spiritual tradition as kataphatically. The intellect,

---

[27] In Spanish, *belleza* and *bella*. Wladyslaw Tatarkiewicz, "The Great Theory of Beauty & Its Decline," *Journal of Aesthetics and Art Criticism* 31, no. 2 (1972) 165–79.

[28] Erwin Schrödinger, *What is Life?* reprint, 1944 (Cambridge: Cambridge University Press, 1967) 163.

on the other hand, "perceives" with the cold light of the immaterially abstract. It perceives "negatively," or apophatically.

Apophatic Beauty and the kataphatically beautiful find poetic image in Hopkins' use of dawn's dappling light. Not the full light of the midday sun, but the texturing light of morning's sunrise reveal another dimension of Hopkins' aesthetics. His poem saw Beauty "fathered-forth" in the shadows and highlights of the dawn's dappling light, revealing and concealing, a "pied" mystery of a world. "Pied" rarely makes an appearance in our vocabulary today. As used in the poem, "pied" designates an interwoven set of contrasts. As one of Hopkin's commentators put it: "Created Beauty is for Hopkins essentially 'pied Beauty'—Beauty that is intricately interwoven with white and black, light and darkness, summer and winter, day and night, heaven and earth."[29] Hopkins apparently wrote the poem as he watched dawn's light slowly fill the English countryside. Such light "dappled" the land transforming what might seem an ordinary landscape at midday into an explosion of beautiful forms and shapes.

The forms and shapes suggested by Hopkins' dawn, however, are "counter, original, spare, [and] strange." Hopkins' pied Beauty is not characterized by obvious clarity of form or shape. Indeed, as such, pied Beauty follows artistic intuition which eschews cliché and tries to situate its works in the originality of the startling and the not-so-obvious. Works of art reveal as much as they delight. Hopkins, however, does not simply assume such an intuition. He offers an explanation for this aesthetic truth. The essential poetic image of "Pied Beauty" is the theological category of mystery.

The relationship between apophatic Beauty and the kataphatic beautiful often appears in the theological tradition as a schoolish telling of the fairy tale known as "Beauty and the Beast." The simplicity and purity of Beauty redeems the chaotic, mixed-up sensuality of the beautiful. Such a struggle only reveals, however, theology's own struggle in what Karl Rahner once described as "one of the most important keywords of Christianity and theology," i.e., mystery.[30] Indeed, mystery reveals God's very nature. As such, Balthasar's description above concerning the nature of theological aesthetics becomes self-evident. Because God is mystery, two crucial principles of theological aesthetics can be articulated. First, God's incomprehensibility belongs to God

---

[29]Peter Milward, S.J., *Landscape and Inscape: Vision and Inspiration in Hopkin's Poetry* (Grand Rapids, Mich.: William B. Eerdmans, 1975) 42.

[30]Karl Rahner, "Mystery," in *Sacramentum Mundi*.

alone. Second, such incomprehensibility does not cease with the vision of God.[31] Mystery, as theologians well know, both reveals and conceals. As such, mystery is not ignorance. Neither would mystery lead us to silence as Wittgenstein's maxim in the Tractatus, no. 7 suggests: "what we cannot speak about, we must be silent about."[32] Something, or rather, Someone becomes known in mystery even as mystery makes us realize how little we know. Similarly, the beautiful allows Beauty to be felt even as Beauty itself slips, in the end, past the grasp of our affection.

The role of mystery, however, reveals the inadequacy of describing apophatic Beauty and the kataphatic beautiful solely in terms of the "quarrel" between the senses and the intellect. If we were to follow the analogy of the quarrel to its logical conclusion, then like the senses and the intellect, beauty and the beautiful, the apophatic and the kataphatic would find themselves opposed to one another. Mystery opposes such opposition. The apophatic and the kataphatic are not opposites in the context of mystery but complement one another. The inadequacy of the argument between the senses and the intellect to address mystery reveals a boundary, a place-between that neither senses nor the intellect wish to claim, yet a place where both find their unity. This place-between has been known in the philosophical tradition as the imagination.[33] Universally seen as "mediator" between the senses and the intellect, its various descriptions bear a striking resemblance to aes-

[31]Ibid.

[32]Ludwig Wittgenstein, *Tractatus Logico-Philosophicau*, translation of: *Annalen der Naturphilosophie*, original work published: 1921, D. F. Pears and McGuiness, trans., with an introduction by Bertrand Russell, reprint, 1922 (London: Routledge and Kegan Paul, 1974).

[33]The literature is vast. Some useful works include Eva Brann, "Ancient Writers," in *The World of the Imagination: Sum and Substance* (Lanham, Md.: Rowman & Littlefield Publishers, 1991) 35–56; Murray Wright Bundy, "The Theory of Imagination in Classical and Mediaeval Thought," *University of Illinois Studies in Language and Literature* XII, no. 2–3 (1927) 7–281; Alex García-Rivera, "Religious Imagination," in *Perspectivas: Hispanic Ministry*, Allan Figueroa Deck, Timothy M. Matovina, and Yolanda Tarango, eds. (Kansas City: Sheed and Ward, 1995) 94–97; Richard Kearney, *The Wake of Imagination: Toward a Postmodern Culture* (Minneapolis, University of Minnesota Press, 1988); Amos Funkenstein, *Theology and the Scientific Imagination: From the Middle Ages to the Seventeenth Century* (Princeton, N.J.: Princeton University Press, 1986); Leonard Lawlor, *Imagination and Chance: The Difference Between the Thought of Ricoeur and Derrida*, Intersections: Philosophy and Critical Theory (New York: State University of New York Press, 1992); John McIntyre, *Faith, Theology and Imagination* (Edinburgh: Handsel Press, 1987); David Tracy, *The Analogical Imagination: Christian Theology and the Culture of Pluralism* (New York: Crossroads, 1981); Mary Warnock, *Imagination* (Berkeley: University of California Press, 1978).

thetic theory. As "imitator" of sensual reality crafting an image for the
abstractive intellect to "appreciate," this view of the imagination resembles
the objective pole of aesthetics. As inventive "expressor" of images from
within the human spirit, the imagination resembles the subjective pole
of aesthetics. There exists, however, another view.

Lawrence Sullivan discovered anew the religious nature of the imagination through his study of the various indigenous societies living in
the Amazon river basin. Sullivan in his ground-breaking work *Icanchu's
Drum* defined the religious dimension of the imagination through his
empirical study of myth:

> Myth does not simply denote a species of narrative; literary or oral gen-
> res are only symptoms of myth. Myth is not a form of lore but a quality
> of *imaginal existence.* Myth is the imagination beholding its own reality
> and plumbing the sources of its own creativity as it relates to creativity
> in every form (plant and planetary life, animal fertility, intelligence, art).
> Myth reveals the sacred foundations and religious character of the imag-
> ination. Myths are . . . *significations that reveal the nature of signifi-
> cance,* they make effective metastatements about imaginal existence
> (emphases mine).[34]

Sullivan's key sense of the religious as "significations that reveal the nature of significance" is hard to grasp but it expresses Sullivan's conclusion that for the religious imagination "understanding a reality requires
that it has a beginning." What Sullivan is proposing is that the imagination concerns the perceptibility of the different structures of reality
as coming from an *origin of differences.* In other words, the imagination
ministers to that place where differences begin and end.

As such, the imagination has its proper role not as artist to the
senses or the intellect but as artist to Original Mystery. Imagination's
artistry makes mystery manifest both to the senses and the intellect.
This affirmation, however, is not philosophical but theological. The
understanding of imagination proposed here is not an epistemology
but a theological aesthetics. Imagination is not so much a servant of
knowledge as it is an aesthetics of mystery. This has an important corollary. If the imagination allows mystery to be made manifest to our
senses and our intellect, then imagination also allows our senses and
intellect to respond to mystery. In other words, the imagination is the
prime mover and movement of the human heart. It allows Beauty to be
appropriated by the human heart, and, as well, allows the human heart

---

[34]Lawrence E. Sullivan, *Icanchu's Drum: An Orientation to Meaning in South
American Religions* (Chicago: University of Chicago Press, 1988) 22.

to respond to Beauty. As such, the imagination is also the natural host-ess to Beauty and the beautiful. The imagination allows apophatic Beauty and the kataphatic beautiful to have an organic connection within the human heart.

Thus, the imagination becomes the apogee of Glory's parabolic path as it emerges out of mystery, becomes appropriated by the human heart and, then, returns to its source. Glory's *exitus* becomes praise's *reditus* through the imagination which represents the human heart. As such, the imagination reveals itself as a human giving and gift, a crea-turely image of Original Giving and Gift. In other words, the imagina-tion has organic affinity to what is known as the *imago Dei,* the image of God. Thus, the imagination is proposed not as a philosophical epis-temology but as essential ingredient in a theological aesthetics. Together with the senses and the intellect, the imagination allows God's Glory to shine forth into the human spirit and return in freedom as praise.

Thus, theological aesthetics cherishes the distinction between and the irreducibility of Beauty and the beautiful. Theological aesthetics re-fuses to fall into the easy answers of a strict dualism or superficial monism for Beauty and the beautiful together form the experience of mystery. Beauty and the beautiful, like mystery, are found where light and darkness meet. Mystery's "dapple," Beauty and the beautiful, more-over, contain another revealing linguistic dimension. Like a candle's light signaling both the hiddenness and the presence of the reserved sacrament, mystery's etymological history suggests the presence of an eucharistic dimension. The Greek *mysterion,* entering Latin usage, be-came the liturgical linguistic equivalent of Beauty and the beautiful, i.e., *mysterium* and *sacramentum.* St. Augustine, for example, used *mys-terium* to refer to the hiddennes of God, and *sacramentum* to God's vis-ibility via the sacramental sign.[35] Thus *mysterium* and *sacramentum* came to refer to the invisible and the visible dimensions of God. As such the linguistic evolution of mystery into mystery and sacrament is more than some arbitrary accident of translation. At work here is something like Sullivan's understanding of the religious imagination, i.e., the significance of signification. At the heart of the connection be-tween mystery and sacrament is symbol or sign. Taking license with Pseudo-Dionysius' penetrating question, I would rephrase it as: *how, then, to speak of mystery?* His answer, like mine, is: through sign and

---

[35]Avery Dulles, "Mystery (in Theology)," in *New Catholic Encyclopedia*, William J. McDonald, ed. (New York: McGraw Hill Co., 1967).

symbol.[36] Hopkins' dappling light discloses another dimension of theological aesthetics: the aesthetic sign or symbol.

FRESH-FIRECOAL CHESTNUT FALLS

Mystery expresses itself in "Pied Beauty" in terms of an explosion of contrasts and "dapplings." Through dawn's mysterious play of light and darkness "all things counter, original, spare, strange" reveal themselves. It is this strangeness that, for Hopkins, points to the presence of God. Like God, the strange is hard to categorize. Language fails and we are forced to break its boundaries. Note, for example, how Hopkins breaks every grammatic rule in the book through his felicitous phrase, "Fresh-firecoal chestnut-falls." Adjective, noun, and adverb mix with abandon trying to name that which cannot be named yet our humanity longs to name. The "magic" of the mix becomes evident as its incantation appears to reveal an underlying sensuous unity.[37] Indeed, the sensuous unity revealed by the poetic craft alerts the well-versed in classical philosophy to a crucial theological aesthetic.

The "many" individuals, in the context of mystery, are also "one." This relationship has long been attributed to Beauty. Richard Bosanquet, for example, believes that aesthetics has always been a way to speak about the relationship between the "One" and the "Many."[38] Most aesthetic theories, in fact, are recognized to be variations of the principle characterized as "unity-in-variety."[39] Indeed, some have seen the history of aesthetics as attempts to answer the question: whence the unity in the varied? Perhaps the most influential answer to this question has been Plato's philosophy of form.

Forms, for Plato, were changeless entities that existed in a world independent of the world of appearances. There they existed eternally not subject to the vagaries of time. Plato's Forms, however, were, in themselves, beyond the senses, i.e., they existed in a world not accessible to the senses. They were, in essence, super-sensible. Plato applied his philosophy of Forms to understand the nature of Beauty. We know Plato's philosophy through a series of dialogues which he wrote to instruct his students in the subtleties of philosophical thought. One of these dia-

---

[36]Pseudo-Dionysius, in other words, saw the divine names as *symbolon*. For an interesting discussion between the theological use of sign, *signum*, and symbol, *symbolon*, see Chenu, op. cit.

[37]Jerome Bump, *Gerard Manley Hopkins* (Boston: Twayne Publishers, 1982) 154.

[38]Bosanquet, op. cit., 32.

[39]Ibid.

logues, Philebus, contains a clear statement of Plato's notion of Beauty. Plato has Socrates telling Protarchus his notion of Beauty:

> I do not mean by Beauty of form such Beauty as that of animals or pictures, which the many would suppose to be my meaning; but, says the argument, understand me to mean straight lines and circles, and the plane solid figures which are formed out of them by turning-lathes and rulers and measurers of angles; for these I affirm to be not only relatively beautiful, like other things, but they are eternally and absolutely beautiful.[40]

Plato's Beauty was "formal," apophatic, non-sensuous Beauty which nonetheless gave delight. As such, it presents a paradoxical situation. Bosanquet puts it:

> exclusion of life and pictures of life, in this passage, from the realm of absolute Beauty, to which regularity and unity are essential, is a striking case of the limitation which we have seen to be inherent in Greek aesthetics. . . . And it is plain that formal Beauty as recognized in such passages as these of which all Greek philosophy is full, is constituted by a symbolic relation—a presentation to sense of a principle which is not sensuous. Such "presentation" . . . may sometimes be called an "imitation"; but it is impossible to "imitate" a non-sensuous principle in a sensuous medium.[41]

Plato's super-sensible forms provided the unity which gave rise to the appearance of the varied beautiful. In this sense, Plato privileges apophatic, intelligible Beauty over the kataphatic, sensually beautiful. Plato's "formal" Beauty relates to the beautiful as form does to "appearance." Beauty's form gives rise to an "appearance" of the beautiful. Yet such a formulation of the relationship between Beauty and the beautiful becomes problematic in theology.

Hopkins, for example, finds Beauty not in the formal but the dappled. As Peter Milward puts it,

> [Hopkins] delights in the variety and profusion of riches in the natural world, which observes a form of balance but with stresses of a far more complex kind than are to be found in the geometry of Euclid. He recognizes that all colours may be resolved into the simplicity of white light; but he prefers to enjoy them for the time being in all their variety. It is as if he feels himself unable to appreciate the rich simplicity of the Creator, until he has fully delighted in the complexity of his creatures.[42]

[40]Electronic text of *Philebus* translated by Benjamin Howett.
[41]Bosanquet, op. cit., 33–34.
[42]Milward, op. cit., 41.

Here subtle distinctions begin to appear. The metaphor of sight could be used to illustrate the differences. Plato and Hopkins both agree Beauty is to be "seen." Plato, however, would insist that true Beauty is "seen" as form and formal Beauty requires the uncompromising apophatic light of the intellect. In other words, Plato's Beauty eschews shadows.

Hopkins, on the other hand, finds Beauty not in spite of the shadows but because of them. Hopkins Beauty jumps out at us in the dappling dawn's light. The difference though subtle is striking. Beauty's true form, for Hopkins, reveals itself in *difference* rather than unity. It is the richness of the unique and individual that provides the unity for its variety. Plato would find the "one" of formal Beauty *in spite* of the appearance of the "many." Hopkins finds the "one" of pied Beauty *because of* the appearance of the "many." Fecundity and the individual provide the theological aesthetic counterpart to the classic aesthetic problem of the "one" and the "many."[43] As such, it suggests a category which is akin to form yet more at home in the world of the fecund and singular rather than the world of the "one" and "many": *difference*.

Difference is a major theme in all of Hopkins' poems. Though many of us are charmed by the Dickensian little villages during Christmas, Hopkins would be repulsed by them. In his time he saw such villages as examples of a dehumanizing undifferentiation of style brought on by the Industrial Revolution. In search for a philosophy which celebrated difference, Hopkins turned to the great philosopher of "difference," Duns Scotus. Scotus taught Hopkins

> that all this variety of mortal beauty must proceed from him whom Saint Paul recognizes as the source of all father hood in heaven and on earth—the immortal source of all that is mortal. Earthly beauty may be fickle; but in its fickleness there is something that charms us by virtue of him "whose beauty is past change." Earthly beauty may be dappled; but in its dappleness there is something that reminds us of him who is perfectly simple and without differentiation. All good attributes of creatures, however diverse among themselves, are somehow—as Hopkins learnt from Duns Scotus—fully present and united in the rich simplic-

---

[43]The influence of Scotus' theory of the individual form (in opposition to Plato and Aquinas) on Hopkins is well known. Scotus developed his philosophy of the individual form to make a foundation for a philosophy of love. Only individuals and not some generic universal, thought Scotus, can be loved. Charles Peirce was also inspired by Scotus in his theory of sign. In another chapter I shall develop the claim that Scotus' individual form leads to symbol rather than form as the essential concept for a theological aesthetics. Bump, op. cit., 38–41.

ity of the divine being. Similarly, all good things and perfect gifts—as Hopkins learnt, not only from Saint James but also from Saint Ignatius Loyola in his "Contemplation for Obtaining Divine Love"—"descend from above, and similarly, justice, goodness, pity, mercy, etc. just as from the sun descend rays, from the fountain waters, etc."[44]

Scotus, like a good Franciscan, felt that the variety of the natural world finds its aesthetic unity in the love God has for God's Creation. Such love, however, could only be based not on knowing the universal form but on knowing the particularity of the individual. Scotus' new philosophy of the individual left behind centuries of theological appropriation of the Platonic form. As such, Scotus' celebration of difference was an antidote to the monotony of Hopkins' industrial age. It becomes for us, however, also a key to understanding the nature of the particularity of human difference, i.e., culture, and its unity in the Creator.

This key, however, begins not with Scotus but with Scotus' theological roots: Augustine's theology. Augustine's *Confessions* have as their motivation his remarkable conversion from Manichaeism to Christianity. The Manichees saw Creation as evil and the soul as "rarefied matter" trying to escape the chains of its corporeal bonds. Augustine, however, was moved by St. Ambrose's depiction of the soul as a "spiritual substance."[45] He describes his aesthetics of a "substantive" soul in this marvelous passage from the *Confessions*:

> And I wondered that I now loved Thee, and no phantasm for Thee. And yet did I not press on to enjoy my God; but was borne up to Thee by Thy beauty, and soon borne down from Thee by mine own weight, sinking with sorrow into these inferior things. This weight was carnal custom. Yet dwelt there with me a remembrance of Thee; nor did I any way doubt that there was One to whom I might cleave, but that I was not yet such as to cleave to Thee: for that the body which is corrupted presseth down the soul, and the earthly tabernacle weigheth down the mind that museth upon many things. And most certain I was, that Thy invisible works from the creation of the world are clearly seen, being understood by the things that are made, even Thy eternal power and Godhead. For examining whence it was that I admired the beauty of bodies celestial or terrestrial; and what aided me in judging soundly on things mutable, and pronouncing, "This ought to be thus, this not"; examining, I say, whence it was that I so judged, seeing I did so judge, I had found the unchangeable and true Eternity of Truth above my changeable mind. And

[44]Milward, op. cit., 46.
[45]Carol Harrison, *Beauty and Revelation in the Thought of St. Augustine*, Oxford Theological Monographs (Clarendon Press: Oxford, 1992) 7.

thus by degrees I passed from bodies to the soul, which through the bodily senses perceives; and thence to its inward faculty, to which the bodily
senses represent things external, whither to reach the faculties of beasts;
and thence again to the reasoning faculty, to which what is received from
the senses of the body is referred to be judged. Which finding itself also
to be in me a thing variable, raised itself up to its own understanding,
and drew away my thoughts from the power of habit, withdrawing itself
from those troops of contradictory phantasms; that so it might find
what that light was whereby it was bedewed, when, without all doubting,
it cried out, "That the unchangeable was to be preferred to the change-
able"; whence also it knew That Unchangeable, which, unless it had in
some way known, it had had no sure ground to prefer it to the change-
able. And thus with the flash of one trembling glance it arrived at THAT
WHICH IS. And then I saw Thy invisible things understood by the
things which are made. But I could not fix my gaze thereon; and my infirmity being struck back, I was thrown again on my wonted habits, car-
rying along with me only a loving memory thereof, and a longing for
what I had, as it were, perceived the odour of, but was not yet able to feed
on.[46]

Though it is obvious that Augustine's aesthetics here are modeled on
Plato's form, Augustine adds a subtle distinction to form. Augustine's
new "form" is described in terms of an ascent of the soul, i.e., an *anagogy*, towards a vision of God. Plato's forms, though also described by
him as an "ascent," were actually more a "separation."[47] Plato's forms
were not so much an ascension within the world to the vision of God
but a universalizing principle which, in the end, separated us from the
world. Augustine's *anagogy*, on the other hand, was a movement within
Creation not one that takes us out of Creation. As such, Augustine's *anagogy* is not the same as Platonic form but something quite different.
Its difference is found in the revealing phrase twice repeated in the passage above: "And then I saw Thy invisible things understood by the
things which are made." Augustine's *anagogy* suggests a visible thing
standing for some invisible other. In other words, Augustine's *anagogy*
has the rudimentary structure of a theory of sign, i.e., a visible signifier
standing for an invisible signified.

---

[46]Augustine, *The Confessions of St. Augustine* (Oak Harbor, Wash.: Logos Research
Systems, Inc., 1995) VII.17,23, CD, Logos Library System.

[47]I am, of course, referring to Plato's famous description of the ascent of the soul
from the shadows of the "cave" to the full brightness of the sun. This ascent of the soul
from the cave, however, was more a separation of the soul from the sensuous appearances of form to another world where form could be contemplated.

Indeed, Augustine was the first to develop a theology of signs.[48] Augustine's theory of signs was inspired by two needs, one personal, the other less so. The less personal need had its source in Augustine's duty as bishop of Hippo to interpret the Scriptures. Compared to the clarity of the philosophical tradition of Augustine's schooling, the Scriptures were obscure and inconsistent. It was not a problem new to Augustine. The Patristic tradition found, in the words of St. Jerome, that the Scriptures were "oceanum mysteriosum Dei, ut sic loquar labyrinthium."[49] Augustine developed his theory of signs as a way to clarify the obscurity and inconsistency of the Scriptures. This, in turn, satisfied his other, more personal need, to find rest for his restless soul not in the rarified atmosphere of the Manicheans but in the Creation-grounded beauty of God. Augustine's theory of signs turned out to be as well an anagogy of the soul towards God.

After Augustine, the theory of signs developed less in the line of an anagogy of the soul but in terms of logical relationships. By the time of Late Scholasticism, Augustine's *anagogical* theory of signs began a momentous shift. The role of the human mind in the process of signifying began to be appreciated. Duns Scotus led the way. Scotus argued that

> To suggest that the object is the only cause of cognition would greatly villify the intellect (n.488). But if the intellect were the only cause, then there would be no reason why it should not always be actively thinking—and this is not so. The intellect and the object together, therefore, form the cause of the knowledge we gain. Two causes which produce a single effect can have various relations.[50]

Expressed in modern terms, it is clear that the key strategy in Scotian realism was to connect a single effect to two causes. Scotus had looked deeply into Augustine's theory of signs and seen a place-between where both the kataphatic and apophatic find their unity. Scotus' strategy, however, was taken up by Ockham who jettisoned the place-between and made a strict separation between objects and intellect. Now the burden of relating the differences between particular objects lay solely

[48]See, e.g., Winfried Nöth, *Handbook of Semiotics*, English-language revised and enlarged edition of a work originally published in German as *Hanbuch der Semiotik* in 1985 by J.B. Metzlersche Verlagsbuchhandlung, *Advances in Semiotics* (Bloomington and Indianapolis: Indiana University Press, 1990).

[49]Jerome, *In.Gen.*, 9.1 quoted in Umberto Eco, *Semiotics and the Philosophy of Language*, Advances in Semiotics (Bloomington: Indiana University Press, 1984) 149.

[50]John Marenbon, *Later Medieval Philosophy (1150–1350)* (London: Routledge & Kegan Paul, Ltd., 1987) 156.

on the intellect. Ockham had transformed the anagogy of signs into a formal logic of relations.

The theory of signs, then, under the influence of Ockham began a process of ossification as formality and cold logic dominated the understanding of signs. The situation of the missionary Church in the Americas, however, began to break the ossified semiotics of Scholastic theory. After several hundred years of little or no missionary activity, the discovery and, unfortunately, the conquest of America gave new life to the theology of signs. Trying to make the Church's faith tradition understood to the indigenous Mexica, Maya, and Inca of America soon proved to be, like Jerome's Scripture, a linguistic and semantic labyrinth. The early missionaries of the Americas turned to their training in the logic of signs and relations for answers. Their pastoral experience, however, transformed their classical training of signs into new thinking about signification.

It became apparent that signs and symbols were more than mental or linguistic gymnastics giving a view of life. Signs and symbols were more than an act of reasoned logic. They guided and participated in the way of life of a people. The connection was made that a way of life and a view of life are intrinsically connected through the work of signs. This realization led to a flowering of the theology of signs through the work of Bernardino de Sahagún and the Jesuit Lafitau.[51] This flowering of semiotics, the science of signs, was nipped in the bud as Europe reeled under the impact of the Reformation. The semiotic work of the early Latin American theologians had allowed a portal through which the Indian's symbols and, thus, their religiosity, could be understood. Rome, fearing more "contamination" of the faith, ordered through King Felipe II that Sahagun's and all other works concerning the meaning of indigenous signs and symbols be confiscated. Indeed, Sahagun's works were not seen again until 1779.[52] The Latin American theological investigation into the nature of humanity and its artistry of signs was abruptly arrested.

Not until the nineteenth century did a new flowering of the study of signs begin again. The great American philosopher Charles Peirce was inspired by Duns Scotus' celebration of difference to once more

[51]Anthony Padgen, *The Fall of Natural Man: The American Indian and the Origin of Comparative Ethnology*, Cambridge Iberian and Latin American Studies (Cambridge: Cambridge University Press, 1986).

[52]Robert Ricard, *The Spiritual Conquest of Mexico*, originally published in French as *Conquête Spirituelle de Mexique*, published as vol. XX of *Travaux et Mémoires de L'institute d'Ethnologie* by the University of Paris, trans. Lesley Bird Simpson, California Library Reprint (Berkeley: University of California Press, 1966) 44–45.

study the logic of relations. Peirce recognized that the most elementary logical relation amounted to a comparison of similarity or of contrast between two objects, mental or physical. Peirce's genius came through, however, in recognizing that such comparison requires a third term, a mediator between the two things being compared which interprets the comparison. This interpretant together with the two objects being compared, the signifier and the signified, compose an elementary relation of understanding that is known as sign. Furthermore, this new sign can now participate in another triadic relation which, in turn, becomes another sign. Thus signs lead to other signs, *ad infinitum*. Peirce's logic of signs, thus, becomes a chain of interconnecting and extending relationships which encompasses the universe. In a sense, Peirce had discovered what I call the Community of the True.

The significance of this rather lengthy exposition is to set a foundation for the startling claim that the uniting category for a theological aesthetics is not form but sign or symbol. This new development in the theory of signs illustrates how signs encompass both Nature and plow, the cosmos and the human spirit. Moreover, the category of sign lends itself more intrinsically to the category of praise. But perhaps, most significantly, the unifying nature of sign reveals the centrality of the incarnation for a theological aesthetics of sign.

The eucharistic sign of bread, for example, is sign and symbol of the body of Christ. Yet sign and symbol unite and interconnect and thus, the eucharistic sign becomes, in turn, another sign which participates in the signification of the entire assembly gathered under such sign. The entire assembly, in turn, participates through its signification by becoming more signs and thus, a community of inclusion and understanding comes to be. It is, in this sense, how the sacramental sign which is the body of Christ becomes the Church which is also known to be the body of Christ. Yet if we allow the logic of sign to have its way, the signification begun with Christ's body now crosses the boundaries of Church and enters the realm of the wider world and, even, the universe. It is in this sense that the Church can also be said to be a sacrament or sacred sign to the world. Thus, theological aesthetics' foundational principle, the incarnation, finds its widest application in the action of sign rather than form. Indeed, a theological aesthetics of sign reveals the Eucharist to be, in its most general sense, the cosmic sign of the body of Jesus the Christ. As such, symbol rather than form appropriates the cosmic sense of the liturgical nature of theological aesthetics' dynamics of Glory and praise. A question, nonetheless, remains. In what sense is a sign or symbol an aesthetics?

SKIES OF COUPLE-COLOUR

"Skies of couple-colour," i.e., blue and white, continues Hopkins' constant use of the image of contrast or comparison. Swift and slow, sweet and sour, adazzle and dim, all these contrasts are relations which, given our discussion above, may be seen as constitutive of sign or symbol. Did Hopkins propose a theory of signs in "Pied Beauty"? No, I don't believe so, but his attempt to describe the Incarnation as sacramental Beauty is not too far away from suggesting a role for sign or symbol in his theological aesthetics. As discussed above, Hopkins' aesthetic principle is not the same as the principle which characterizes the aesthetics of form: "unity-in-variety." An aesthetics of form does not do justice to Hopkins' "Pied Beauty." What Hopkins proposes is an aesthetics of contrast.

The aesthetics of contrast were worked out, in a sense, by a disciple of Charles Sanders Peirce, the American philosopher Josiah Royce. Royce, like Peirce, had come to realize that there is a continuity between our thoughts and our acts. Royce, however, was interested in the ethical context of that continuity. In other words, Royce was interested in thought done in the context of the "garden of good and evil." By the "garden of good and evil," I mean the theological category of sin active in the world and represented by the biblical metaphor of the garden of Paradise where Adam and Eve ate the fruit of the tree of knowledge of good and evil. Thinking done in the context of the garden of good and evil relates to our actions in a special, i.e., ethical, way. Royce's great insight into the relationship between thought and act, i.e., human art, is that it contains not only a logical but also an ethical component. Royce also believed with Peirce that the relationship between thought and act becomes incarnated in the interpretation of the triadic sign. As such, Royce introduces another key insight for a theological aesthetics. Interpreting signs in the context of the garden of good and evil is a social act of the Good. In other words, in the interpretation of signs an ethical dimension is discovered which forms a society, a community which has made a decision for the Good. Royce, similar to Peirce, had discovered another dimension to the social act of interpreting signs, the Community of the Good.

Royce also discovered a key component of this book's project, the aesthetic roots of the logic of signs. Royce was persuaded by Peirce to undergo a long study of logic. In his studies, Royce discovered a marvelous relationship between geometrical form and logical order. A geometrical form (a line segment, for example) can be transformed into a set of unique, individual members of an infinite set. Such a set has the marvelous property of Peirce's famous triadic sign but is also capable of using such triadicity to form complex and subtle polyadic relationships. Royce had discovered the logical equivalent of complexity by marrying geometrical form and logical order. Furthermore, Royce observed that a "negation," i.e., two individuals so related that one is the opposite of the other, placed inside such a system undergoes a transformation in value judgement. A pure logical negation has no value attributed to it but under the conditions of a complex polyadic system of relationships, the context of such relationships begin to "draw out" of the simple, pure negation the sense of a "higher" and a "lower." Royce compared this process to the mystic's experience of the divine. The mystic in the "negative" experience of the transcendent experiences nonetheless a sense of "higher" and "lower."

Royce's discovery of the polyadic relationships of sign opens up the possibility to describe the religious experience. Moreover, it reveals the roots of such an experience as a semiotic aesthetics. Royce, however, confided he knew little about aesthetics and apparently did not notice what I consider a great aesthetic discovery, the aesthetic underpinnings of logical order in the polyadic sign. Royce demonstrated in a clear though technical manner what von Balthasar described in a more poetic but less clear metaphor, "seeing the form." As such, a tantalizing possibility suggests itself. The logic of signs of Peirce and Royce may have an undiscovered affinity with the classical, almost mystical, approach of von Balthasar's theological aesthetics. Such affinity, I believe, is found in the work of the semiotician, Jan Mukarovsky and his semiotic aesthetics of "foregrounding."

Mukarovsky studied the semiotics of poetry in the 30s and 40s of this century. Belonging to what is known as the Prague school of Aesthetics, Mukarovsky realized that there is good and bad poetry. Indeed, poetry possessed a norm. The aesthetic norm, however, was not some inviolable law. The aesthetic norm subversively announces its normative character by violating it. Central to the subversive aesthetic norm is the elementary act of artistic production, "foregrounding," i.e., the lifting up of a piece of background and, then, giving it value, therefore "foregrounding" it. The subversive aesthetic norm and the aesthetic principle of "foregrounding" was discovered by Jan Mukarovsky when he wondered how it is that a poem converts a bunch of words, even a meaningful bunch of words, into something more, into something of Beauty.[53] Mukarovsky noticed that the sense of Beauty was cre-

---

[53]I am referring to that school of semiotic aesthetics known as the Prague School of Semiotics whose most prominent figure was Jan Mukarovsky. Mukarovsky saw the es-

ated in the poem through the sensuous foregrounding of sound through rhythm and cadence. Poetic "foregrounding" contrasts the background prose by giving accent, i.e., value, to selected words. As such, "foregrounding" consists of an elementary contrast and, thus, a sign. "Foregrounding," in Mukarovsky's analysis, becomes not only an aesthetics but also a semiotics. Through his work, Mukarovsky identified, perhaps for the first time, an alternative aesthetic principle other than "unity-in-variety," i.e., the aesthetic principle of "foregrounding." Indeed, many artists identify more with the semiotic aesthetics of "foregrounding" than with the aesthetics of "unity-in-variety."

"Foregrounding" also resembles the role of the imagination in Sullivan's sense. The act of "foregrounding" is also the elementary act of *difference*. The separation of foreground and background reveals the structure of the anthropological imagination at work. It is the elementary human work of art. Moreover, "foregrounding" emphasizes what the two poles of philosophical aesthetics overlook. Whether art imitates or expresses, it must become embodied in some sensuous medium. Art, as discussed above, possesses a formative dimension. "Foregrounding" has as its heart this formative dimension. "Foregrounding's" essential dimension of embodiment makes it an analogy of the incarnation. It implies that all human "foregroundings" are, in a sense, an image of the incarnation, and as such possess a redemptive character. The value of "foregrounding" is of the nature of redemption. The redemptive value of "foregrounding" is seen most clearly in Mary's role in the drama of redemption.

The "couple-colour" of Hopkins' skies, blue and white, are, as discussed above, also the colors of Mary. The secret to Hopkins' use of aesthetic contrast lies within the role he himself most appreciated of Mary, the medium in which God became human. For Hopkins that role is exquisitely expressed in the Magnificat.[54] A closer look at this, Mary's hymn, identifies a revealing phrase

---

sential semiotic element in aesthetics (poetry was his example) as "foregrounding," selecting a piece of the background and making it prominent through nondiscursive means such as rhythms or uniqueness. See, e.g., Jan Mukarovsky, "The Esthetics of Language," in *The Prague School Reader of Esthetics, Literary Structures, and Style, Selected and Translated from the Original Czech*, Paul L. Garvin, ed. (Washington, D.C.: Washington Liguistic Club, 1955).

[54]Hopkins, e.g., wrote a poem celebrating the Magnficat. Gerard Manley Hopkins, "The May Magnificat," in *Gerard Manley Hopkins, Poems and Prose*, Penguin Classics (London: Penguin Books, 1985).

He has shown strength with his arm; he has scattered the proud in the thoughts (diánoia) of their hearts. He has brought down the powerful from their thrones, and lifted up the lowly (Luke 1:51-52).

Mary's aesthetics reveals the principle of "foregrounding." Not only are those who have been kept in the "background" "lifted up" into the "foreground," but also those who had previously achieved "foregrounding" through the abuse and misuse of power now become part of the "background." Mukarovsky's semiotic principle of "foregrounding" now becomes the biblical principle of "lifting up the lowly." As such, it reveals what I call the Community of the Beautiful.

The Community of the Beautiful describes a theological aesthetics which can say with Prince Myshkin in Doestoevsky's "The Idiot," "the world will be saved by Beauty."[55] In a world that has seen the ovens of Auschwitz and the *favelas* of Brazil, this claim may seem impossible, perhaps, obscene. Yet without this fundamental conviction, how else, in light of the pain and troubles of this world, can we even attempt, like Hopkins, to "Praise Him"? Thus, the stakes are high. "Foregrounding" attempts to give account for such a conviction. It echoes over and over again in the Scriptures. From the Creation of the Cosmos out of chaos, through the psalmist's praise in the midst of agony, the Prophet's call to the wicked, Wisdom's song to the hidden beloved, the Magi's gifts to a helpless child, even the cruel "lifting up" the Son of Man for the sake of the world, "foregrounding" appears as aesthetic counterpoint to the lowly settings of the Biblical narrative. For me, Mary's song gives voice to the redemptive nature of this theological aesthetics. God's Beauty embodies itself as a "lifting up the lowly," creating the Community of the Beautiful.

WRAPPING UP

As such, "lifting up the lowly" comes at the end of a long historical trajectory that, as mentioned above, has its roots in the Americas. The long repressed theology of signs, however, begun by the early missionaries in the Americas burst again into the scene with the *aggiornamiento* of Vatican II. With the charter of the Medellín documents, Latin American and Hispanic/Latino theologians began anew to discover the power of a theology of signs. This book places itself as a continuation of this trajectory. Like Hopkins, I see the beautiful of the American experience as "pied Beauty." God's gracious gift to the people

[55]Quoted in Harrison, op.cit., 270.

and the land of the Americas can only be discerned in the dapple of mystery. To the extent that the American imagination participates in this mystery, the lowly shall be lifted up. "Lifting up" is also a central liturgical act whether raising our arms in prayer or lifting up the host. More significantly, "lifting up" is at the heart of the paschal mystery. God born out of the lowly "lifted up" into human existence, crucified into the darkness by being "lifted up," and "lifted up" once again from the cave of his tomb reveals an original Imagination, an aesthetics which has love and not simply delight as its aim. "Lifting up the lowly" does not avoid either the tragedy of suffering nor the joy of the resurrection. As such, it provides an aesthetics that does not harmonize away suffering nor lead us into despair. "Lifting up the lowly," in sum, reveals what moves the human heart. As such, "lifting up the lowly" reveals God's gracious Glory shining forth into the darkness of the fallen human spirit only to lift up the human heart back towards itself creating the Community of the Beautiful so that songs of praise may be heard once again, even, amidst the tombstones.

2

A Different Beauty

If Hopkins saw Beauty father-forth inspiring scenes of English countryside, then people from Spanish-speaking America see Beauty mother-forth a beautiful Lady, *Nuestra Señora de Guadalupe*. According to legend, Our Lady appeared to a young Indian man going to catechism class in the misty, cold dawn of a December Mexican day. Juan Diego was walking near an ancient sacred site, a hill known in Nahuatl (the native Mexican language) as Tepeyac, when he heard birds singing beautiful songs. Then, on a fateful dawn of mid-December in 1531, Juan Diego heard his name called. Beauty called in the form of a beautiful lady dressed in a blue mantle filled with stars. She was standing by a rose bush in full bloom though it was winter. Juan noticed she wore a black ribbon around her waist, Indian fashion, to signify she was with child. But there was something not quite Indian about her. She was neither Indian nor Spanish and, somehow, both! She was, indeed, a different beauty. Our Lady of Guadalupe's beautiful difference came at a time when Juan Diego's people were dying by the thousands of disease brought in the wake of the Spanish conquest. That Mary would appear resembling, in part, an Indian was wondrous. Even more surprising, her beauty included the Spanish as well. An Indian Mary might raise eyebrows with pious Spaniards. Yet such Spaniards might tolerate it. An Indian-Spanish Mary, a half-breed, the incarnation of human difference, would be a scandal.[1] Nonetheless, this Lady's beauty charmed even the Spanish and continues to have profound influence on all the people of the New World.

---

[1] The Spanish Reconquista refers to the recovering of Spanish lands lost to the Moors in the eighth century. The reconquest or *reconquista* took place over several centuries until Fernando and Isabela conquered the last Moorish stronghold in Spain in

   Thus, a different beauty appeared in the Americas. This book is, in a sense, an attempt to understand not so much Our Lady of Guadalupe *per se*, but, rather, the nature of the beauty she so graciously possessed, a beauty many of us believe truly came from God. Like the Lady herself, the theological aesthetics suggested by such beauty, the beauty of difference, contains within itself elements of an Old World sensitivity to measure, proportion, and color[2] while, at the same time, incorporating elements of a New World sensitivity to the Cosmos, Song, and Flowers.[3] Perhaps even more promising is the challenge Our Lady's beauty poses to traditional understandings of aesthetics. Guadalupe's beauty, after all, comes to be perceived through the signs and symbols that she embodies. The aesthetics of "different" beauty perceives not only by form but by signs and symbols. At the heart of this claim lies the issue and nature of "difference."

1492. The prolonged encounter with Moors led to a mixing of races and cultures. For example, there existed *Mozárabes*-Christians adopting Moorish culture, *Mudéjares*-Moors living as vassals of Christians, *Muladíes*-Christians converted to Islam, and *Tornadizos*-Moors converted to Christianity. This racial and cultural plurality led to a very diverse Spain needing to be unified. Fernando solved the problem through the means of insisting on one single faith. Under the newly reconquered Spain, to be Spanish was to be Catholic. Thus, under the new kingdom, Roman and natural law mixed and the phrase *la pureza de sangre* ("purity of blood") became a reference to both one's cultural and biological "nearness" to Christian faith. A "half-breed," then, would also mean a diminishment of one's claim to the Christian faith. A "half-breed" Mary, then, would be scandalous.

[2]I am referring to the classical aesthetic principles of measure, proportion, and color based, in part, on Wis 11:21. Some fine histories of aesthetics include Bernard Bosanquet, *A History of Aesthetic* (Cleveland: World Publishing, Meridian, 1957) and Katharine Everett Gilbert and Helmut Kuhn, *A History of Esthetics* (New York: The MacMillan Company, 1939). The Wisdom reference may be found, in particular, in Carol Harrison, *Beauty and Revelation in the Thought of St. Augustine*, Oxford Theological Monographs (Oxford: Clarendon Press, 1992).

[3]Mesoamerican religious sensibility emphasized the role of flower and song, *flor y canto*, as dialogue or prayer with God. Aztec ways of thought are expertly discussed in Miguel León-Portilla, *Aztec Thought and Culture* (Norman, Okla.: Oklahoma University Press, 1963). The issue of difference as developed here can be taken a step further if the response of the Western World to the Nahua people is measured. See, e.g., Benjamin Keen, *The Aztec Image in Western Thought* (New Brunswick, N.J.: Rutgers University Press, 1990) and Antonello Gerbi, *The Dispute of the New World: The History of a Polemic, 1750–1900*, trans. of: *La disputa del Nuovo Mono: Storia di una polemica, 1750–1900*, original work published: Italy: 1955, trans. and revised by Jeremy Moyle (Pittsburg: University of Pittsburgh Press, 1973).

"DIFFERENCE"

Most Latin Americans born before the 1960s will feel their greatest "difference" with English-speaking North Americans at Christmas. Our "big" day of gift-giving came January 6, the feast of the Epiphany, when the Three Kings brought presents and placed them under our beds. In contrast, English-speaking North America celebrates gift-giving on December 25 and a "Santa Claus" places presents under a pine tree. Such "difference" might be explained in terms of climate. "Santa," a Nordic figure, is appropriate for northern climates where snow abounds. The Three Kings, on the other hand, makes "sense" in southern climes where sand reigns. Such comparison shows its poverty to anyone who has traveled to South America. The Andes are hardly deserts or beaches. The "south" Americas also know of snow. There is, perhaps, a deeper reason for our "differences."

Sometime around the eighth century, the saintly bishop of Seville, Isidore, ingeniously attributed the variety of races in the known world to geography and the Bible. Origins fascinated Isidore. His book, the *Etymologies*,[4] claimed that the three major regions of the Earth, i.e., Europe, Asia, and Africa, had been originally settled by the three sons of Noah: Shem, Japheth, and Ham. Isidore's book was instantly popular and became extremely influential as the Middle Ages took their course. A hundred years later, a tradition spread celebrating the famous visitors to the Christ child. Though Scripture says little about these visitors, the popular tradition fixed their number at three, Melchior, Gaspar, and Balthasar. It does not take much reflection to realize Isidore's influence on this tradition. The three sons of Noah had metamorphized via the infancy narratives of the Scriptures into what would become the Three Kings of Latin America's Christmas.[5]

Though perhaps seen as an innocuous tradition, it was not so in the sixteenth century. The discovery of the continent of America had added a fourth major geographic region to the known world, which messed up the neat synthesis the revered Isidore had conceived. Worse, it appeared that this new fourth region was home to a new race of human beings. What had been a sacred geography began to experience an unprecedented challenge. Ironically, the symbol of the variety of

[4]E. Dressel, "De Isidori Originum Fontibus," *Rivista di Filologia e di Instruzione Classica* 3 (1875) 207–68.

[5]Henri Baudet, *Paradise on Earth: Some Thoughts on European Images of Non-European Man* (Middletown, Conn.: Wesleyan University Press, 1988).

races, the Three Kings, becomes, in the Americas, the symbol against accepting a different race of human beings.[6]

Indeed, "difference" may have been the theme most discussed by Latin America's first intellectuals. Fernando de Oviedo observed, e.g.:

> In my opinion, these animals are not tigers, nor are they panthers, or any other of the numerous known animals that have spotted skins, nor some new animal [of the "old world"] that has a spotted skin and has not [yet] been described. The many animals that exist in the Indies that I describe here, or at least most of them, could not have been learned about from the ancients, since they exist in a land which had not been discovered until our own time. There is no mention made of these lands in Ptolemy's *Geography*, nor in any other work, nor were they known until Christopher Columbus showed them to us. . . . But, returning to the subject already begun . . . this animal is called by the Indians *ochi*.[7]

Perhaps, the most astute of these new observers of "difference" was the Jesuit de Acosta. He, among all the other commentators on "difference," realized the radical break such "difference" made with the categories of the past. De Acosta makes the explicit observation that

> what I say of the guanacos and pacos I will say of a thousand varieties of birds and fowls and mountain animals that have never been known [previously] by either name or appearance, nor is there any memory of them in the Latin or Greeks, nor in any nations of our [European] world over here. . . . It is well to ask whether these animals differ in kind and essence from all others, or if this difference be accidental. . . . But, to speak bluntly, any one who in this way would focus only on the accidental differences, seeking thereby to explain [away] the propagation of the animals of the Indies and to reduce them [to variants] of the European, will be undertaking a task that he will not be able to fulfill. For, if we are to judge the species of animals [in the Indies] by their essential properties, they are so different that to seek to reduce them to species known in Europe will mean having to call an egg a chestnut.[8]

---

[6]Tzvetan Todorov, *The Conquest of America*, Richard Howard, trans. (New York: Harper & Row Publishers, 1984) 4.

[7]Fernandez de Oviedo, *De la Natural Hystoria de las Indias*, facsimile ed., reprint, 1526 (Chapel Hill: University of North Carolina Press, 1969) 11 as quoted in Jonathan Z. Smith, "What a Difference a Difference Makes," in *To See Ourselves as Others See Us: Christians, Jews, "Others" in Late Antiquity*, Jacob Neusner and Ernest S. Frerichs, eds., Studies in the Humanities (Chico, Calif.: Scholars Press, 1985) 3–48.

[8]Jose de Acosta, *Historia Natural y Moral de las Indias*, critical ed., O. E. Gorman reprint, 1590–1608 (Mexico City: N.p., 1940) 44 as quoted in Smith, op. cit., 44.

Thus, religion scholars such as Jonathan Z. Smith conclude that the first intellectuals of Latin America saw "the 'new world' not merely 'new,' not merely 'different'—it is 'other' *per essentiam*."[9] Such "difference," radical "difference," becomes the source for Latin America's greatest gift to human thought: a new concern for the treatment of the poor and a new study of the relationship between symbols and culture.

The question of the "other" became more than a question for observant intellectuals. The "difference" of the American Indian soon began to have political and, even, theological consequences. Pope Alexander VI, the notorious Borgian pope, had graciously "donated" the new lands to Spain's Crown. His famous bulls of donation, *Inter caetera* and *Dudus sidiquem*, contained the formula, *donamus, concedimus, et assignamus*, which donated, granted, and assigned American lands to Spain. Unfortunately, these lands had been given before much thought was given about their inhabitants. Indeed, these new vassals of the Crown began to be treated much as their land had been treated. America's indigenous were also "donated," or, more precisely, *encomendados* to the colonial authorities. For food, clothing, shelter, and education, the American *encomendado* was supposed to do manual labor. This system of human "donation" and "assignation" became known as the *Encomienda*.

It soon became clear, however, that such a system amounted to little less than slavery. The first Latin American theological statement may be attributed to the Dominican Fray Antón de Montesinos. On the fourth Sunday of Advent, December 21, 1511, Montesinos preached on the words of John the Baptist:

> *I am the voice that cries in the desert* . . . It has been given to you to have me ascend [this pulpit], I who am the voice of Christ in the desert of this island, and so, it behooves you to pay much attention, not simply listen, but listen with all your heart and your senses, to this voice you shall hear . . . With this voice says [John the Baptist] that all of you are in mortal sin and in it you live and die, because of the cruelty and tyranny with which you abuse these innocent people . . . These, are they not men? Don't they have rational souls? Aren't you obliged to love them as you would love one another? . . . Have it for certain that in the state [your soul] is in you are no more capable of your own salvation than are the Moors or the Turks that do not have nor want the faith of Jesus Christ.[10]

[9]Smith, op. cit., 44.

[10]Bartolomé de las Casas, *Historia de las Indias*, 2d ed., Agustín Millares Carlo, prepared by Lewis Hanke, Cronistas de Indias por la Biblioteca Americana (Mexico, D.F.: Fondo de Cultura Economica, 1965–1986) II, 441–44.

Montesino's sermon began a Latin American theological tradition that was at once prophetic and incisive. Montesinos had characterized the *Encomienda* as an unjust social structure. Any colonist participating in such a system committed mortal sin and was in grave danger of losing his (or her) soul. Montesinos' sermon made manifest a perspective and dynamic which characterizes the Latin Church of the Americas to this day. This new perspective, born out of the dynamics of "difference," sees sin as not only having a personal dimension but a social one as well. As such, Montesinos' sermon profoundly shook the Crown. In March 1512, Montesinos' provincial superior, Alonso de Loysa, sharply reprimanded him. He warned Montesinos not to delve into theological matters which "are no concern for monks." Montesinos' act would eventually become a paradigm for almost all theologians reflecting from the Americas. Soon, the famous Bartolomé de las Casas would follow in his footsteps. Five hundred years later, Gustavo Gutiérrez continues this basic Latin American locus.

Loysa's reprimand to Montesinos, however, also points out the second dynamic emerging out of the context of "difference." In one sense, Jose de Acosta, Montesinos, even, Las Casas were not "official" intellectuals. They, of course, had been educated through the process of formation of their corresponding religious orders. Nonetheless, the Church had "official" theologians and neither de Acosta, Montesinos, nor Las Casas could claim such status. Yet they were coming aware of a new approach to intellectual inquiry. Even monks or missionaries are capable of doing theology because theology, in the context of "difference" which eschews traditional categories, lies less in arbitrary authority than in lived experience. No one felt the truth of this claim more than the early missionaries to the Americas.

A NEW FAITH SEEKING UNDERSTANDING

The early missionaries faced a major challenge: the "difference" of language. The challenge of such "difference" had three dimensions. First, the missionaries either had to teach the new converts Spanish or they themselves would have to learn a completely unknown language. This meant discovering tools not simply for learning how to speak in Nahuatl but for analyzing the structure of the language itself. Moreover, it was not simply language but languages that was the greater challenge. Jose de Acosta had called Mexico a "forest of languages."[11]

---

[11]The variety of dialects and the strategic problems it presented to the early evangelization efforts of the missionary friars is ably presented in Robert Ricard, *The*

Learning all native languages was practically impossible. Adopting a *lingua franca* in order to facilitate communication became a necessity. Finally, the translation of words from one language to another was one thing, the translation of equivalent concepts was another. Catechism proved to be most susceptible to this last challenge. There were dogmatic concepts which had no equivalent or analogy in the Mexican conceptual universe. On the other hand, there were Mexican concepts that had no equivalent in the Western scheme of things.

Sin and redemption, e.g., were two notions that had very different meanings to indigenous and Spaniards. Redemption for the missionaries involved the notion of a moral conversion away from sin. Redemption for the indigenous, on the other hand, involved keeping cosmic order. Jacques Soustelle, e.g., tells us that the "Aztecs were above all 'the people of the sun.'" They saw cosmic order in apocalyptic terms:

> The Mexicans, like some other Central American peoples, believed that several successive worlds had existed before ours and that each of them had fallen in ruins amid cataclysms in which mankind had been wiped out. These were the "four suns," and the age in which we live is the fifth. Each of these "suns" is shown on monuments such as the Aztec calendar or the stone of the suns by a date, a date which is that of its end and which evokes the nature of the catastrophe which ended it: in this way the fourth epoch, for example, the "sun of the water," which was drowned in a kind of Flood, has the date *naui atl*, "four-water." Our world will have the same fate. . . . At that moment the appearance of reality will be ripped open like a veil and the *Tzitzimime*, the monsters of the twilight who await the fatal hour beneath the Western sky, will swarm out and hurl themselves upon the last survivors.[12]

To avoid a premature end, the Aztec priests ritually "fed" the sun with human blood to keep it moving on its course. As Soustelle put it: "Everytime that a priest on top of a pyramid held up the bleeding heart of a man and placed it in the *quauhxicalli* the disaster that perpetually threatened to fall upon the world was postponed once more."[13] The

---

Spiritual Conquest of Mexico, originally published in French as *Conquête Spirituelle de Mexique*, published as volume XX of *Travaux et Mémoires de L'institute d'Ethnologie* by the University of Paris, trans. Lesley Bird Simpson, California Library Reprint (Berkeley: University of California Press, 1966) 46–51.

[12]Jacques Soustelle, *Daily Life of the Aztecs: On the Eve of the Spanish Conquest*, Originally published as *La vie quotidienne des aztèques à la veille de la conquête espagnole*, Paris: Hachette, Patrick O'Brien, trans. reprint, 1955 (Stanford: Stanford University Press, 1961) 95–96.

[13]Ibid.

missionaries, then, had a tremendous conceptual gap to cross if their notion of sin was to have some meaning in the culture of the Aztecs and the neighboring tribes.

Such linguistic challenges led to a dilemma. On the one hand, if Spanish became the *lingua franca*, the preaching of the Gospel would be unintelligible to the Mexican. On the other hand, if Nahuatl was adopted, the precision of the Church's dogmatic precepts would be lost; their meaning quite possibly altered. The missionary solution to this dilemma was as creative as it was astounding. Dominican, Augustinian, Franciscan, and Jesuit missionaries all, in their own way, managed to merge Christian and indigenous signs and symbols via aesthetics. The missionary turn to an aesthetics of symbol aimed to communicate Christian concepts less with the precision of language than with the incision of the aesthetic sign. Dramas, music, and paintings all were called into missionary service.[14] As if responding to a genuine communication, the indigenous response was striking. Almost instantaneously, native Americans began to make such aesthetic and symbolic catechesis their own.[15] Such symbolic aesthetics allowed Western and indigenous elements to co-exist; neither usurping the traditional meaning of the other yet, at the same time, creating a new understanding at once traditional and new.

The *piñata* seen at birthday parties, for example, began as a way to teach about sin and grace. The *piñata* began as an effigy of the devil upon which the new catechists were encouraged to battle in the manner of St. Michael the Archangel. Later, the *piñata* was stuffed with fruit and sweets and began to symbolize sin and the goodies inside, grace or virtue. One fought against sin and grace and virtue would pour out as reward for heroic resistance. The *piñata*, in fact, began to take the form of temptations that might distract the Christian from a virtuous life. Thus, seductive women, *burros* (a sign of wealth), and food all were represented as temptations to the would-be saint. The name *piñata* comes from one of the fruits favored in representation, the *piña* or pineapple. The *piñata* was hung from a limb and the person blindfolded so that they may experience the ambiguities of the virtuous life and the disorientation that sin causes. In other words, missionary evangelization took the form of aesthetic symbolic productions aimed at

[14]Ricard, op. cit.

[15]See, for example, my discussion of the Latin American shepherd's play, *La Pastorela*, in Alex García-Rivera, "The Whole and the Love of Difference," in *From the Heart of Our People: Latino/a Explorations in Systematic Theology*, Orlando Espín and Miguel Díaz, eds. (Maryknoll, N.Y.: Orbis Press, forthcoming).

surpassing the limitations of language, or, as a semiotician would say, the linguistic sign.[16]

Though the symbolic aesthetics of missionary and indigenous invention was constructed "on the way," a tradition of intellectual inquiry into the nature of signs and symbols flowered in the early missionary years. One particularly gifted missionary was the Franciscan Bernardino Ribeira, better known as Bernadino de Sahagún. In his famous work *Historia general de las cosas de Nueva España*, he compares himself to a physician who must come to understand the behavior of the old Mexican religion because "the physician would be unable to treat his patient properly unless he knew from the beginning the humor and causes of the disease."[17] The medical reference, at first glance, suggests a suspicious, perhaps even, hostile missionary determined to undercut indigenization of the gospel. Such a picture, however, seems to me to be incomplete.[18] Sahagún no doubt was suspicious that non-Christian indigenous symbols were being introduced in new convert practices. He also was deeply concerned that the Gospel be appropriated by the Indians in their own way. Because of this, I believe Sahagún's famous study of the Mexican language and Mexican religious symbols reveals a new intellectual endeavor that was more than a linguistic achievement (though it was that).

The reference to the study of symptoms as a means for understanding something not immediately perceptible is as ancient as Galen of Pergamum (139–199 B.C.).[19] Galen encouraged the physician to study the *semeion*, signs, or *sema*, signals, of the disease. As such, Galen

[16]J. Trinidad Martínez Solís, Pbro., "Piñatas y Colación," in *Las Posadas con lecturas Biblicas*, An educational pamphlet containing *las posadas* for parochial use (Los Angeles: Librería San Pablo, n.d.).

[17]Bernardino de Sahagún, *Historia general de las cosas de Nueva España*, Angel Maria Garibay K., ed., reprint, 1956 (Mexico: Editorial Porrúa, 1981) 27.

[18]Many scholars have shown that Sahagún apparently believed that the Indians were descendants of the lost tribes of Israel and that their language descended from ancient Hebrew. His linguistic efforts, then, were motivated by Franciscan millennial aspirations such as those described in John Letty Phalan, *The Millennial Kingdom of the Franciscans in the New World* (Berkeley: University of California Press, 1970). Nonetheless, the awareness that New Spain was actually a continent and not a land extension of Asia began to grow as explorers such as Magellan and others circumnavigated the world. The belief that the Indians were just that, Indians, was losing ground rapidly in Sahagún's day.

[19]See the account on Galen in Winfried Nöth, *Handbook of Semiotics*, English-language revised and enlarged edition of a work originally published in German as *Hanbuch der Semiotik* in 1985 by J. B. Metzlersche Verlagsbuchhandlung, Advances in Semiotics (Bloomington and Indianapolis: Indiana University Press, 1990).

was indicating that experience not authority be a physician's guide. The process of correlating symptoms with disease continues today in modern medical practice.[20] Galen called the process *semiosis*. Like Galen, Sahagún calls attention to the study of experience. Perplexing customs and behavior, he intuits, are akin to symptoms. In other words, Sahagún believed that the customs and ways of the peoples they were evangelizing were symptoms of profound religious experience (even if he felt such religion was false and idolatrous). As such, Sahagún offers more an epistemological insight than a call to mistrust the Indian.

Moreover, Sahagún realized he had entered new territory. Past missionary practices inadequately presented the Gospel. To make the Gospel intelligible, credible, and authoritative, the Nahuatl language and their use of signs and symbols must be understood in order to truly inculturate the faith. To do so, the emphasis in theology must shift from abstract theory to reflection on experience. Sahagún himself became the prime model for such a new theological orientation. He consulted with Mexican priests of the ancient religion. He invented the method of cultivating informants that would answer questions of custom or behavior. He even wrote his *Historia general* in the Nahuatl language first and, then, translated it into Spanish. No wonder, then, Jonathan Z. Smith attributes Sahagún's method the first instance of a modern ethnographic study.[21] Sahagún's genius, I believe, however, lies less in his ethnographic contributions than in his semiotic endeavor.

Historia general developed into a work of twelve volumes. Though all the volumes concern the nature of native symbols and their correlation to cultural behavior, the tenth and eleventh books, in particular, address the relationship between linguistic signs and cultural customs. The French translators of Sahagún's book, D. Jourdanet and Remí Siméon, described these books as a "dictionary in action."[22] The correlation of linguistic sign and cultural act provided, indeed, a dynamic dictionary. It is here, perhaps, that one can recognize the true nature of Sahagún's achievement. More than a linguistic analysis of Nahuatl, Sahagún developed the beginnings of what I have called the semiotics of culture. Sahagún's achievements, however, have taken a long time to be recognized. The story behind this fact reveals one more element in

---

[20]Indeed, many medical schools of fifty years ago offered courses on "medical semiotics."

[21]Smith, op. cit., 43.

[22]Bernardino de Sahagún, *Histoire générale des choses de la Nouvelle-Espagne*, trans. D. Jourdanet and Remí Siméon, trans. (Paris, 1880).

the journey that has brought Hispanic theology to concentrate on a theological aesthetics.

AN UNFORTUNATE REPRESSION

The days of missionary creativity and intellectual inquiry into the nature and use of signs and symbols, however, were soon coming to an end. The Reformation began to sweep Western Christendom with full force and fury. Moreover, there was the dawning realization that New Spain was not really a land extension of Asia but an actual, new, continent. Spain, the soul of the Counter-Reformation, became increasingly sensitive to matters of orthodoxy and doctrine. With an apparently new people threatening Isidore's orthodoxy on one hand, and a rebellious Northern Europe, on the other hand, a great feeling of mistrust began to be placed against the lands and the people whose faith Spain had cultivated since the beginning of the sixteenth century. No bishops from Latin America were allowed to participate in the Council of Trent perhaps in fear that heresies heard there might spread to Latin America.[23] The indigenization of the clergy was abruptly stopped and, then, reversed. More and more episcopal appointments were given to Europeans. It did not take long before European suspicion reached the creative work of the missionaries themselves.

In 1557, Felipe II prohibited any works describing or explaining the cultural behavior of indigenous Americans. The Inquisition further forbid the translation of Sacred Scripture into native languages. Most devastating was the injunction to collect all the sermons, catechisms, and music written in native languages in order to be burned.[24] The Inquisition, itself, arrived on Mexican soil in 1570. No sooner had Sahagún finished *Historia general* that it was confiscated by the Inquisition. Sahagún's *magnum opus* did not see the light of day again until it resurfaced in 1779. Ironically, the physician who began a study of the symptoms of a disease, did not recognize the symptoms of a virulent pestilence. Such pestilence stifled **official** creative theological thought in the Americas for four centuries even as **unofficial** creative theological thought raged on in the popular religion and exceptional

---

[23]Indeed, the pre-Vatican II Latin American Church has been observed to be less a Tridentine Church than a fifteenth-century Church. See Orlando O. Espín, *The Faith of the People: Theological Reflections on Popular Catholicism* (Maryknoll, N.Y.: Orbis Press, 1997) 70.

[24]Ricard, op. cit., 56–58.

individuals of the new and vibrant Latin Church of the Americas.[25] It would not be until the fresh winds of Vatican II that Latin American theological reflection would burst forth from its suppressed but lively non-traditional setting into the once inaccessible halls of academic theological inquiry. In this new form, Latin American theological inquiry emerged as a "new way of doing theology," another form of theological reflection at once very traditional yet very "un-modern."

Latin American theological reflection, and its Hispanic counterpart, resurfaced with renewed vigor in the wake of Vatican II revealing a vitality and vibrancy whose source appeared non-modern. Indeed, the new academic inquiry into the faith of the Latin Church of the Americas has turned out to be not so much an assimilation of the Latin American faith to Modernity but the faith of the Latin Church of the Americas itself questioning the assumptions of Modernity. Nowhere can this be seen so clearly as in the first Latin American Bishop's Council that took place at Medellín, Colombia, in 1968.

MEDELLÍN

If one asked Roman Catholic theologians what event in the twentieth century most affected the Church, most would univocally answer: Vatican II. Vatican II had as spiritual aim an *aggiornamiento*, i.e., "opening up the windows," of the Tridentine Church to let in the "fresh air" of the Spirit. The aim was to renew an institution much battered by the challenges of Modernity. Some might comment that it was not so much "fresh air" but a "hurricane" that swept the Church. Whatever one's judgement of the council might be, it did have one salutary effect on the Latin church of the Americas. For the first time in nearly four hundred years, academic theological inquiry began to assert itself. This as-

---

[25]Many who have read previews of this chapter have pointed out to me that the picture of a dearth of intellectual reflection in colonial and pre-Vatican II America is inaccurate. Fr. Allan Deck, for example, has pointed out the inculturating work of Father Kino, the Jesuit, in the Southwest and the intellectual reflections by Sor Juana de la Cruz. I agree. I wish not to be misunderstood, however. Intellectual thought, even, theological thought such as in the reflections of Sor Juana de la Cruz, continued after the suppressions of 1550 (see, e.g., Electa Arenal and Stacey Schlau, *Untold Stories: Hispanic Nuns in Their Own Words*, Amanda Powell, trans. (Albuquerque: University of New Mexico Press, 1989)). It continued, however, under conditions of isolation and lack of official academic support. Nor do I wish to deemphasize the profound non-official reflection present in popular religion. My point here is to emphasize the fresh explosion of *official* theological reflection that took place after Medellín due, in great part, to an openness to the implicit reflection that had taken place beforehand.

sertion, however, did not spring up *ex nihilo* from the intellectual soil of the Americas. It had been a long time growing. Vatican II in "opening up the windows" of the Tridentine Church also "opened up the windows" of a vibrant and lively ecclesial tradition that had developed distinct from Modernity. The Latin American *aggiornamiento* took place under the auspices of the Latin American bishops (CELAM)[26] in 1968 at Medellín, Colombia. Vatican II attempted an *aggiornamiento* of the Tridentine Church to Modernity. Medellín, though ostentatiously convened for the same reason, disclosed two distinct currents that did not neatly fit either the Tridentine Church nor Modernity. The *documentos* of this famous council reveal a pair of complementary themes whose roots begin before the origins of the Tridentine Church and Modernity. A first theme calls for justice; the other for theological reflection on the experience of popular Catholicism.[27]

One can hear in Medellín's call for justice, the voices of Montesinos and Las Casas. One can also hear in the call for theological inquiry into the phenomenon of popular Catholicism the voice of Sahagún. Thus concerns academically repressed for four hundred years are taken up again by the Latin Church of the Americas. These concerns, however, are taken up with one big difference. Another nation joined the Spanish in the Americas and, subsequently, conquered (in part) the conqueror. In the 1800s the United States took territory settled by Spanish colonialists. Medellín took place in the shadow of a powerful new conqueror. In the heart of that shadow, left behind by the vagaries of war, a part of the Latin Church of the Americas remained. This remnant Church, the Hispanic or Latino Church of the United States, participated in Medellín only superficially.[28] Nonetheless, it found the concerns raised up at Medellín as its own. A curious development then took place.

Latin American theologians took up the first theme of Medellin as their clarion call but, for some reason, neglected the second. Gustavo Gutiérrez, for example, published that same year his book, *Teología de la Liberación*, which would become one of the most influential

---

[26]CELAM stands for *Consejo Episcopal Latinoamericano*, the Latin American Bishops' Conference. Emerging in 1955, they have had official meetings in 1968 (Medellín, Colombia), 1979 (Puebla, Mexico), and 1992 (Santo Domingo).

[27]Consejo Episcopal Latinoamericano (CELAM), *Medellín: Conclusiones*, 14ª edición (Bogotá, 1968).

[28]Fr. Virgilio Elizondo, a founder of Hispanic theology, participated in Medellín as a guest observer.

theological reflections in the twentieth century.[29] Since then, the literature on liberation theology spread at an amazing pace, influencing
people far beyond the regions of Latin America. Meanwhile, the other
theme of Medellín, the theological inquiry into the popular religion of
the Americas went relatively unnoticed. The reasons are many but some
may be counted as crucial. First, the vastness and systemic nature of
poverty in Latin America had created what Jose Miguez Bonino called a
"revolutionary situation."[30] The need of justice could simply not be ignored. The greatness of the problem led soon to a critical theological
perspective. Shall the poor of Latin America be seen as the object or the
subject of liberation?[31] The poor as object of liberation was espoused by
a majority group who often spoke of a "minority" Church, a Church of
enligthened elites who would educate the masses into a liberative
praxis.[32] Only a minority took the perspective of seeing the poor as subject of liberation. This minority saw the popular religion of the poor as
a "homemade" liberation theology.[33] Thus, one theme was taken up full
force and another relatively neglected.[34] Fortunately, the neglected
theme was taken up by the Hispanic Church in the United States.

POPULAR CATHOLICISM

Popular Catholicism is difficult to define.[35] It is not, however, a
challenge only to the Latin Church of the Americas. Nor is it, even, a

[29]Gustavo Gutiérrez, *Teología de la liberación*, edition no. 7, With a new introduction, "Mirar Lejos," reprint, 1968 (Lima: Centro de Estudios y Publicaciones, 1990).

[30]Jose Miguez Bonino, *Doing Theology in a Revolutionary Situation*, William H.
Lazareth, ed., Confrontation Books (Philadelphia: Fortress Press, 1975).

[31]See the fine analysis in Michael R. Candelaria, *Popular Religion and Liberation: The
Dilemma of Liberation Theology* (Albany: State University of New York Press, 1990).

[32]Juan Luis Segundo would be an example of this view. See, e.g., Juan Luis Segundo,
Faith and Ideologies (Maryknoll, N.Y.: Orbis Books, 1984).

[33]An example would be Juan Carlos Scannone, *Sabiduria Popular, Símbolo y
Filosofía: Dialogo Internacional en Torno a una Interpretación Latino Americana*
(Buenos Aires: Editorial Guadalupe, 1984).

[34]This assessment, of course, has in mind the early days of liberation theology. Since
then Latin American theologians have begun to take seriously the issue of culture and
theology and popular religion. See, e.g., Gutierréz recent writings such as *Las Casas: In
Search of the Poor of Jesus Christ*, Robert Barr, trans. (Maryknoll, N.Y.: Orbis Books,
1993).

[35]The reader is referred to chapter 6 of Robert J. Schreiter, *Constructing Local
Theologies* (Maryknoll, N.Y.: Orbis Books, 1985) and to Alex García-Rivera, *St. Martin
de Porres: The "Little Stories" and the Semiotics of Culture*, foreword by Robert Schreiter
and Virgilio Elizondo, Faith and Cultures (Maryknoll, N.Y.: Orbis Books, 1995) and,
also, Espín, op. cit.

new challenge. Augustine, for example, had to face the issue of popular Catholicism with none other than his mother, Monica. The following letter to Monica's bishop illustrates the issue.

> It had been my mother's custom in Africa to take meal-cakes and bread and wine to the shrines of the saints on their memorial days, but the door-keeper would not allow her to do this in Milan. When she learned that the bishop had forbidden it, she accepted his ruling with such pious submission that I was surprised to see how willingly she condemned her own practice rather than dispute his command. . . . She used to bring her basket full of the customary offerings of food, intending to taste a little and give the rest away. For herself she never poured more than a small cupful of wine, watered to suit her sober palate, and she drank only as much of it as was needed to do honour to the dead. . . . For her purpose was to perform an act of piety, not to seek pleasure for herself. But she willingly ceased this custom when she found that this great preacher, this holy bishop, had forbidden such ceremonies even to those who performed them with sobriety, both for fear that to some they might be occasions for drunkenness and also because they bore so close a resemblance to the superstitious rites which the pagans held in honour of their dead.[36]

One can ask various questions after reading the passage. Was the bishop's request reasonable? Why did Monica consider her funerary meals an act of piety and the bishop an occasion for drunkenness and superstition? Was Monica clinging to some pagan superstition inappropriate to her faith? Or was she simply a naïve faithful Christian who did not know any better until the bishop had enlightened her?

These are questions asked about popular Catholicism no more in the fourth century than in the twentieth. It is instructive to note, however, that Augustine was deeply moved by his mother's "naïve" faith. Augustine wrote a letter to her bishop at Carthage while he was still a priest at Hippo Regius. He advised toleration even as he urged the ban of copious drinking and eating at graves. In his letter, Augustine suggested a policy that showed a sensitivity to the complexity of the issue. The Church, he wrote, when faced with practices not directly opposed to the Gospel should exercise her authority not in an imperial or harsh manner but more teaching than commanding, more admonishing than threatening. Not surprisingly, Bartolomé de las Casas appealed to this letter in his defense of the Indians.[37]

---

[36]Aurelius Augustine, *Confessions*, R. S. Pine-Coffin, trans. (Hammondsworth: Penguin Classics, 1961) 112–13.

[37]Bartolomé de las Casas, *Apologiae Adversus Genesium Sepulvedam*, vol. 9 of *Obras Completas*, Angel Losada, ed., reprint, 1550 (Madrid: Alianza Editorial, 1988).

The reader, by now, might be exasperated. This is all very fine but what does it have to do with theological aesthetics? As answer, I beg the reader's patience. I have outlined the twin driving issues of Latin American theology: redemptive liberation and aesthetic inculturation. We have seen how the former found forceful voice in the early reflections of Latin American theologians while the latter found itself in neglect. It is this latter concern, the symbolic aesthetics of the early missionaries, however, that is the *raison d'etre* of this book. The next step is to show how symbolic aesthetics began to have an effect on the reflections of Hispanic and Latino theologians. That reflection begins with the popular Catholicism of the Latin Church of the Americas. The questions asked about Monica have become questions of Hispanic theologians and most, if not all, have given reply in terms of a theology of symbols and, an increasing number, in terms of a theological aesthetics.

HISPANIC THEOLOGY AND AESTHETICS

It takes some courage to describe the burgeoning field of Hispanic or Latino theology.[38] It is a field in creative flux. Moreover, Hispanic theology is not monolithic. There are diverse and distinctive directions present in this growing body of theological reflection. Nonetheless, it can be described in imprecise though accurate strokes. As mentioned above, Hispanic theology appears to have taken the subject of liberation most seriously. As approach to this basic issue, two major approaches stand out: the symbolic-cultural and the practical-theological. Both approaches have been pioneered by Mexican-Americans. Virgilio Elizondo, founder of the Mexican American Cultural Center and former rector of the San Fernando Cathedral of San Antonio, pioneered the symbolic-cultural approach. Allan Deck, S.J., on the other hand, pioneered the practical-theological approach. The difference between the approaches may be due to the emphasis one puts on either theme of Medellín in an approach to the subject of liberation.

A practical-theological analysis favors an emphasis on the justice theme while a symbolic-cultural analysis favors an emphasis on the inculturation theme. The practical-theological analysis centers on changing the conditions of the subject of liberation while the symbolic-cultural centers on the identity of the subject of liberation. Neither of these emphases are mutually exclusive and they are simply distinguished here to identify

---

[38]I shall, from now on, use the single term "Hispanic" than both terms "Hispanic" and "Latino" in order to keep confusion of terms to a minimum.

them. In other words, Father Deck's approach has as much to say about inculturation as Father Elizondo's approach. Similarly, the symbolic-cultural approach has as much to say about justice as the practical-theological approach. They are complementary rather than antagonistic approaches. They are distinguished here to demonstrate the range and distinctiveness of Hispanic theological inquiries at present.

Father Deck's practical-theological analysis is the most empirical of the two approaches. Like that other Jesuit, Jose de Acosta, Deck attempts to "see" for himself the reality of the Hispanic Church in the United States using a social-scientific analysis. Demographics, class structures, cultural patterns, historical information all come together in Deck's penetrating analysis of Hispanic faith formation. In insisting on actual data for his theological reflection, Deck displays the tough minded approach to cultural and social reality that distinguished the very first Latin American theologians.[39] This tough minded approach has borne much fruit. Deck has successfully launched a myriad of highly effective programs aimed at organizing, educating, and preparing the Hispanic faithful.[40] Deck is not alone in using this approach. Others, if not directly inspired by him, have used a practical-theological approach with a social scientific-analysis. The Hispanic feminist theologian, Maria Pilar Aquino, for example, uses a practical-theological analysis in her pioneering study of Latin American women as subjects of liberation.[41]

The symbolic-cultural approach has been, in a sense, defined by Father Elizondo, who was at the Medellín conference in 1968. A native of San Antonio, Texas, Elizondo felt in the bishop's deliberations a deep resonance. The call for justice of Medellín was a call that also needed to be heard in the borderlands of Texas. The call for understanding the popular Catholicism of the Latin Church of the Americas, however, stirred him deeply. As a Hispanic, he had been raised in the popular Catholicism typical of Latin America. It was, however, a popular Catholicism which grated roughly with the English-speaking Church

[39]For a fine analysis and review of Father Deck's works, see Alfred T. Hennelly, S.J., *Liberation Theologies: The Global Pursuit of Justice* (Mystic, Conn.: Twenty-Third Publications, 1995) 128–50.

[40]Among these one might include his highly effective certificate program for Hispanic lay ministry education based at Loyola Marymount of Los Angeles and the very successful national organization for Hispanic pastoral agents known as National Catholic Council for Hispanic Ministry (NCCHM).

[41]Maria Pilar Aquino, *Our Cry for Life: Feminist Theology from Latin America* (Maryknoll, N.Y.: Orbis Books, 1993).

of the United States. In seminary, his boyhood faith had been challenged and depreciated.[42] His experience parallels the experience of almost every Hispanic Catholic in the United States. The cause of this experience, Elizondo soon recognized, was more than ignorance or simple prejudice on the part of the English-speaking Church in the United States. The popular Catholicism of ordinary folks had yet to be understood as authentic faith. Unspoken but always near the surface, the popular faith of ordinary folks was considered childish, superstitious, or, worse, inauthentic.

At Medellín, Elizondo realized an opportunity had come that had been buried for hundreds of years. Somehow, the symbols of popular Hispanic faith contained within themselves a profound understanding of faith. After Medellín, Elizondo turned to these symbols. It was then he rediscovered a different beauty. As Elizondo himself describes it:

> In 1531, ten years after the conquest, an event happened whose origins are clouded in mystery, yet its effects have been monumental and ongoing. . . . According to the legend, as Juan Diego, a Christianized Indian of common status, was going from his home in the "barriada" near Tepeyac, he heard beautiful music. As he approached the source of the music, a lady appeared to him and speaking in Nahuatl, the language of the conquered, she commanded Juan Diego to go to the palace of the archbishop of Mexico at Tlatelolco and to tell him that the Virgin Mary, "Mother of the true God, through whom one lives" wanted a temple to be built at that site so that in it she "can show and give forth all my love, compassion, help, and defense to all the inhabitants of this land . . . to hear their lamentations and remedy their miseries, pain, and sufferings." After two unsuccessful attempts to convince the bishop of the Lady's authenticity, the Virgin wrought a miracle. She sent Juan Diego to pick roses in a place where only desert plants existed. She arranged the roses on his cloak and sent him to the archbishop with the sign he had demanded. As Juan Diego unfolded his cloak in the presence of the archbishop, the roses fell to the ground and the image of the Virgin appeared on his cloak.[43]

---

[42]See his moving account in Virgilio Elizondo, *The Future Is Mestizo: Life Where Cultures Meet* (Bloomington: Meyer-Stone Books, 1988).

[43]Virgilio Elizondo, "Our Lady of Guadalupe as a Cultural Symbol," in *Liturgy and Cultural Traditions*, Herman Power and David Schmidt, eds. (New York: Seabury Press, 1977) 25–33.

The story of Guadalupe has stirred Mexican hearts for centuries. It is an example of "difference" encountered in the form of a "story as beautiful as it is simple."[44] As Jose Luis Guerrero put it:

> The "Guadalupan Event" is a premier example of how [it] is possible, even in the worst of circumstances, as it was in the case of two peoples, Spaniards and Indians, confronting a mutually total distrust of each other and separated by a human chasm of insuperable lack of comprehension, to be able to unite so effectively, with a union that is not only genetic, but also psychological and axiological, and gave birth to a new people, the mestizo, the Mexicans of today. This has happened without transgressing these peoples human limitations but activating the little they had in common and de-emphasizing (without denying) the great difference that separated them.[45]

As such, Guerrero judges the "Guadalupan Event" described by Elizondo as a "Salvific Act." The "difference" that divided two peoples became an act of union which was, at its heart, redemptive. This redemptive act, this union of "difference," takes the form of a symbol, or, rather, a set of symbols and signs, known as Our Lady of Guadalupe. It is this redemptive act of "difference" through symbols that also suggests the proposal for a reconceived theological aesthetics.

It was Elizondo who first recognized the promise of a new approach to popular Catholicism through its symbols. His analysis has become a classic in Hispanic theology. He begins with a symbolic-cultural analysis. Like Sahagún before him, Elizondo goes back to indigenous sources for help in interpretation:

> Upon reading the legend, the first striking detail is that Juan Diego heard beautiful music, which alone was enough to establish the heavenly origin of the Lady. For the Indians, music was the medium of divine communication. The Lady appeared on the sacred hill of Tepeyac, one of the four principal sacrificial sites in Meso America. It was the sanctuary of Tonantzin, the Indian virgin mother of the gods. The dress was a pale red, the colour of the spilled blood of sacrifices and the colour of Huitzilopopchtli, the god who gave and preserved life. The blood of the Indians had been spilled on Mexican soil and fertilized mother earth, and now something new came forth. Red was also the colour for the East, the direction from which the sun arose victorious after it had died for the night. The predominant colour of the portrait is the blue-green of the

---

[44]Jose Luis Guerrero, *El Nican Mopohua: Un intento de exégesis* (Mexico, D.F.: Universidad Pontificia de Mexico, A.C., 1996) 7.
[45]Ibid.

mantle, which was the royal colour of the Indian gods. It was also the colour of Ometéotl, the origin of all natural forces. In the colour psychology of the native world, blue-green stood at the centre of the cross of opposing forces and signified the force unifying the opposing tensions at work in the world. . . . The Lady wore the black band of maternity around her waist, the sign that she was with child. She was offering her child to the New World. The Lady was greater than the greatest in the native pantheon because she hid the sun but did not extinguish it. The sun god was their principal deity, and she was more powerful. The Lady was also greater than their moon god, for she stood upon the moon, yet did not crush it. However, great as this Lady was, she was not a goddess. She wore no mask as the Indian gods did, and her vibrant, compassionate face in itself told anyone who looked upon it that she was the compassionate mother.[46]

As such, Elizondo's analysis offers us understanding the symbol of Guadalupe in its indigenous dimension. A cultural anthropologist could have done as much. Elizondo's originality breaks through when he continues the analysis with a striking observation.

Not only did the Lady leave a powerful message in the image, but the credentials she chose to present herself to the New World were equally startling. For the bishop, the roses from the desert were a startling phenomenon; for the Indians, they were the sign of life. . . . At the time of the apparition, the Spanish were building churches over the ruins of the Aztec temples. The past grandeur and power of Tenochtitlán-Tlatelolco (the original name for present day Mexico City) was being transformed into the glory of New Spain, which was to supplant native Mexico. The tearing down and the building up was symbolic of the deeper struggle to destroy a people, even if the intention was to rebuild it. Juan Diego dared to go to the city of power and with supernatural authority—the native lady had commanded—he demanded that the powerful change their plans and build a temple—a symbol of a new way of life—not within the grandeur of the city in accordance with the plans of Spain, but within the *barriada* of Tepeyac in accordance with the desires of the native people of this land. The hero of the story is a simple conquered Indian from the barriada who is a symbol of the poor and oppressed refusing to be destroyed by the dominant group. The purpose of the story was to lead the archbishop, the symbol of the new Spanish power group, to a conversion so as to turn the attention of the conquering group from building up the rich and powerful center of governments, knowledge and religion, to the periphery of society where the people continued to live in poverty and misery.[47]

[46]Elizondo, "Our Lady of Guadalupe as a Cultural Symbol," 126–28.
[47]Ibid., 130–31.

Medellín's influence on Elizondo shows up clearly here. The concern for justice, the tradition of Montesinos and Las Casas, emerge in this liberation-type account of the significance of Our Lady of Guadalupe. It emerges, however, out of a previous analysis of the cultural symbolic nature of this popular devotion. Elizondo brought together symbols and history, the synchronic and the diachronic, to demonstrate the liberative dimensions of the symbols of Hispanic popular Catholicism. As such, Elizondo more than any other Latin American theologian brought together the twin challenges raised at Medellín.

The recognition of the redemptive nature of symbols by Elizondo electrified the Hispanic intellectual community. Elizondo opened up the relationship between liberation and popular religion with his insightful analysis of the signs and symbols contained in the popular image of our Lady of Guadalupe. Elizondo's ground-breaking work defined the task for a new generation of Hispanic theologians. How does one conceive the connection between the redemptive dimensions of the Gospel and its cultural incarnation? Two important Hispanic theologians that have tried to answer this question include Orlando Espín and Roberto Goizueta.

Orlando Espín has single-handedly defined the field of Hispanic popular religion in the United States. He has worked tirelessly to bring popular religion to the attention of the academic community. In doing so, Espín has identified the dynamics and perspectives that must be taken into account when commenting on popular religious practices. Espín, through his careful scholarship, has helped lay a careful fundament on the grounds of popular religion from which a symbolic-cultural analysis may flourish.[48] Roberto Goizueta has taken such a fundament to heart in his theological reflection. Of all the Hispanic theologians, Goizueta has been the most willing to appropriate insights from all others towards synthesizing a new Hispanic theology. His most creative reflection, however, has been his original contribution that an aesthetics may be a decisive approach for symbolic-cultural analysis. Thus, Goizueta proposes a "theo-poetics" of "accompaniment."[49]

I have profited from all these great thinkers now rising in the Hispanic Church. It was Virgilio Elizondo, however, who most inspired me. As a graduate student I took Robert Schreiter's course "Constructing

[48]See his fine analysis of popular Catholicism in Espín, op. cit.
[49]Roberto S. Goizueta, *Caminemos con Jesús: Toward a Hispanic/Latino Theology of Accompaniment* (Maryknoll, N.Y.: Orbis Books, 1995).

Local Theologies." There, Professor Schreiter suggested that it was possible to articulate a "semiotics of culture." In other words, Schreiter believed that culture could be treated as a linguistic text which consisted of a "grammar" of signs. Schreiter's suggestion intrigued me. If one can treat culture as a "text," then that "text" could both be a cultural incarnation as well as a "word" of redemption. Yet, such conceptualizing of culture bothered me. I could not see how culture may be reasonably compared to a language. In a culture, many people are speaking at the same time. Have you tried to follow a conversation where three or more people speak at once? I struggled with Schreiter's suggestion of a semiotics of culture with little insight until one day I happened to see the movie *Amadeus*.

In the movie, Mozart tries to explain to the emperor why he wrote the opera "The Marriage of Figaro":

> It's a piece about love . . . The end of the second act . . . starts out as a simple duet, just a husband and a wife quarreling, suddenly the wife's scheming little maid comes in . . . the duet turns into trio, then the husband's valet comes in, he's plotting with the maid, trio turns into quartet . . . [the] gardener comes in, quartet becomes quintet, and so on and on and on, sextet, septet, optet!! . . . only opera can do this, in a play if more than one person speaks at the same time, its just noise . . . no one can understand a word, but with opera, with music . . . with music you can have twenty individuals all talking at the same time and it's not noise it's a perfect harmony.

It then dawned on me. Culture is not so much a language as it is an aesthetics! Culture can support various conversations at once because like an opera, they complement one another.

The idea of a cultural aesthetics energized me. I now realized the power and potential of Schreiter's suggestion for a theology of culture. I also realized that this meant converting Schreiter's suggestion of culture as a linguistic text into culture as an aesthetic work. Thus, I began to pore over the literature of both Latin American and Hispanic theology as well as on the theory of signs, i.e., semiotics. My reading over the Hispanic theological literature was both rewarding and sobering. It was rewarding because other Hispanic theologians had begun to see cultural aesthetics as a fruitful approach to theology. It was sobering because the literature reminded me of the long, tragic history of oppression and suffering both of Latin Americans and Hispanics. Harmonizing suffering away is an obscene not an aesthetic act. Only a cultural aesthetics which can face up to suffering, even find its aesthetic force there could adequately describe Hispanic and Latin American experience.

This book emerges as a response to that experience. It is a search for a theology that does justice to the authenticity and originality of the Latin Church of the Americas found in the signs and symbols of its popular religion yet also discloses which of these signs and symbols are transformative and redemptive. These twin dimensions frame this particular attempt to articulate a theological aesthetics. In the struggle to articulate such a theological aesthetics, I have learned a great deal as well from the English-speaking culture that now constitutes part of my Hispanicity. The writings of the Anglo-American philosophers Charles Peirce and Josiah Royce mix synergistically in my mind with Latin American theology. Their semiotic pragmatism have great affinities with this Latin American and Hispanic project and reveal that a quest for a theological aesthetics is, in a larger sense, an original American contribution. This American contribution, however, I believe will also be of great significance to the wider Church as it struggles with the issues that appear in all corners of the world: a hunger for spiritual identity and a cry for liberation. These twin issues have lately been seen as antonyms. The theological aesthetics proposed here, I hope, will reveal these two challenges for the Church to have an intrinsic unity.

Thus, I have tried to help the reader know the historical and intellectual context for this project. Like Elizondo, I see myself as standing in that long tradition of Latin American theology as articulated at Medellín. The call for justice and the symbolic enactment of faith will always be a part of the Latin American theological tradition. I would further argue that it has always been a part of the Church's wider tradition if not at the heart of its expression of faith. Hispanic theology has taken seriously Guadalupe's "different" beauty. Beauty, as Hispanic theologians increasingly recognize, reveals its theological dimension in "difference." As the next chapters will demonstrate, such "difference" is at the heart of sign. Peirce and Royce will demonstrate how the "difference" of sign reveals the True (Peirce) and the Good (Royce). I will argue with the help of von Balthasar's notion of form that the "difference" of sign also reveals the Beautiful.

3

Seeing the Form

Von Balthasar, in his intellectual autobiography, introduces the transcendentals of Being, the True, the Good, and the Beautiful, in a captivating image:

> The infant is brought to consciousness of himself only by love, by the smile of his mother. In that encounter, the horizon of all unlimited being opens itself for him, revealing four things to him: (1) that he is one in love with the mother, even in being other than his mother, therefore all being is one; (2) that that love is good, therefore all Being is good; (3) that that love is true, therefore all Being is true; and (4) that that love evokes joy, therefore all Being is beautiful.[1]

These attributes of Being, the One, the True, the Good, and the Beautiful, are called transcendentals because they are coextensive with Being even as they transcend any one creature. As such, they promise an analogy implicit in the image of the love between mother and infant that allows the insuperable difference between creature and God to be crossed. Indeed, it is only the transcendentals that allow for such an analogy. If so, then the modern state of affairs is in deep trouble.

A world that knows the Holocaust has little use of the transcendentals. What is Truth under the gallows of Auschwitz? Indeed, what is Good? Only now are we experiencing the full force of the nihilism unleashed in the misery of two world wars. Our contemporary nihilism, more importantly, is already at work in destroying a belief in Beauty itself. Von Balthasar speaks eloquently about the implications of such a loss:

[1]Hans Urs von Balthasar, *My Work: In Retrospect,* originally in German, *Mein Werk—Durchlike,* Johannes Verlag, Freiburg, reprint, 1990, Communio Books (San Francisco: Ignatius Press, 1993) 114.

No longer loved or fostered by religion, beauty is lifted from its face as a mask, and its absence exposes features on that face which threaten to become incomprehensible to man. We no longer dare to believe in beauty and we make of it a mere appearance in order the more easily to dispose of it. . . . We can be sure that whoever sneers at her name as if she were the ornament of a bourgeois past—whether he admits it or not—can no longer pray *and soon will no longer be able to love.* . . . In a world without beauty . . . the good also loses its attractiveness. . . . Man stands before the good and asks himself why *it* must be done and not rather its alternative, evil. For this, too, is a possibility, and even the more exciting one: Why not investigate Satan's depths? In a world that no longer has any confidence in itself to affirm the beautiful, the proofs of the truth have lost their cogency. In other words, syllogisms may still dutifully clatter away like rotary presses or computers which infallibly spew out an exact number of answers by the minute. But the logic of these answers is itself a mechanism which no longer captivates anyone.[2]

The "linchpin" of the transcendentals, then, according to von Balthasar is the beautiful. Without the beautiful, we "soon will no longer be able to love." Without the good, evil will become an equally plausible alternative, and without the true, we shall fall into a "logic" of answers that "no longer captivates anyone." In short, the loss of belief in beauty is the unraveling of the transcendentals that manifests itself as nihilism. Indeed, isn't nihilism the reigning paradigm of our days? Does not despair contaminate all aspects of our culture? Hasn't von Balthasar's prophecy already come true?

Maybe, but there is hope. People are still moved by the likes of Mother Teresa whose life has been described as "something beautiful for God." Somehow, the true, the good, and the beautiful refuse to be annihilated. Thus, von Balthasar's call for a theological aesthetics. Theological aesthetics attempts to recover a belief in the reality of the beautiful and, thus, of all the transcendentals. It proposes to do so by delineating the long theological tradition of beauty as a transcendental encapsulated in the phrase "seeing the form." I intend in this chapter to expose von Balthasar's aesthetics of "seeing the form" so that it may act as guide and prompt in the chapters that follow. Beginning with my version of a Platonic dialogue, Albertus (Einstein) and Sophia (Wisdom) set up the issues involved in a philosophical aesthetics. The transition from a philosophical aesthetics to a theological aesthetics will then be proposed in von Balthasar's terms, i.e., the incarnation. The incarnation reveals the intrinsic capacity of the human creature to

[2]Hans Urs von Balthasar, *Seeing the Form*, op. cit., 18–19.

know and love God. A theological aesthetics concerns this *capax Dei*. The human *capax Dei*, however, knows many dimensions and each of these will be explored culminating in von Balthasar's great aesthetic insight "seeing the form." Finally, von Balthasar's aesthetics will be examined in light of Hispanic theology's aesthetics of signs. The possibility of an aesthetic shift from form to sign will be proposed.

FROM A PHILOSOPHICAL TO A THEOLOGICAL AESTHETICS

An attempt to lay out in the space of a few paragraphs the immense field of philosophical aesthetics would be a foolish undertaking. It might be possible, however, to help the reader understand by the means of a simple dialogue what the essential issues are that concern a philosophical aesthetics. The following Platonic dialogue concerns the issue about the relationship between an original work of art and its copy. In this issue, my hope is to flesh out the basic concerns that intersect both philosophical and theological aesthetics. As such, I make no claim that the dialogue exhausts the field of philosophical aesthetics nor that I have represented it fairly. I merely wish to set up for the reader the distinction between a philosophical and a theological aesthetics and the concerns common to both. Moreover, I want to raise the issue of aesthetics in terms of the issue of difference which is vital to Hispanic theology. Towards that end, our dialogue finds Albertus and Sophia discussing the marvelous invention known as a material hologram. A material hologram is unabashedly modeled after the famous "Holodeck" of Star Trek fame. It is capable of reproducing a material entity in (almost) perfect fidelity. It is this almost but not perfect fidelity that raises the issue of difference in aesthetics.

ALBERTUS AND SOPHIA: A DIALOGUE

The eyes, though hollowed in marble, pierce through the viewer. His right hand looms large and strong poised for a graced movement of terrible strength. Thus Michelangelo envisions at the moment of decision to strike Goliath. Michelangelo's *David* strikes most Westerners as an example of superb beauty. As such, it serves the purpose of asking the question: what exactly makes *David* a beautiful work of art? Is it a matter of the exquisite proportions incarnate in its marbled body? Could it be the effectiveness with which Michelangelo expresses his own inner feelings? Or is *David's* beauty simply a conditioned response of Westerners to a historical, well-defined style of representation? Following my own training in science, let me ask the reader to consider, in the contemporary style of theoretical physics, a "thought" experiment presented in the form of an older theoretical physics, a Platonic dialogue such as Galileo's "Dialogue concerning two new sciences."[3]

Albertus: "Good morning, Doña Sophia. Say, did you see the wonderful exhibit of material holograms at the Silicon Valley Museum of Technology yesterday?"

Sophia: "Why, yes. It is marvelous, isn't it."

Albertus: "Indeed, it is! Imagine being able to take raw energy and by using the right conversion factors convert that energy into any material shape you wish. Someday we will be able to shine a flashlight into a machine and a steak ready for dinner will pop out."

Sophia: "That could very well be true, dear Albertus, but do you think it will be as tasty as a real steak?"

Albertus: "I don't see why it shouldn't as long as the right conversion factors are included."

Sophia: "Well, you might be right. I don't think, however, that everything can be so conveniently reproduced."

Albertus: "Again, I don't see why not. As long as accurate measurements are made of an object, anything can be reproduced exactly by the material hologram."

Sophia: "That is what I love about you, Albertus. You love to argue."

Albertus: "I was not aware that I was arguing, my dear Sophia. I am simply stating a fact."

Sophia: "Let me then propose to you an object that might not be able to be exactly reproduced by the material hologram."

Albertus: "And what might that object be?"

Sophia: "A great work of art."

Albertus: "Why not any work of art?"

Sophia: "All art has predecessors and similarities with other pieces of art but a great work of art stands out among these similarities and precedents on its own. Its beauty shines through as particular and unique. Say, Michelangelo's *David*, for example."

Albertus: "Go on, you intrigue me."

---

[3]Galilei Galileo, *Dialogues Concerning Two New Sciences,* trans. Henry Crew and Alfonso de Salvio, introduction by Antonio Favaro, reprint, 1914 (New York: Dover, 1954).

Sophia: "Okay. Assume you measure every inch of Michelangelo's *David*, from the distance between the wrist and the elbow of David's right arm to the distance between the first right-hand knuckle of its index finger and the second. Now suppose you plug these numbers into the material hologram and a copy of the statue comes out based on the measurements made. Now ask yourself the question: can these numbers reproduce the particular and unique sense of the beautiful found in the original statue? Unless, my dear Albertus, one loves numbers more than the reality they represent, you must agree that even an excellent copy built from scratch in the garage does not do justice to the original. The original apparently possessed 'something' now lacking in the copy."

Albertus: "Wait a minute, Sophia! You're trying to pull a fast one. It is true that an imperfect copy of Michelangelo's statue would be inadequate but what about a 'perfect' copy? If every detail of Michelangelo's *David* were measured, a perfect copy could be re-created. Indeed, a naïve viewer gazing at a perfect copy would experience the same feelings of the beautiful as another viewer gazing at the original."

Sophia: "Given the technological marvel of the material hologram, my curmudgeon friend, you do persuade. A 'perfect' copy appears 'doable.' Unless, of course, you ask the nitty-gritty question of how a copy is actually made. Copies are, even in a material hologram, reproductions of measurements of difference. The difference between two points on an original are then reproduced on a similar pair of points on a copy. You argue that a reproduction of measurable 'differences' can, in principle, be made. What you fatally ignore is that though the difference between two points can be perfectly reproduced, the way that difference is interpreted, i.e., the way one draws the line or curve between those two points, cannot!"

Albertus: "Okay, my wily Sophia, I must agree. A perfect copy cannot, in actuality, be made. One, however, can come fairly close! One can, for example, make the difference between two points so small that there is little room for interpretation in the copy. Thus, even though a material hologram of Michelangelo's *David* cannot, in actuality, be made perfectly identical to the original, I doubt an ordinary person would sense a difference and would cherish the copy as much if not the same as the original. I, for one, would feel no shame to display a material hologram of *David* in the living room of my home."

Sophia: "Granted, my insightful friend. A good copy has value. Nonetheless, the value of a copy will always be measured by its original. The closer a copy follows the original, the more valuable it is. And, thus, we return to the original observation of our experiment. No matter how good a copy you have, the original possesses 'something' that a copy cannot."

Albertus: "You still haven't met my practical challenge, my evasive Sophia. If one can get as close as one wants to reproducing an original's details, then, practically, the copy will come as close as one wants to having the same value. A material hologram of Michelangelo's *David* can make such an exquisite reproduction that if, for example, one would offer the original at one million dollars and a material hologram of the statue at, say, two hundred and fifty dollars, a rational person would opt for the two hundred and fifty dollar copy and forget the original."

Sophia: "Oh, Albertus, you do press the point. Let's take your example and reverse it. Suppose you gave a material hologram *David* to a friend without telling her that it was a copy. Your friend, a skilled art historian, does not detect any sign that this *David* is a copy. She is thrilled and wonders at the magnanimity of your generosity. Now suppose that later she learns that the original *David* is currently in display at the Louvre. What do you suppose her reaction to your gift will be?"

Albertus: "I shudder to think."

Sophia: "That's right. She most probably will be offended that you did not mention it was a copy. She will interpret your generosity as a deception and her estimation of you and your material hologram will be immediately diminished. Dear Albertus, the value of a work of art is not economic. Its value lies elsewhere. Yet, I fear I may be misleading you. I do not wish to claim that the value of a great work of art lies in the original."

Albertus: "Well, now I am truly disoriented. I thought your whole point was that reproducing an original work of art fails to reproduce its value."

Sophia: "Please, Albertus, bear with me. Suppose the great artist and good friend of Michelangelo, Raphael, had made a copy of the *David*. Suppose, further, that it was this copy that you had given your art historian friend. What would her reaction now be, if you 'confessed' that you had not given her an original but a copy made by Raphael?"

Albertus: "Hmmm!"

Sophia: "You seem confused."

Albertus: "Not confused but wary of your charming deceptions, Sophia. Yes, my friend would not be angry at learning that it was a copy."

Sophia: "Indeed, she might even find it more valuable than the original!"

Albertus: "Yes, but there is something amiss here. Raphael's copy could not possibly be as exact as my material hologram. If one measured the proportions, i.e., the differences, of Raphael's copy of *David*, one would find many variances."

Sophia: "That is my point, my illumined Albertus. Raphael's 'copy' would now become another 'original.'"

Albertus: "Yes, that's true. Now there would be two *David*'s, one by Michelangelo and one by Raphael."

Sophia: "That's right. Raphael's 'copy' was able to reproduce the value of the Michelangelo original but only by becoming an 'original' itself."

Albertus: "I see that."

Sophia: "That's right, my dear Albertus, it is about 'seeing.' Beauty, above all is 'seen.' Both Raphael and Michelangelo can 'see' the beauty of *David* and through their genius allow others to 'see' as well. Unless your material hologram can 'see' and then allow others to 'see' as well, it will never be able to 'copy' a great work of art."

Albertus: "I cannot contest your reasoning. Yet, my victorious Sophia, I come back to the original issue of this delightful discussion. What is this 'something' whose presence does not allow reproduction?"

Sophia: "Why, my most gracious friend, it is simply seeing the form."

THE TWO POLES OF PHILOSOPHICAL AESTHETICS

The dialogue between Sophia and Albertus revolves around the issue of *mimesis* or copying a great work of art.[4] It is instructive as it reveals two poles a philosophical aesthetics may take in explaining its subject matter: imitative representation or interpretative origination.[5]

[4]The dialogue also concerns the issue of artificial intelligence. The reader might be interested in how I have handled the issue of mimesis in the context not of a work of art but in the case of artificial intelligence. See Alex García-Rivera, "Artificial Intelligence, 1992, and Las Casas: A 1492 Resonance," *Zygon* 28, no. 4 (1993) 543–50.

[5]The famous philosopher of aesthetics, Bernard Bosanquet, saw these two poles as characterizing much of philosophical aesthetics. As such, it may be an over-characterization reducing the many position and subtleties contained in that field. Nonetheless, it serves the purpose of providing background for the reader uninitiated in the field and as contrast to the unique claims a theological aesthetics. For the reader interested in a deeper and more nuanced discussion of philosophical aesthetics, I recommend the following: Bernard Bosanquet, *A History of Aesthetic* (Cleveland: World Publishing, Meridian, 1957). Wladyslaw Tatarkiewicz, "The Great Theory of Beauty & Its Decline," *Journal of Aesthetics and Art Criticism* 31, no. 2 (1972) 165–79; Katharine Everett

As such, the two poles reveal the close connection between cosmology, one's view of the universe, and aesthetics. The pole known as imitative representation corresponds to a cosmological position known as Monism. Greek Monism, for example, perceived a thoroughly material, i.e., "visible," world. Such a belief happily embraces the famous aesthetic principle *ars simiae naturae*, "art imitates nature." In other words, beauty is "given." The artist does not create beautiful objects but, rather, skillfully re-presents what is already beautiful. Thus, the world of beauty consists of imitative representation.[6] The artist, then, is seen more as craftsman. This is the sense of the artistry of the wonderful machine invented above. The "material hologram" is the product of an artistry thoroughly "technical," in the sense of a mechanical but skillful imitative representation. As such, beauty reveals itself as purely formal, i.e., as "consisting in certain very abstract conditions which are satisfied, for example, in elementary geometrical figures as truly as in the creations of fine art."[7] The pure formality of a monistic world leads to a purely sensual and formal beauty. In the case of our material hologram machine, such sensual formality corresponds to the conversion factors which accurately recreate Michelangelo's *David*. Such an aesthetics, however, has religious implications. If the world contains only objects that can be visibly imitated, then beautiful objects cannot refer to an invisible reality. This leaves us with a sensual but purely formal beauty, a beauty without spirit, without life. Anyone with religious sensitivities would recoil from such a view of the beautiful. One who did was the deeply religious philosopher Plato.

The other pole known as interpretative origination corresponds to a cosmological position known as Dualism. Platonic dualism, for example, presupposes two distinct realities, or, rather, two different worlds, the world of Being and the world of Becoming. The world of Being corresponds to an invisible world of Forms. The world of Becoming corresponding to the visible world of Appearances. Indeed, the world of Forms is responsible for the world of Appearances in which the unreflecting must live. Appearances give witness to the

---

Gilbert and Helmut Kuhn, *A History of Esthetics* (New York: The MacMillan Company, 1939); Bendetto Croce, *Aesthetic: As Science of Expression and General Linguistic*, rev. ed., trans. Douglas Ainslie (New York: Noonday Press, 1922); George Santayana, *The Sense of Beauty: Being the Outline of Aesthetic Theory*, reprint, 1896 (New York: Dover, 1955); Umberto Eco, *Art and Beauty in the Middle Ages*, Hugh Bredin (New Haven, Conn.: Yale University Press, 1986).

[6]Bosanquet, op. cit., 11.

[7]Ibid., 18.

Forms responsible for their "appearance" as shadows give witness to the sunlight which streams into a cave. Yet Forms are more than shadows. Forms must be "seen" in original light not in secondary reflections and projections of light. Forms "exist" in the world of direct sunlight. Beauty corresponds to such a Form. How, then, can such Forms be "seen"? Can human eyes perceive original light? Plato answers No! Human eyes cannot perceive Forms illumined by original light. Our sensual eyes only see appearances caused by reflected or projected light. Original Forms, however, can be "seen" by the "eye" of reason which can perceive original light. In other words, our minds are the means by which the Forms may be "seen." The mind, another organ, a faculty, "ascends" from the shadows that are appearances to the world of original light where it can bask in the glory of the Forms. Such a cosmology leads to an aesthetics aptly named interpretative origination.

Such sight, however, presents a curious "aesthetics." What sort of art is it that foregoes appearance? Is not art by its very nature sensual? Indeed, if Forms cannot be "seen" by sensual vision, what type of vision is a Form? What does a Form illumined by original light "look" like? It is here where the religiosity or spirituality of Plato's philosophy manifests itself. To the extent we may associate the spiritual as an invisible reality, Plato places the Forms in what Christians might interpret as the world of spiritual realities. No wonder Christian theologians found Plato so congenial! Plato is after a vision of the invisible, i.e., the spiritual! As such, Platonic dualism brings to sharp focus the issue of spirituality in a work of art.[8]

In the language of spirituality, one can categorize the Monistic aesthetics of the Early Greeks as *kataphatic*, i.e., as sensual perception. The

---

[8]Christian spirituality, however, rejects a strictly Platonic spirituality. The very sacramentality of Christian vision asserts at the same time that invisible realities become present through visible signs or appearances. As such, Christian spirituality also rejects a purely sensual view of spirituality. Indeed, Christian spirituality can be situated between two poles that correspond to the two poles found in philosophical aesthetics. *Kataphatic* spirituality resembles the philosophical aesthetics of imitative resemblance. As in one of the spiritual exercises of Ignatius of Loyola instructs, one attempts to imitate Jesus by "smelling" what Jesus might be smelling, or "seeing" what Jesus might be "seeing." *Apophatic* spirituality, on the other hand, resembles interpretative origination. Like *The Cloud of Unknowing*, *apophatic* spirituality attempts to get rid of any sensual experience in order to enter a more original, direct experience with the divine. Of course, there is no purely *kataphatic* or purely *apophatic* spirituality. Both of the examples above contain elements of both. Nonetheless, emphasis towards one pole or the other can be noted. See, e.g., Urban T. Holmes, III, *A History of Christian Spirituality: An Analytical Introduction* (New York: Seabury Press, 1980).

Dualist aesthetics of Plato, on the other hand, may be categorized as *apophatic*, perception without the use of the bodily senses. Plato pits *apophatic* Beauty against the *kataphatic* beautiful and demonstrates forcefully the spirituality of the former and the mechanical lifelessness of the latter. Thus, Platonic dualism answers Albertus' final question to Sophia in the same way it answers Socrates' question to Xenophon, "can the invisible be imitated?"[9] *Apophatic* vision, the vision of the invisible spiritual, is original. Imitations, copies of an original, only "darken" such vision. Notice, however, that Platonic dualism also leads to a purely formal account of Beauty. Beauty is a pure Form apprehended apophatically.[10]

At the heart of Albertus and Sophia's dialogue beats the issue concerning the meaning of difference. Does true "difference" exist? And if it does, is it meaningful? Either of the two poles of a philosophical aesthetics ignores the issue of "difference." Both poles consider "difference" as superficial as "appearance." A monistic approach to the relation between original and copy, for example, makes their difference superficial. A copy may not be as "good" as the original but, for all practical reasons, a copy can be made as close to an original as desired and this is where its value can be found. Likewise, a dualist approach to the relation between copy and original also makes their difference superficial. The

---

    [9]*Memorabilia*, III, 10 quoted in Bosanquet, op. cit., 44.
    [10]Interpretative origination has a modern counterpart. The world of Forms now becomes transformed into the inner invisible world of the artist-creator. The artist-creator attempts to contact the very origins of an inner world in order to express it. The modern artist-creator, like Plato, answers Socrates' question about imitating the invisible with a resounding No! They add, however, a distinctly modern element. The invisible cannot be imitated but it can be expressed! Indeed, the most modern of artist-creators aim for pure expression. Modern manifestations of interpretative origination reveal the other dimension of a Dualist theory of aesthetics. A purely *apophatic* vision supports either form without expression or expression without form. A Platonic pre-Modern aesthetics supports an *apophatic* split between expression and form in favor of form. A Platonic Modern aesthetics supports an *apophatic* split between expression and form in favor of expression. It is for this reason, I believe, that we are more comfortable speaking of a modern art than a modern aesthetics. This has important implications for a philosophical aesthetics. Pure expression, after all, is, in essence, apophatic. It strives to communicate the invisible by striving to be invisible. Modern art seeks the anti-Form. The modern spiritual search for the expression of invisibility convinces many that Beauty is a chimera. There is art but not Beauty. The religious implications reveal why atheism is a characteristic modern phenomena. What kind of God can be conceived without Beauty? If pure expression successfully conveys the spiritual, then God can't be named only expressed. Indeed, liturgy cannot be response to the divine but God created in the human expression of art.

copy is eschewed in favor of the original. Their difference has no meaning. Meaning resides entirely in the original.[11] As such, these two philosophical poles illumine a theological aesthetics even as they fail to effectively engage the very special "difference" that a Christian theology presents, the "difference" described in the doctrine of the incarnation.

THE DECISIVE DIFFERENCE: THE INCARNATION

The incarnation is, in a sense, a very special type of "appearance." The incarnation is "appearance" not as phenomenon to the senses but as epiphany to the heart. As such, incarnation's epiphany contains, at once, kataphatic and apophatic dimensions. It is mystery. The mystery that is the incarnation raises Socrates' question, "can the invisible be imitated?", to a new level. How can the "image of God," the human being, give rise to his and her archetype, the original God? How can Jesus Christ be the "last Adam" and the God who created Adam? It is this particular relation between copy and original, a revelation more than an observation, that places theological aesthetics squarely as an attempt to understand the meaning of "difference." Indeed, the incarnation suggests that all "difference" is a gracious epiphany, a loving revelation. Thus, theological aesthetics distinguishes itself from philosophical aesthetics in its approach to the aesthetic relation between copy and original. Theological aesthetics asks the question of "difference" rather than the question of "identity." For only the question of "difference" asks about the nature of true love, a freedom making possible a sacrificial transcendence of identity. None, in our century, have made this point so clearly as the great Jesuit theologian Hans Urs von Balthasar.

Balthasar's justification for the centrality of the incarnation in a theological aesthetics is well worth quoting in full:

[11]I would argue that these attitudes towards "difference" emerge from modern Western cosmology. Newton's (and Leibnitz') calculus proposed a cosmos whose spatial and temporal dimensions could be envisioned in terms of the "differential" between two points in space or time rather than their "difference." The differential between two spatial or temporal points makes the difference between these two points ever smaller until the difference ideally vanishes and a single value emerges. Thus, the notion of the differential idealizes space and time. Such approach to the cosmos disengages our experience of the cosmos from our theories of the cosmos. See, e.g., Funkestein's discussion of the notion of "inertia" in Amos Funkestein, *Theology and the Scientific Imagination: From the Middle Ages to the Seventeenth Century* (Princeton, N.J.: Princeton University Press, 1986) 44.

Unity of nature, distinction of persons: this formula, . . . reminds us
above all that in Christ the one, concrete divine nature becomes revealed
and manifested in the world, precisely where this revelation is given as *a
sending and a being sent,* a remaining in the *background* and a coming
into the *foreground,* a remaining above and a descending and re-ascend-
ing. God's nature reveals itself in this twofoldness, and this in turn
points further to a selfhood which is also in the line of distinctions: it
points to *a third Reality* which unites the Sender and the Sent in a vital
way. The one God, who is invisible by nature, appears, but not in the
manner to which we are accustomed with worldly reality, namely, that
the same being, identical to itself (which may be a person), appears
while not appearing and enters visibility while at the same time remaining a ground that rests in itself. Rather, the one invisible God appears in
such a way that this polarity reveals itself to us as a personal relationship
within God's very nature. This is where God is an absolute mystery for
us, precisely in his revelation . . . what occurs is that the incomprehensible mystery . . . itself appears and becomes visible within God's manner of becoming manifest. This event cannot be reduced to any worldly
categories of Beauty, although it makes use precisely of the double ves-
sel offered by the world—form and its proper glory, on the one hand,
love and its glory, on the other—in order to make itself present. **Thus,
the categories of aesthetics are not simply annihilated, but rather raised
above themselves** in an incomprehensible positive way *(non destruit, sed
elevat, extollit, perficit naturam)* in order to contain something which is
infinitely greater than themselves (emphases mine).[12]

Thus, the "categories of aesthetics" are "raised above themselves"
through the decisive difference of the incarnation. A theologian approaches aesthetics differently than a philosopher. The aesthetics of the
theologian concern the human capacity to know (and love) the un-
knowable, to name the unnamable, to make visible the invisible. The
aesthetics of the theologian elevate the human capacity for the beautiful into the human capacity to know and love God, i.e., the *Capax Dei.*

THE *CAPAX DEI*

Some Catholics may associate the theology of Hans Urs von
Balthasar as a conservative theology opposite the progressive theology

---

[12]The emphases in the quote highlight the theme of the triadic nature of the incarnation, and the themes of foreground and background. These themes, as will be seen
later, will become essential in this proposal of a semiotic aesthetics. Von Balthasar,
Seeing the Form, 609–10.

of Karl Rahner. Von Balthasar's prolific writing culminates in an awe-some trilogy of theological aesthetics, *Theologik, Theodramatik* (trans-lated into Theo-Drama), and *Herrlichkeit* (translated into The Glory of the Lord). This trilogy represents, of course, the transcendentals, the True, the Good, and the Beautiful. Overall, they contain over a dozen volumes of breathtaking breadth and aguilar scope. Indeed, Louis Dupré, reviewer of von Balthasar's greatest work, *The Glory of the Lord*, exclaims

> With a feeling of great awe the reader closes the final volume of this last great *summa*, so original and so traditional, in which Tridentine theol-ogy attains its final, perhaps most beautiful expression.[13]

Dupré's assessment may explain why Rahner and not von Balthasar gripped the attention of those attending the Second Vatican Council. If Balthasar's theological aesthetics represents an impressive synthesis of Tridentine theology, then Rahner's transcendental anthropology repre-sents a progressive opening into the modern world. Rahner's theology served the interests of the Council well.

I would like, however, to suggest a re-assessment. Hans Urs von Balthasar belonged to a movement originating in France known as *ressourcement*, a return to the sources. Led principally by Jesuits at Fourviére and Dominicans at Le Saulchoir, *ressourcement* swept into its dynamic waters theologians such as Henri de Lubac, Yves Congar, Marie-Dominique Chenu, Jean Daniélou, and, of course, von Balthasar. *Ressourcement* believed that the Church ought to address the contem-porary situation but the conditions for doing so lay in faithful recovery of the tradition's sources. It was felt that the Tridentine church ossified such sources and prevented the Church from vitally interacting with the modern world. Indeed, the theologians of the *ressourcement* paved the way for the Second Vatican Council. None were so heroic in this at-tempt as von Balthasar. Dupré's assessment notwithstanding, von Balthasar sounded the Church's treasury of theological reflection for an original yet traditional synthesis. Such synthesis is less Tridentine than it is traditional. Furthermore, von Balthasar's aesthetic theological syn-thesis may still serve the needs of the contemporary Church.

Ironically, such synthesis of traditional sources may be more rele-vant in the postmodern world of today than in the modern times of Vatican Council II. Whereas modernity rejected the sources of its own

---

[13]Louis Dupré, "Hans Urs von Balthasar's Theology of Aesthetic Form," *Theological Studies* 49, no. 2 (June 1988) 314.

tradition, postmodernity now calls into question modernity's sources. As such, postmodernity calls for a re-look at traditional sources in order to re-think or go beyond modern assumptions. Rahner's work may have ushered the Church through the abyss of Modernity, but, von Balthasar's work, I believe, may help guide the Church out of the morass of postmodernism.[14] Von Balthasar's work does so through his retrieval and rethinking of aesthetic form.

I have shown how the issue of difference gave rise to Latin American and Latino theology. In the difference between the American Indian and the European Spaniard lay hell or redemption. From human difference as experienced in the Americas rose the twin issues of justice and differing visions of God. As such, von Balthasar (probably much to his surprise) joins Hispanic theology as a welcomed conversation partner. The issue of human difference as posed in the Americas, after all, is not very different than the issue of human nature which launched von Balthasar's aesthetic project. Both, in essence, refer to the human capacity to know and love insuperable difference, the "capacity" for God, the *Capax Dei*.

Von Balthasar's theological aesthetics have their roots as an attempt to rethink the relationship between nature and grace. Nature and grace may be seen as the locus for both a theological aesthetics and a theology of human difference. The relationship between nature and grace determines, e.g., how faith understands or explains the human capacity to "see" God, i.e., the *capax Dei* of a theological aesthetics. The relationship between nature and grace determines, as well, how faith might understand or explain the human capacity for differing "visions" of God, i.e., a theology of human difference. Thus, von Balthasar and Hispanics have similar if not identical projects. Both Hispanics and von Balthasar seek to understand how God may be "seen," and "seen" through differing visions. Hispanics, however, ask a further question. Can these visions change the world? The first question took von Balthasar to form. The second has generated a renewed interest among some Hispanics in the aesthetics of sign.

---

[14]Defining modernity or postmodernity would involve writing another book. In terms of my own understanding of these terms, I refer the reader to Alex García-Rivera, "Creator of the Visible and the Invisible: Liberation Theology, Postmodernism, and the Spiritual," *Journal of Hispanic/Latino Theology* 3, no. 4 (1996) 35–56.

The First Dimension of the Capax Dei: Intrinsic Grace

What greater difference can be imagined than between Creator and creature? Indeed, what other relationship can be as profound a well of meaning than this insuperable difference? Thus begins von Balthasar's investigation into a theological aesthetics. Von Balthasar first asked the question of creaturely difference through the influence of his mentor and teacher, Erich Przywara. Erich Przywara (1889–1972), a philosopher of religion from Munich, was von Balthasar's teacher during his philosophy studies (1931–1933) in the Jesuit seminary at Pullach. Przywara, along with Maréchal, were major critics of the neoscholastic orientation predominant in advanced Catholic studies of their time. Their criticism centered around a neoscholastic understanding of grace known as "extrincism."

Extrincism saw human nature as self-contained. Humans as creatures have self-sufficient resources to accomplish their goal of being human. In other words, humans can be human without any further assistance from God. Such a view makes grace extrinsic, an "addition," an undeserved "supplement," to human nature. As such, grace serves to add an additional "supernatural" aim to being human. Extrincism suggests that while it is true we do not need any further assistance from God to be human, we can be transformed through grace beyond this purely "natural" goal to a greater, an over-and-beyond existence, a "supernatural" human goal. Extrincism encourages a "two-story" view of human nature. Though human nature is capable of a "supernatural" goal, it is perfectly happy with its natural one. Thus, human nature appears neutral and indifferent to grace. Indeed, one can ask whether grace is needed at all.[15]

In response to extrincism, Maurice Blondel argued in *L'Action* (1893) that grace is an *intrinsic* rather than an *extrinsic* demand of the human spirit.[16] Blondel's view of grace led to two separate approaches against extrincism. One approach emphasized the subjective unity between Creator and creature, the other their objective difference. Rahner's theological anthropology, through Maréchal, is an example of the first approach. The notion of the subjective unity of all reality is a

[15]Hans Urs von Balthasar, *The von Balthasar Reader*, eds. Medard Kehland, S.J., and Verner Löser, S.J., trans. Robert J. Daly, S.J., A Crossroad Herder Book (New York: The Crossroad Publishing Company, 1997) 17–18.

[16]Maurice Blondel, *Action: Essay on a Critique of Life and a Science of Practice*, translation of: *L'Action*, original work published: Presses Universitaires de France, 1950 <1893>, trans. Olive Blanchette (Notre Dame, Ind.: University of Notre Dame Press, 1984).

theme of German idealism (Kant, Fichte, Hegel). Rahner exploits the theme by making connections between German idealism and Thomistic metaphysics using the model of the mystical uniting of God and human subject. To do so, Rahner demonstrates the unity of natural and spiritual realities. Thus, Rahner conceived and developed a transcendental anthropology; human beings are "spirits in the world."[17] As such, human and divine realities meet in the subjective reality of the individual spirit. In other words, God becomes present to human experience as the transcendental horizon which makes possible all human knowing and willing. Thus, God is always present in human experience "not as object [but] in the self-realization of the human spirit."[18]

The Second Dimension of the Capax Dei: The Analogy of Being

The other approach developed by Przywara and exploited by von Balthasar emphasizes the difference rather than the unity between Creator and creature.[19] Przywara's key concept is known as the *analogia entis*, the analogy of being. Although a difficult concept, it is nonetheless worth explaining. Rahner's transcendental theology may be seen as an answer to the thoroughly subjective question of human nature: *who am I?* It is a natural place to start for modern thinkers who wish to find a religious foundation to human being. Given a mechanical, Newtonian universe, where else but in the subjective spirit of the human can one find the motivation, the possibility of transcendence required for religious vision? Another possibility, however, remains. A more objective way to ask the question about the nature of being human might be to ask: *what am I?* It is an objective question requiring an objective answer. It is an approach, however, that grates hard against modern ears. How can something as transcending, as spiritual, as necessary of freedom, be found in the objective whatness of the universe? Yet this is the approach of von Balthasar and Przywara. They wish to show that the universe is more than a Newtonian watch untouched by divine hands except for that one time when a few words set the giant mechanism ticking. Hidden in the question the *what*, you see, an element of awareness waits to make its presence known. The very asking of the question, *what am I?*, presupposes a presence, that is, *that*

[17]Karl Rahner, *Spirit in the World,* trans. William Dych (New York: Herder and Herder, 1968).
[18]von Balthasar, *The von Balthasar Reader,* 18–19.
[19]Ibid., 18–20.

I am. The assertion *that I am* is the assertion of the philosophy of being, i.e., ontology.[20] The assertion *that I am* distinguishes itself from the assertion *what I am* in that it requires no explanation simply awareness. It is an act not a question. *What I am,* however, calls for explanation, for elaboration.

The significance of this approach is that it can be applied to everything in the universe. Thus, the objective approach transforms the human question into a cosmic one. This cosmic question answers that two assertions can be made of every creature in the universe: *that it is* and *what it is.* As such, these two assertions make paradoxical claims. *That things are* makes the claim that all creatures have something in common. They all participate in *being what they are. What things are,* on the other hand, makes a seeming antithetical claim that each creature possesses a unique particularity that makes it what it is. As John Riches points out,

> Conscious experience is experience of being in a world, being a part of a whole; and to experience another entity is to experience it likewise as a part of a whole. Thus the fundamental cognitive moment is the apprehension of participation, the participation of beings in being . . . . But if I am genuinely aware of the world as contingent, a different consequence suggests itself. I participate in the world, but I am not a function of the whole; I am aware of my own unique, non-necessary concrete being as distinct from the "necessity" of the world around. Yet all particular subsistents have the same characteristic of participation in the whole in a unique, non-functional manner.[21]

Thus, unique particularity as *beings* and universal participation in *being* are paradoxical cosmic claims made by the distinction between *what things are* and *that things are.* These cosmic assertions correspond to Aquinas' famous *real distinction* between being and essence.

The *real distinction,* i.e., the distinction between *that things are* and *what things are,* between presence and essence, sets up a divine analogy. God's "whatness" is also God's "isness." God is the "I am." God's presence

[20]Ontology has fallen into hard times and there are doubts that it can become a viable conversation partner for theologians. I do not agree with this assessment, but I do agree that ontology when it does rise itself from its contemporary ashes will have a very different form than its classical formulation. In any case, those who would disagree that the question of *what things are* does not necessarily raise a further question, *that things are,* must agree that if you do ask the question between *what things are* and *that things are,* their distinction can be appreciated even if, like Scotus, not fully accepted.

[21]John Riches, "Balthasar and Rahner," in *The Analogy of Beauty: The Theology of Hans Urs von Balthasar,* ed. John Riches (Edinburgh: T. & T. Clark Ltd., 1986) 21–22.

is God's essence. If all things can claim a real distinction between *what
they are* and *that they are,* then the **distinction** between "whatness" and
"isness" in things finds a kind of analogy in the **unity** of "whatness" and
"isness" in the divine "I am." As Erich Przywara himself put it:

> In this form the creaturely realm is the "analogy" of God. It is similar to
> God through its commonality of unity between its "being-what-it-is"
> [*Sosein:* that is, its essence] and its "being-there-at-all" [*Dasein:* that is,
> existence]. But even in this similarity, it is essentially dissimilar to God
> because God's form of unity of essence and existence is an "essential
> unity" while that of the creature is a "unity in tension." Now since the re-
> lation of essence and existence is the essence of "being," so God and crea-
> ture are therefore similar-dissimilar in "being"—that is, they are
> "analogous" to one another: and this is what we mean by *analogia entis,*
> analogy of being.[22]

Thus, the analogy between the real distinction in creatures and the divine unity of the "I am" corresponds to the analogy of being. As such,
the analogy of being is a complex and difficult notion. It attempts to express the Christian conviction of a participation of all things in the divine while, at the same time, preserving the difference between the
divine and the creature. In other words, the analogy of being expresses
the famous formula of the Fourth Lateran Council of 1215: "As great as
may be the similarity, so much greater must the dissimilarity between
creator and creature be preserved." In this the analogy of being has an
ancient ally: Pseudo-Dionysius.

Pseudo-Dionysius refers to Dionysius of Mars' hill, Paul's Athenian
convert, the Areopagite of Acts 17. His writings apparently date from
the sixth century (A.D. 540) and are associated with the Neoplatonism
of Proclus. Von Balthasar, however, rejects the claim that the system of
Pseudo-Dionysius is simply Christian Neo-Platonism. In perhaps his
most brilliant essay, von Balthasar claims Pseudo-Dionysius as an original Christian thinker who borrowed from Neo-Platonism but only to
create a brilliant and original synthesis. Pseudo-Dionysius also spoke of
the "dissimilar similarity" between creatures and the Creator.
"Dissimilar similarity" made all creatures *symbolon* or symbols in relation to the divine and allowed human beings to know and love God. As
Dionysius himself explains it:

---

[22]Erich Przywara, *Religionsphilosophie katholischer Theologie* (1926) quoted in
Edward T. Oakes, S.J., *Pattern of Redemption: The Theology of Hans Urs von Balthasar*
(New York: Continuum, 1997) 33.

Now there are two reasons for creating types for the typeless, for giving shape to what is actually without shape. First we lack the ability to be directly raised up to intelligible contemplations. We need our own upliftings that come naturally to us and which can raise before us the permitted forms of the marvelous and unformed sights. Second, it is most fitting to the mysterious passages of Scripture that the sacred and hidden truth about celestial intelligences be concealed through the inexpressible and sacred and be inaccessible to the *hoi polloi*.[23]

In ["dissimilar similarity"], one can "behold *[epistrophé]* the sacred forms attributed to it by the scriptures . . . so that we may be uplifted *[anagogé]* by way of the mysterious representations to their divine simplicity."[24] Thus,

To "behold" is to view the highest mysteries most reverently, indeed with "supramundane vision . . . the focus does not long remain on the descriptions themselves since the goal of their consideration, of this hermeneutical method is "that we may be uplifted." The beholder's spiritual movement "upward" is not an active ascent but rather a passive elevation. The contemplator of these sacred formations will not thereby climb upward but will be uplifted by another force. This uplifting takes place by means of the formation: the movement is not *away* from the images as undesirable, *but* precisely *through* them as the means to a higher realm. The Scriptural symbols are not disparaged but are rather valued in their temporary but indispensable role in the uplifting process. Yet the movement here described is not just vaguely or metaphorically "up": it is "to their divine simplicity."[25]

Pseudo-Dionysius makes plain the explanatory power of emphasizing the difference between the Creator and creatures. The difference makes possible an "uplifting," an "anagogy," which consists of a participation of the creature in the Creator made possible precisely because of its distance from the Creator. Thus, "dissimilar similarity" is, at once, a participation and a distancing. As such, Pseudo-Dionysius sets up a "dynamic" analogy, an anagogy. The "dissimilar similarity" of the creature creates a "dynamic" analogy, the anagogy of the lowly creature being lifted up into a grand vision of God.

This is exactly what von Balthasar wished to demonstrate through Przywara's analogy of being, without, of course, falling into some sort

---

[23]Pseudo-Dionysius, *The Divine Names*, in *Pseudo-Dionysius: The Complete Works*, ed. John Farina, Classics of Western Spirituality (New York: Paulist Press, 1987) II.140AB.

[24]Ibid., II.117AC.

[25]Paul Rorem, *Biblical and Liturgical Symbols Within the Pseudo-Dionysian Synthesis* (Toronto: Pontifical Institute of Medieval Studies, 1984) 55.

of Neo-Platonic emanationism. The analogy of being brings the human being into the incomprehensibility of God through the sensuality and presence of the natural objects of the world. All finite things in one way or another reveal something about God even while, as St. Augustine described, they give witness that "I am not He who made me." Indeed, it is because of the analogy of being that there could even exist a language about God. At the same time, however, the very act of conceptualizing God, of attempting to speak about God reveals God's utter otherness.

As such, von Balthasar's analogy of being works against Rahnerian transcendence, i.e., a privileged place (a horizon) from which one might contrast God and God's creation. The analogy of being plants the human being firmly in creation and from there God must be found and known. Thus, against Rahnerian transcendence, von Balthasar's analogy of being demands the human creature contemplate the Creator from within the very stuff of creation rather than from some transcendental horizon. As such, the analogy of being creates a "dynamic" analogy. Our very finitude becomes the means to contemplate the infinite only to realize the infinite breaking through any form, any concept, any symbol our finitude provides. Thus, von Balthasar provides an alternate view of the relationship between nature and grace. The "difference" between Creator and creature sets up a "dynamic" analogy dear to the human spirit. Our "dissimilar similarity" of creature to Creator allows the human spirit to participate in the knowledge and the love of God but only by having every concept, form, or symbol irrupted in the very act of knowing and loving God. Nowhere is this dynamic "analogy," the analogy of being, more radically demonstrated than in the incarnation, the Word become flesh.

The Third Dimension of the Capax Dei: The Word Became Flesh

As presented above, the incarnation raises philosophical aesthetics to a level only theology can occupy. "No one has ever seen God. It is God the only Son, in the bosom of the Father, who has revealed him" (John 1:18). Jesus, the Word become flesh, reveals the Father. Jesus affords human beings the "sight" of God, beauty itself. That the Word brings sight raises a question for a theological aesthetics about the relationship between "seeing" and "hearing." Indeed, as von Balthasar's masterly interpreter, Edward Oakes, points out, theological aesthetics is to be understood not simply as a theology of "sight" but also of "hearing." It is the "aesthetics" of music that inspire von Balthasar not the "aesthetics" of a painting. Why?

> The eye is the organ with which the world is possessed and dominated, the immediate reflection—in the sphere of the senses—of the rational intellect that comprehends. Through the eye, the world is *our* world, in which we are not lost; rather, it is subordinate to us as an immeasurable dwelling space with which we are familiar. The other side of this material function denotes distance, separateness. All the other senses touch their object in some direct manner, and they have at least an instinct to come as closely as possible to this object. Only the eye needs separateness, in order to see. It is not through a close encounter that it comes to terms with things but through the look from a distance that tames them—the way trainers stare down wild animals in a circus ring.[26]

In other words, sight implies perceptive control and conquest, while hearing implies surrender to the perception. The latter cannot choose (we can't stop our hearing) what to hear, the former can. As such, "hearing" becomes the central act of theological aesthetics. Sight, on the other hand, belongs more to the eschatological, e.g., the beatific vision. Some day we may "see" God face to face, but in our pilgrimage here on earth we must, instead, strive to "hear." The point here is not a call to be submissive to the point of being victims, but, rather, to emphasize the ability to perceive God while, at the same time, emphasizing that the "typeless" and "shapeless" God makes all perceptions relative. "For the beauty of hearing sounds, especially the sounds of words and music, is that sounds always remain ever evanescent, and therefore ungraspable, even as they communicate."[27]

What, then, is the relation of "hearing" to "seeing"? Is von Balthasar denigrating the sense of sight in favor of the sense of sound? The answer, of course, is no! Von Balthasar has no interest in denigrating sight over sound. Rather, he reveals an important theological relationship. Von Balthasar's theological aesthetics uses the metaphor of sight extensively. Nonetheless, the metaphor of sight must be located within theology. For von Balthasar, the metaphor of sight aptly applies to the act of faith. Faith "sees" the form. As such, the relationship between "seeing" and "hearing" becomes clear. Faith "sees" but only in having "heard." The Word becomes flesh but only when Mary hears the Word. In other words, von Balthasar is not after a theology of "hearing" but rather he is after a theology of "seeing" that most resembles "hearing." As Peter Casarella has so aptly pointed out, Von Balthasar finds such a model in language.

---

[26]Hans Urs von Balthasar, *Spouse of the Word,* vol. 2, *Explorations in Theology* (San Francisco: Ignatius Press, 1991) 474 quoted in Oakes, op. cit., 136.

[27]Oakes, op. cit., 137.

> Central to Hans Urs von Balthasar's trinitarian theology is the notion
> that the person of God the Word is the "exegesis" of God the Father. . . .
> By reading and interpreting God the Word, those possessing the eyes of
> faith see the dynamism and fecundity of the Father expressed in a con-
> crete, human form. As Bonaventure states, the Son is the very language
> of the Father. Once can deduce from this doctrine that human expres-
> sion is an adequate analogue to the perfectly unique mode of expression
> by which the word exegetes the Father. In other words, language imitates
> the outpouring within the divine Trinity in that it manifests a unique
> gift for self-expression.[28]

As such, the generation of God the Word from the silent ground of the
intra-Trinitarian expression of loving difference reveals that the expression of the Word is inseparable but distinguishable from its form. Thus,
von Balthasar can say: "the Father is Ground, the Son appearance."[29]

This dynamic polarity between expression and form of God-the-
Word holds analogously to human words as well. Human speech does
not point statically to some mental word but, rather, "makes what is
meaningful in the world really present through the expressiveness of
speech itself."[30] Clifford Geertz makes the point with his famous example of considering the difference in meaning between a "twitch" and
a "wink."[31] Twitches and winks may be similar expressions but there is

---

[28]Peter J. Casarella, "The Expression and Form of the Word: Trinitarian
Hermeneutics and the Sacramentality of Language in Hans Urs von Balthasar's
Theology," *Renascence* 48, no. 2 (Winter 1996) 111–35.

[29]Hans Urs von Balthasar, *The Glory of the Lord: A Theological Aesthetics*, eds. Joseph
Fession and John Riches (New York: Crossroads, 1983) 610.

[30]Casarella, op. cit., 111.

[31]This is a reference, of course, to Clifford Geertz' proposal that culture be seen as
". . . essentially semiotic. Believing, with Max Weber, that man is an animal suspended
in webs of significance he himself has spun, I take culture to be those webs, and the
analysis of it to be therefore not an experimental science in search of law but an interpretive one in search of meaning." His famous example for demonstrating this point
was the difference between a *twitch* and a blink:

> Consider he says, two boys rapidly contracting the eyelids of their right eyes. In one, this is
> an involuntary *twitch;* in the other, a conspiratorial signal to a friend. The two movements
> are identical . . . yet the difference . . . between a *twitch* and a *wink* is vast . . . Suppose,
> he continues, there is a third boy, who "to give malicious amusement to his cronies," paro-
> dies the first boy's *wink,* as amateurish, clumsy, obvious, and so on. Here, too a socially es-
> tablished code exists . . . only now it is not conspiracy but ridicule that is in the air . . .
> [The] point is that between what Ryle calls the "thin description" of what the rehearser . . .
> is doing . . . and the "thick description" of what he is doing . . . lies the object of ethnog-
> raphy: a stratified hierarchy of meaningful structures in terms of which twitches, winks,
> fake-winks, parodies, rehearsals of parodies are produced, perceived, and interpreted.
> Clifford Geertz, *The Interpretation of Cultures* (New York: Basic Books, Inc., 1973) 5–7.

a world of difference in what is being expressed. At the same time, both twitches and winks are expressed as they are because of what they wish to express, i.e., their form. As such, expression and form in human communication are, as in God-the-Word, distinguishable yet inseparable. Von Balthasar, however, would go further. The polarity of form and expression is at the heart of the real distinction. As Peter Casarella puts it: "Through its participatory being, creaturely being is 'caught' between its expressed form (its definable essence) and its expressivity of being itself *(esse ab alio)*. The act of being a creature is irreducible to either its form (essence) or its source of expression because essence coincides with the pure act of being in God alone."[32] Thus, the polarity of expression and form that has its grounds in the generation of God the Word from the outpouring of loving difference of the Trinity has its analogue in the being of creatures.

The distinction yet inseparability of expression and form goes to the heart of Albertus' and Sophia's dialogue. The unity between form and expression does not allow expression to be a blind copy of what is being expressed. Expression is not an epiphenomenon of form. Thus, a "wink" by an actual human being is experienced quite differently than a "wink" by a human being on a TV screen. A material hologram copy of Michelangelo's *David* assumes that the expression is the form. As such, it is "blind" to the form. The distinction between form and expression, on the other hand, allow Raphael to successfully "copy" what Michelangelo's *David* wished to express. Raphael's copy "sees" the form. In other words, a successful copy of a great work of art requires that the relation between form and its expression, i.e., both their unity and their inseparability, be preserved. The unity and the distinguishability between expression and form describe the phenomenon of "seeing" in the aesthetic sense. The material hologram cannot "see" the form of Michelangelo's *David*. It is "blind" in the aesthetic sense because it cannot distinguish between the form and its expression. Raphael, however, can "see" the form. He is affected and shaped by the expression of the form of Michelangelo's *David*. Only then can he go on and "reproduce" a copy. It is as if Michelangelo's *David* had to be imprinted on Raphael's soul before it could be expressed again. This is, in fact, the model von Balthasar uses and it has its origins in the theology of Bonaventure and in the relation between mystical and ordinary experience.

The example demonstrates the semiotic roots of some of von Balthasar's claims which will be developed further.

[32]Casarella, op. cit., 119.

The Fourth Dimension of the Capax Dei: "Seeing the Form"

Von Balthasar rails against the loss of the "full" Christian experience. Such loss lies in the history of the Christian concept of experience which too easily unites mystical and "ordinary" experience. Such unreflected unity lay itself open to the anti-spiritual acids of Modernity that questioned such unquestioned unity. Von Balthasar agrees that it is false to insist on an uncalled for unity between "ordinary" and Christian experience. Nonetheless, he points out that there is an important continuity between the two. Von Balthasar tells us that mystical experience is

> an experience which prolongs another experience by deepening, purifying, clarifying, transcending, and crowning it. . . . Only if the integral Christian experience can be shown, if not to initiate, then surely to prepare for mystical experience, can it be proven that the latter is not a degenerative phenomenon. Only if Christian experience does not stand over against mystical experience in heterogenous fashion will authentic Christian living not be undervalued or mystical experience overvalued. This way of stating the question is of decisive importance. Despite all that is said in Scripture and the tradition of the Fathers, Christian experience has not been sufficiently investigated in itself because it was simply confounded with mystical experience; in consequence men sought either to rediscover in normal Christian life an experience of the mystical type (so the heretics) or to deny its existence (so the Catholics).[33]

Thus mystical experience "deepens" ordinary experience. It does so not as the private experience of an individual but as an experience "within the context of the Church." It is "a spiritual becoming which is incarnate and is lived within the Church's own process of becoming."[34] As such, mystical experience combines with "ordinary" experience in the understanding of the *capax Dei*. Nowhere is this clearer than in the mystical experience of the crucified seraph suffered by St. Francis.

The Feast of the Holy Cross found St. Francis praying fervently in his cell in Mt. Alvernia. Francis implored the Lord to let him experience some of the pain he had undergone in his agony. At that moment, St. Francis had a vision. The story is told by St. Bonaventure:

> On a certain morning about the feast of the Exaltation of the Cross, while Francis was praying on the mountainside, he saw a Seraph with six fiery and shining wings descend from the height of heaven. And when in

---

[33]von Balthasar, *Seeing the Form*, 300.
[34]Ibid., 300–01.

swift flight the Seraph had reached a spot in the air near the man of God, there appeared between the wings the figure of a man crucified, with his hands and feet extended in the form of a cross and fastened to a cross. Two of the wings were lifted above his head, two were extended for flight and two covered his whole body. When Francis saw this, he was overwhelmed and his heart was flooded with a mixture of joy and sorrow. He rejoiced because of the gracious way Christ looked upon him under the appearance of the Seraph, but the fact that he was fastened to a cross *pierced his soul with a sword* of compassionate sorrow (Luke 2:35). He wondered exceedingly at the sight of so unfathomable a vision, realizing that the weakness of Christ's passion was in no way compatible with the immortality of the Seraph's spiritual nature. Eventually he understood by a revelation from the Lord that divine providence had shown him this vision so that, as Christ's lover, he might learn in advance that he was to be totally transformed into the likeness of Christ crucified, not by the martyrdom of his flesh, but by the fire of his love consuming his soul.[35]

St. Francis' impression by the crucified seraph describes what von Balthasar calls the "fundamental experience" of Bonaventure.[36] It is the experience of the dissimilar similar. The incongruity between the "infirmity of the Passion" and the "immortality of the seraphic spirit" result in the experience of joy, compassion, and wonder. Indeed, it is in that "perplexity" that St. Francis encounters enlightenment. Such enlightenment, however, involves a "consuming fire of the soul" which transforms St. Francis into the express image of Christ crucified. Thus, St. Francis, in ecstatic wonder, becomes "imprinted" with the crucified seraph. His body now, in turn, becomes the expression of the impression of a marvelous image.

Von Balthasar sees in this "fundamental experience" of Bonaventure a reshaping of the Pseudo-Dionysian tradition. "It is significant that although the power of the expression goes out from the crucified, the bodily sign is imprinted only because Francis . . . had already himself become in spirit an expression of the love of the crucified."[37] What von Balthasar refers to is St. Francis' embracing of poverty as preparing the way for the "imprint" by the crucified seraph. Pseudo-Dionysius' *via*

---

[35]Bonaventure, "The Life of St. Francis," in *Bonaventure*, trans. Ewert Cousins, preface by Ignatius Brady, O.F.M., The Classics of Western Spirituality (New York: Paulist Press, 1978) 305–06.

[36]Hans Urs von Balthasar, *Studies in Theological Style: Clerical Styles*, vol. 2 of *The Glory of the Lord: A Theological Aesthetics*, trans. of *Herrlichkeit: Eine theologische Ästhetik, II: Fächer der Stile, I Klerical Stile*, ed. John Riches, trans. Andrew Louth, McDonagh, and Brian McNeil (New York: Crossroads, 1984) 270.

[37]Ibid.

negativa transforms into Franciscan poverty, the "stripping away of all things" so that the "simplicity" of God if not the conceptualization of God can become one with Francis. As such, a certain relationship between subject and object is proposed that sounds alien to modern (and postmodern) ears. "The crucified seraph is not only the object of contemplative loving meditation: he is also active and expresses himself by impressing himself, which is to say his wounds, in Francis."[38]

This expression by impression speaks of a certain kind of epistemology that was quite familiar to the classical tradition. Beauty comes to St. Francis as Wisdom. The six wings of the crucified Seraph represent the six paths to wisdom. Indeed, "the whole tradition from Augustine, Denys, Bernard, and the Victorines understood the divine glory as the beauty of his Wisdom."[39] Wisdom *(sapientiae)* differs from philosophical or scientific knowledge *(scientiae)*. If *scientiae* requires confidence in the certainty of its truth, *sapientiae* requires humility before its knowledge. In order to experience wisdom, there must be a kind of poverty—a receptivity for that which is other. Bonaventure identifies this receptivity with Franciscan poverty. As such, Francis' poverty makes him receptive to Beauty's wisdom by allowing him like warm wax to be shaped into a receptable ready to receive the crucified seraph's wounds. Thus, Bonaventure adds the notion of being "impressed" in order to become "expressed" into the loving ecstasy of God's beauty. This is Bonaventure's "anagogy." If Pseudo-Dionysius "anagogy" lifted up the creature in an almost pre-determined way, Bonaventure's *anagogicus excessus* (anagogical ecstasy) requires a certain receptivity of the creature, a poverty towards being "shaped," **a receptivity for that which is other.**

It is this receptivity that explains, in part, what von Balthasar means by "seeing" the form. "Seeing" the form, like the act of hearing, is not a selective or controlling act, but an act of surrender to that which is "seen." But what, exactly, is "seen"? Perhaps only in this act of receptivity can von Balthasar's unique sense of form may best be described. For what is being received is the form of that which is other. The reception of that which is other makes unique demands. To receive that which is other means that the other must be received wholly. That which is other can only be experienced in its fullness. Any diminishment of its "otherness," any reduction of detail, any attempt at selectivity is to lose the experience altogether. For it is in the experience of otherness that the

[38]Ibid., 271.
[39]Ibid., 270.

inbreaking of God's glory becomes possible. Thus, form, for von Balthasar, is inseparably tied to the experience of otherness and the experience of otherness refers to the experience of a unique whole. The crucified seraph, for example, must be experienced in its unique otherness. Its difference must be experienced whole. Form constitutes such experience. As such, form concerns the wholesome uniqueness that is other. Form, in von Balthasar's words, is

> a totality of parts and elements, grasped as such, existing and defined as such, which for its existence requires not only a "surrounding world" but ultimately being as a whole: in this need it is . . . a "contracted" representation of the "absolute," in so far as it transcends its parts as members and controls them in its own confined territory.[40]

"Seeing" the form, then, amounts to the capacity to receive the whole of a unique difference. That capacity depends on our willingness to be "formed" by the requirements of that which is other. Having been "shaped" to that which is other, the other in its total otherness becomes an experience of *excessus,* of being transported out of oneself. Thus, "seeing" the form is the expression of the impression which the form makes with its glorious splendor on the beholder who is taken out of him and herself in an anagogy, a "lifting up," towards God. "The form of the beautiful is the glory of God *(kabod, doxa)* whose splendor seizes and enraptures."[41]

Von Balthasar's theological aesthetics, then, cannot be separated from the experience of difference. It involves two key concepts, form and "seeing." Form concerns the authentic communication of that which is other by keeping its unique difference intact from any reductionism or generalization. "Seeing" is, paradoxically, an *act* of *receptivity* to that which is other. As such, "seeing," in von Balthasar's sense, describes what I call an epistemology of "objective affection." In order to receive the form of the beautiful our affections must be "shaped" or "formed" toward the form. This "shaping" of the affections occurs objectively in that it is not the psychology of the subject that crafts the shape of the affections but, rather, it is the form itself in its otherness to the subject that provokes and initiates the receptacle that becomes the subject's affections. Thus, von Balthasar introduces a radical objectivity

[40]Hans Urs von Balthasar, *The Realm of Metaphysics in Antiquity,* op. cit. 29.

[41]Angelo Scola, *Hans Urs von Balthasar: A Theological Style,* originally *Hans Urs von Balthasar: Uno stile teologico* (Milan: Editoriale Jaca Book, 1991); *Ressourcement: Retrieval and Renewal in Catholic Thought* (Grand Rapids, Mich.: William B. Eerdmans, 1995) 2.

that takes theological aesthetics far away from a merely subjective or psychological analysis.

FROM FORM TO SIGN

But how can such a radical objectivity be analyzed? It is this question that, I believe, exposes the greatest weakness of von Balthasar's theological aesthetics. The move towards objectivity has as one of its greatest motives the reconciliation between faith and reason. Von Balthasar's theological aesthetics takes us to that crucial intersection in a poetic and awesome *tour de force* of the theological tradition. Like Dante who was led by Virgil (Reason) through the Purgatorio to meet beautiful Beatrice (Faith), von Balthasar takes us to the threshold between Reason and Faith. There stands the radical objectivity of the form, at once accessible to Reason and Faith. But is ecstasy reasonable? Is rapture? More important, are there deceptive ecstasies? If so, how can one tell between a deceptive or false ecstasy and a true one? Or does von Balthasar believe all ecstasy is true and good?

The answer to these questions is hard to discern in von Balthasar's theological aesthetics. I would like to suggest that answers to these questions requires a closer examination of the nature of that radical objectivity as it relates Faith and Reason. This, I believe, can be done if one makes the move from concentrating on the traditional notion of form to the more general notion of sign. The notion of sign has potentially aesthetic development. A sign, after all, also refers to making visible the invisible. Towards such a development, we shall continue our development of von Balthasar's initial insight into theological aesthetics by bringing into conversation the great American philosophers of signs, Charles Sanders Peirce and Josiah Royce. Their development of the logic of signs reveals a fundamental aesthetic orientation of sign that may elucidate the relationship between Faith and Reason that is central to the radical objectivity of a theological aesthetics.

4

The Community of the True

I remember a dark time. While I was pastor of a struggling Hispanic congregation in the Pennsylvania Dutch town of Allentown, an ambitious Italian-American city council woman decided to run for mayor on the strength of a popular universal. She stood on a street corner not far from where I lived, a Hispanic *barrio,* and began her press conference. "Ninety-nine percent of the crimes committed in the city of Allentown are committed by Hispanics." A generalization had been made. A universal had been claimed of me, this particular Hispanic, Alex Garcia-Rivera.[1] I also remember another dark time: the death of my father. Generalizations were also made but this time I felt comfort. My father possessed intelligence, kindness, and a contagious happiness. I nodded with agreement. These, indeed, described my father.

---

[1] The official outcry was, of course, predictable. The police department gave out figures which contradicted the hopeful mayor-to-be's generalization. No actual figures, however, could dissuade the conviction of her supportive constituency. This was their belief if not their experience. Not soon after the press conference, I received a phone call from outraged Hispanics. "Will you join us on a march to her house?" The request chilled my blood. Such an action could only end in violence. I begged my friend to wait. I had another plan. Quickly I called religious leaders, Protestant and Catholic, and we agreed. The next day we would hold a public exorcism at the very corner from which this evil generalization had been launched. Indeed, the next day, a Lutheran bishop, a dozen religious leaders, and myself began a march from my church to that terrible corner. Along the way we picked up supporters. By the time we arrived, over a hundred marched with us. While the cameras whirred, the bishop began those powerful words:

Both these experiences concern universals, claims of an invisible but common nature applicable to a collection of individuals.[2] Universals have fallen on hard times. We know them today as stereotypes, ideologies, abstractions, and generalizations (in the pejorative sense). Yet my experience above with two very different types of "universals" leads me to suspect this current characterization of universals. After all, one universal rang true while the other was patently false. Nonetheless, one cannot ignore the reasons why our current society has lost faith in universals. The reality of stereotypes, for example, provides a good reason for believing that universals are illusionary. Stereotypes, in the name of universality, distort reality and bring suffering to the world. Yet it is this very nature of the stereotype that raises the question. If stereotypes, ideologies, abstractions, and generalizations, by their very nature, are falsehoods, distortions of particular reality, then why not attack their very falsehood rather than throw away, indeed, despair over the possibility of universals? If stereotypes are falsehoods, then they are not universals. Ideologies do not claim a reference to the true, but service to a dominant power. Because falsehoods exist that lie about their claim to universal reality does not mean that universals are not real. Indeed, how else can one respond to such falsehoods? If we cannot love justice, then what motivates us to expose the stereotype? If we cannot experience kindness, then how can we reject the lies of the cruel?

If we do not believe in universals, then we are forced into a never-ending, despairing struggle with falsehoods, cruelty, and chaos. We shall never know prophetic challenge against powerful claims, heroic good shaming cowardly cruelty, and joy in the midst of suffering giving lie to the cynical implications of evil. What, then, has driven us to abandon the project of discovering the reality of the universals? At heart, I believe, is despair over understanding the meaning of difference. Faced with the reality of difference, we see only the difference it-

---

"I adjure you evil serpent. . . ." The exorcism done, we went back to our work. That same night, the hopeful city councilwoman appeared in the news once again. "I can't understand why the bishops think I am an evil person. I don't deserve that kind of treatment. I was trying to wake up this town to a menace it is facing . . . ," and so on. The result was a happy one. There was no violence. The city councilwoman lost the election, and for quite a long time never made outrageous generalizations about Hispanics again. The exorcism, apparently, worked!

[2]In the case of my father, kindness is a virtue not solely possessed by him but also by other individuals.

self and not the meaning of the difference.[3] If difference, and, human difference in particular, has no meaning but is simply difference itself, then despair and cynicism fill in the void of our lack of understanding. And when despair and cynicism inform our experience of difference, then abusive power is soon to follow. Arbitrary difference has little defense against arbitrary power. Meaningful difference, on the other hand, can not be manipulated so easily. The meaning of difference, however, is the heart of the reality of the universal.

The crisis in the belief of the reality of the universal is, in a sense, a crisis in confidence in the reality of the invisible.[4] The singular individual can be seen with the eyes of our senses. Universals, on the other hand, are invisible to our organic eyes. One does not "see" goodness, for example, through the vitreous humor of our bodily eyes. It is this "invisibility" that makes universals so difficult to demonstrate. Nonetheless, there was a time when their reality was unquestioned. Though not seen by the eyes of the body, they were felt to become visible through the "eyes" of the soul.[5] This conviction has lost its force among the educated of Western society. The intellectual cosmology of the twentieth century has become a dichotomy of what C. P. Snow called the "two cultures."[6] I would describe the situation as a Platonism without the reality of the Forms. Whatever the actual situation may be, it appears that

[3]Leonard Lawlor makes this point in comparing Ricoeur and Derrida. Recognizing the reality of true difference, Derrida opts for a type of knowing based on the difference itself while Ricoeur argues for knowing as the meaning of difference. If the significance of difference is simply the difference itself, then meaning is composed arbitrarily. As such, power plays the most significant role in shaping social meaning. Arbitrary difference lends itself to manipulation. Meaningful difference, on the other hand, is not so open to being manipulated arbitrarily. Leonard Lawlor, *Imagination and Chance: The Difference Between the Thought of Ricoeur and Derrida*, Intersections: Philosophy and Critical Theory (New York: State University of New York Press, 1992).

[4]What do we mean when we confess in the Nicene Creed that we believe in the Creator of all things, visible and invisible? Can we today believe in an invisible creation, in the reality of the invisible? Such are the theological stakes. For a more thorough discussion on the theological implications of the invisible creation, see Alex García-Rivera, "Creator of the Visible and the Invisible," op. cit.

[5]I am referring to the long tradition known as the "spiritual senses." For an excellent summary, see Karl Rahner, "La doctrine des 'Sens Spirituels' au Moyen-Age," *Revue d'Ascétique et de Mystique* 14, no. 55 (1933) 263–99.

[6]By the two cultures, Snow refers to the two main intellectual movements of the century, the humanities and the natural sciences. The intellectual heritage of Western society is, at present, divided among these two major intellectual ways of life. C. P. Snow, *The Two Cultures: And a Second Look* (Cambridge: Cambridge University Press, 1969).

either the invisible exists only as construct of our mind, or the invisible exists only as some reality counter to our experience.[7] Thus, it takes some courage to call for a reconsideration of the reality of universals. Yet the experiences described above convince me that such an enterprise may be rather fecund.

At stake in such a belief stands a special set of "universals," the true, the good, and the beautiful. First encountered in the chapter on von Balthasar, the transcendentals are, in a sense, "universals" of the Whole. Transcendentals cannot be confined to any one group of individuals. They surpass (*transcendere*) all limits. Scotus, for example, defined the transcendentals as "whatever cannot be contained under any genus."[8] Thus, all that is participates in the true, the good, and the beautiful.[9] Theologians prize the transcendentals in the deep conviction that they constitute as well names for God who is True, Good, and even, Beauty itself. The loss of belief in the transcendentals, in von Balthasar's opinion (and mine), has led to a contemporary nihilism with its social ramifications of despair. Thus, von Balthasar calls on an awesome lineup of testimony from Augustine to Hopkins as witnesses to the true, the good and the beautiful. Indeed, one comes away from reading such testimony thoroughly awed by their eloquence. We leave von Balthasar's advocacy for a theological aesthetics inspired. At least, I was. Nonetheless, such inspiration leads to frustration without a clear idea of how theological aesthetics "works." Von Balthasar inspires but gives precious little insight on how a theological aesthetics might take concrete form and become viable for us today. Inspiring as it is, von Balthasar's theological aesthetics

---

[7] I am referring to Amos Funkestein's brilliant analysis of the roots of modern science which he describes as the method of the "counterfactual conditional." When we roll a ball on the ground, for example, our experience is that such a rolling ball always comes to a stop. The law of inertia, on the other hand, claims that, barring other forces, a ball set in motion will continue in motion. Inertia, then, describes a reality counter to our experience. See, Amos Funkestein, *Theology and the Scientific Imagination: From the Middle Ages to the Seventeenth Century* (Princeton, N.J.: Princeton University Press, 1986).

[8] *Oxoniensis*, 1, d.8, q.3, n.19, IX, 598a: *Ita transcendens quodcumque nullum habet genus sub quo contineatur* as quoted in Allan B. Wolter, O.F.M., *The Transcendentals and Their Function in the Metaphysics of Duns Scotus*, Philosophy Series (St. Bonaventure, N.Y.: The Franciscan Institute, 1946) 8.

[9] The number of transcendentals has varied. Almost all agree that unity, truth, and goodness belong to the "necessary notes of being." As necessary notes of being, the transcendentals are distinct but not separate. Each presupposes the other. Johannes Baptist Lotz, "Transcendentals," in *Sacramentum Mundi*, Karl Rahner, ed. (London: Herder and Herder, 1970) 285. The beautiful, nonetheless, is explicitly called for by St. Bonaventure.

becomes a caged spirit unless it can be shown how it engages the concrete challenges raised by the powerful nihilism of our day.

Part of this task necessitates facing head on the loss of belief in the reality of the invisible. At the heart of the problem is the philosophy of being that guides and founds von Balthasar's theological aesthetics. Since Heidegger, theology's reliance on the philosophy of being (now known derisively as "onto-theology") has come under devastating attack. The response of theologians to this postmodern devastation might be characterized by two extremes: retrenchment and abandon. Retrenchment characterizes that response to the call for the death of onto-theology by a dogmatic fundamentalism about the ontological tradition. Like an ostrich that buries its head, retrenchment heads quietly underground and hopes that the storm against ontological thought blows by. The merits of this position include recognizing the value of a long and fruitful tradition. Its failings might be a lack of confidence in the viability of the tradition itself. Ontological thought has not weathered intellectual squalls for these hundreds of years by going underground. Abandonment, on the other hand, characterizes a response fully engaged in the call for the death of onto-theology. Theologians like Jean Luc Marion, for example, call for a theology based on the *God without Being*.[10] Such theologians courageously face the storm of nihilism by demonstrating theology at home even in the emptiness of a world without being. They do so, however, in reaction to a storm rather than the flowering of a tradition. It is theology taking cover from the rain, rather than using the rain to water its gardens. Between the Charybdis of retrenchment and the Scylla of abandonment, there lies, however, a third possibility.

A more fruitful response than retrenchment or abandonment would be an approach appreciating the insights of a philosophy of being even as it transforms it. No one has done this more masterly than the American philosopher Charles S. Peirce. Peirce recognized through his study of Ockham, Scotus, and Kant that at the heart of the modern loss of belief in the reality of the universals was the issue of difference. Can something real be said about two very different individuals that somehow applies to both of them without destroying their individuality? Ockham, through his nominalism, said no. Kant finessed the question (on the side of nominalism) with his transcendental philosophy.

---

[10]Marion, Jean-Luc, *God without Being* (Chicago and London: University of Chicago Press, 1991).

Scotus, however, provided precious insights that allowed Peirce to develop what has become a major field of study in philosophy and linguistics: semiotics, the science of signs. Peirce's notion of sign was meant as a philosophically responsible response to the lack of belief in the reality of the universal. The sign corresponds to a triadic relation issuing from the difference between two individuals and an *interpretant,* the carrier of generality which allows the two individuals to be compared or contrasted. The significance and implications of Peirce's notion of sign for a theological aesthetics is a major project of this book. It provides, I believe, the philosophical substance that complements the theological inspiration of von Balthasar's "seeing the form." It is Hispanic theology's insight into the redemptive nature of sign, however, that will prove to be the most effective response to today's nihilism. Together with Peirce and von Balthasar, Hispanic theology closes a circuit of systems full of intellectual and inspirational energy. The result, I hope, will be a set of concepts and relationships that may be less a system than a semiotic domain, i.e., a pool of semantically related notions with the power and force to convince.[11] Thus closing the circuit, my hope soars towards the revitalizing of a theological aesthetics that affirms an ecclesial tradition born in the Americas and recovers an ancient, even beautiful, tradition.

CHARLES SANDERS PEIRCE

Charles Sanders Peirce (1839–1914), though making his major contributions in the nineteenth century, could very well be the philosopher that provides the notional structures that take us into the twenty-first century. Little appreciated in his own century, he is hailed today by many as one of the most original and productive thinkers in the history of thought. Not only a philosopher but also a scientist, he was that rarity of modern philosophers, a philosopher who held a deep respect for thought while at the same time having an equally deep respect for the "otherness" of Nature. He was, like Scotus, a subtle thinker and much of his thought was misunderstood by his contemporaries. Peirce founded, for example, the philosophy of pragmatism only to rename it pragmaticism against those (William James, for one) who developed pragmatism into something he himself could not recognize. Indeed, if

---

[11]See my discussion on semiotic domains in chapter 3 of Alex García-Rivera, *St. Martin de Porres,* op. cit.

today pragmatism has a bad name, it is not because it was ill conceived. The pragmatism with the bad name is not the pragmatism of Peirce. Thus, a return to study Peirce's pragmatism is not an attempt to revitalize a worn-out nineteenth century doctrine but, rather, to rediscover a subtle and profound insight by one of this world's greatest minds. Peirce's pragmatism is the inevitable conclusion of his theory of signs which he named semiotics. Peirce's theory of signs, in turn, responds to Ockham's razor. Peirce saw Ockham's nominalism contaminating every nook and cranny of intellectual thought in his day and exemplified in the philosophy of Kant. It was, in fact, his study of Kant that convinced him to return to the medieval sources which were Kant's conversation partners. There he found Aquinas, Ockham, and, most significantly, Duns Scotus.

A DIFFERENT RAZOR

If the philosophy of being has lost its ancient force, it may be because Modernity and its postmodern conclusions have been bewitched by Ockham's razor.[12] Ockham, the great Franciscan medieval philosopher, eschewed interminable scholastic speculation. "Get to the point," might be his motto. Thus, he slashed at intricate philosophical arguments by insisting that the simpler argument was the most logical one. One can ascertain the significance of Ockham's razor by regarding the considerable sympathy his battle cry holds for us today. "Get to the

---

[12]I realize there are many opinions concerning the proper relationship between Modernity and Postmodernism. I hold that Postmodernism is the ultimate expression of Modernity. As such it is not different from Modernity but its fullest expression or, at least, the consequence of its foundational presuppositions. On Ockham's thought, the reader can consult the following: Eugene R. Fairweather, ed. and trans., *A Scholastic Miscellany: Anselm to Ockham*, The Library of Christian Classics, vol. X (Philadelphia: Westminster Press, 1956); Frederick Copleston, *Ockham to Suárez*, vol. 3 of *A History of Philosophy*, The Bellamine Series, vol. XIV (London: Burns and Oates, 1968); Michael J. Loux, trans., *Ockham's Theory of Terms*, vol. 1 of *The Summa Logicae* (Notre Dame, Ind.: University of Notre Dame Press, 1974); Alfred J. Freddoso, trans. and introduction, Henry Schurrman, trans. *Ockham's Theory of Proportions*, vol. 2 of *The Summa Logicae* (Notre Dame, Ind.: University of Notre Dame Press, 1980); William of Ockham, *Philosophical Writings: A Selection*, Philotheus Boehner, trans. and introduction reprint, 1957, The Library of Liberal Arts, founder Oskar Piest (Indianapolis: Bobbs-Merrill, 1964); Etienne Gilson, *The Spirit of Medieval Philosophy*, A. H. C. Downes, trans. (New York: Scribner's, 1940); Norman Kretzmann, Anthony Kenny, and Jan Pinborg, eds., *The Cambridge History of Later Medieval Philosophy* (Cambridge: Cambridge University Press, 1982).

point" still holds today. The modern mentality has little patience with "long-winded" explanations, long "artistic" films, and "rambling" arguments. Instead we have "fast" food, sound "bites," and pamphlets that must make their point in less than a paragraph. Our society's enchantment with Ockham's razor demonstrates its affinity with his thought. Indeed, Peirce believed Ockham's thought permeated all modern thinking. Taking its cue from Ockham, Modernity, Peirce would say, sliced reality into twos: mind and matter, nature and culture, materialism and idealism, feelings and thought. Ockham's razor sliced to pieces what is in actuality a continuum. As such, Ockham's razor may have brought comfort to the impatient, but it also had the unfortunate consequence of reducing the subtlety and intricateness of being. Indeed, the modern epoch may be characterized as one that opted for simplicity over subtlety. In losing its taste for the subtle, however, modernity left itself open to nihilism.[13]

Ockham's razor goes hand in hand with Ockham's legacy: nominalism. Nominalism was conceived as a response to the furious medieval debate over the reality of the universal. This debate took the form of a question: What's in a name? In other words, do names refer to actual realities independent of our mind, or do they refer to an idea only made possible by our mind which, nonetheless, describes an actual reality? Put another way, is Paul called human because there is, in addition to the reality that is Paul, a human reality independent of our minds? Or is Paul called human because when Paul is compared to Peter, our mind makes a valid logical connection relating Peter and Paul and signified by the name human? The issue, once again, is the meaning of difference. Is the difference between two unique individuals understood as a meaningful reality or a meaningful mentality? The former position leads to a subtle but rich reality; the latter to a reality sliced asunder by Ockham's razor. The former concerns a reality based on the subtlety of the number three (the two individuals and another meaningful reality); the latter concerns a reality based on the simplicity of the number two (the physical and the mental).

Ockham's razor, in a sense, presupposes an anthropocentric epistemology, a view of knowledge centered solely on the human creature,

---

[13]Einstein's famous quote, "God is subtle, but He is not malicious," is appropriate here. Subtlety counters the sense of chaos, of arbitrariness in the world. Though things may seem to be falling apart around us, a belief in the subtlety of reality lends itself to the feeling of hope in discovering a reason for the apparent chaos. Without a belief in the subtlety of reality, a belief in the order, the goodness of the world, is problematic. Ronald W. Clark, *Einstein: The Life and Times* (New York: Avon Books, 1971) 38.

who becomes aware of the physical world through the senses. This data of the senses then becomes organized into concepts through the action of the mind. Thus, Ockham's human creature knows only percepts (the data of the senses) and concepts (the constructs of the mind). This dyadic epistemology has serious implications as to how one understands the meaning of difference. If the meaning of difference begins with comparing two unique, particular individuals (say an apple and a pear), then these physical individuals give rise to percepts (red, round, sweet, oblong), which the mind must then organize into meaningful connections, i.e., a concept (fruits). As such, it is the concept that carries the meaning of the difference between the two unique individuals. Thus, Ockham places the burden of the meaning of difference on the concept. Notice, however, that in Ockham's epistemology, the concept itself has reality only to the mind; it is not found in the physical world. Such an epistemology has consequences for an aesthetics.

Aesthetics, after all, refers to perception. Ockham's epistemology accounts for the meaning of difference at the expense of percepts. It amounts to saying that the meaning of a work of art lies less in our perception than in our conception. In other words, it is saying that to appreciate a work of art, one must also become an art critic. Said this way, Ockham's epistemological consequences for an aesthetics appear reasonable. Isn't art criticism a necessary element in the fine arts? Yes, but only if you believe that aesthetics or art is found solely in museums. What can art criticism contribute, for example, to the sense of beauty felt as one overlooks the northern Cascade mountains? How can critical thought illumine the beauty sensed in the "ugly" work of art that was Mother Teresa's ministry to the poor of Calcutta? Obviously, there are works of art that are not found in museums. There are beautiful objects not made by human hands. Indeed, there exist ways of life that amount to works of art. There are other arts besides fine arts. Yet modernity, through Ockham's razor, has, in a sense, "caged" the beautiful inside the halls of the modern museum. There is an alternative, however, to Ockham's razor.

Duns Scotus provided a different solution to the problem of the meaning of difference.[14] Like Ockham, Scotus emphasized the physical reality of the individual. Also like Ockham, Scotus believed in the autonomy of the human mind to make sense of the world outside its

---

[14]Duns Scotus was called the "subtle doctor" with good reason. His thought is nuanced and difficult to understand in a single reading. Some excellent commentaries on his thought include: Gordon Leff, *The Dissolution of the Medieval Outlook: An Essay on*

domain. Scotus, unlike Ockham, adds a third element to reality. There exists the physical world of the individuals. There also, exists the conceptual world of the mind. There exists, however, a further third reality, a metaphysical reality that has one foot in the physical world and the other foot in the mental world. This metaphysical reality, the Common Nature, is part of the reality found alongside the physicality of the unique individual even if it can only be "seen" by the mind. If the physical individual corresponds to a visible reality, then the Common Nature corresponds to an invisible reality, a reality independent of the mind and only "seen" by it. The two feet of the Common Nature corresponds to Scotus' most controversial proposal: the formal distinction. The formal distinction was, in a sense, a way to assure the reality of the universal. It is a subtle concept and deserves some explanation.

By the end of the thirteenth century, the Aristotelian revolution in Western philosophical thought had defined the universal as "that which is in many and predicable of many (*unum in multis et de multis*)."[15] Such a definition presents two extremes of interpreting the nature of the universal. One extreme would find the universal only in physical, individual things (*unum in multis*); the other only in the mind (*unum de multis*). In other words, one extreme position would make the universal a physical thing with the subsequent error of trying to reify something whose nature is not "thing-like." The other extreme, on the other hand, would make the universal a mental abstraction from the many with the subsequence that the universal would lose any claim to a reality independent of the mind Scotus takes these two extremes to make a distinction over the nature of universals. There are universals,

---

the *Intellectual and Spiritual Change in the Fourteenth Century* (New York: Harper & Row, Harper Torchbooks, 1976); John Marenbon, *Later Medieval Philosophy (1150–1350)* (London: Routledge & Kegan Paul, Ltd., 1987); Kretzmann, Kenny, and Pinborg, op. cit; Wolter, op. cit; Maurice J. Grajewski, O.F.M., *The Formal Distinction of Duns Scotus: A Study in Metaphysics*, Ph.D. diss. (Washington, D.C.: The Catholic University of America Press, 1944); John F. Boler, *Charles Peirce and Scholastic Realism: A Study of Peirce's Relation to John Duns Scotus* (Seattle: University of Washington Press, 1963); Efram Bettoni, *Duns Scotus: The Basic Principles of His Philosophy*, trans. B. Bonansea (Washington, D.C.: The Catholic University of America Press, 1961); C.R.S. Harris, *Duns Scotus* (Oxford: Clarendon Press, 1927); Etienne Gilson, *Jean Duns Scot: introduction à ses positions fondamentales* (Paris: J. Vrin, 1952); Etienne Gilson, *History of Christian Philosophy in the Middle Ages* (New York: Random House, 1955).
[15]This is Scotus' definition found in *In Metaph.*, VII, q.18, n.5 quoted in Boler, op. cit., 40. The perceptive reader may see already in this definition the relevance to our aesthetics project. The unity found in the many and from the many parallels the traditional aesthetic principle of "unity-in-variety."

he says, that properly belong to logic. The logical universal, i.e., the *unum de multis*, concerns the truthfulness of our statements, the correspondence between what we say about a thing and the thing itself. It does not exist *per se*. It is an act of the mind. There exists, however, another type of universal that grounds our concepts such as *human*. As such, this type of universal can be investigated or discovered much like one would discover a new species in biology. This universal, Scotus claims, carries the real *commonness* between two particular individuals. i.e., the *unum in multis* or Common Nature. The difference between these two universals is the difference between real existence and existence in the mind. Nonetheless, the real existence of the Common Nature cannot be simply identified with the real existence of a physical, particular individual. Though real, it only manifests itself in the mind. Thus, it has one foot in the world of the physical, particular thing and the other foot in the mental world of logical relationships. This is the formal distinction.[16]

As such, Scotus' formal distinction introduces into the notion of being, three different modes of being: the physical, the metaphysical, and the logical. There is physical being, the particular individual, an *ens reale*. There is logical being, the logical act of the mind, an *ens rationis*. There is, however, also metaphysical being, an *ens reale* that can only be seen by the "mind," a reality that bridges the chasm between the mechanically passive physical and the free act of the mind. Scotus, unfortunately, did not work out the consequences of this third reality for an aesthetics. Certain implications for an aesthetics, however, present themselves. A world that is experienced not simply by percepts and concepts but also by a reality invisible and "in-between" is a world that can entertain aesthetics not simply as passive perception of beauty nor the purely active act of mind but as a making visible the invisible, an act that involves not simply the mind nor simply the percepts but the whole creature. As such, an invisible reality allows room for the spiritual. An invisible metaphysical reality makes the mind's act a spiritual act of "seeing" rather than a mechanical "connecting" of perceptions. Making visible the invisible is neither a logical machination nor an arbitrary act of will. It is, however, a will shaped by the "difference" of that which it attempts to understand. Indeed, making visible the invisible involves that which is "other" making its demands on both our logical capacity for truth and our ethical capacity for willing good. Thus, the three modes of being set up in the human creature its very life in the

[16]Boler, op. cit., 37ff.

three transcendentals. To be human is to participate with logical mind and spiritual heart in the true, the good, and the beautiful. If there is nobility in the human creature, then here is where it may be found.

Scotus' view on universals may seem far afield from our previous discussion of von Balthasar. They both, however, hold something in common: the concern with the meaning of difference. Von Balthasar approached the meaning of difference through the real distinction; Scotus through the formal distinction.[17] Von Balthasar's approach depended on an analogical reality, the analogy of being; Scotus on a metaphysical reality, the real universal. Von Balthasar's approach takes us to theology rather quickly; Scotus' approach takes us to spirituality in a robust manner. At the heart of the tantalizing parallels and differences of the thought of these two great thinkers is the nature of "difference." Von Balthasar's analogy of being, on the one hand, concerns the difference between Creator and creature. Scotus' real universal, on the other hand, concerns the difference between creatures themselves. Von Balthasar's difference rises vertically from the cosmic; Scotus' travels horizontally along the cosmos. As such, these respective approaches to difference reveal the possibility of a fruitful complementarity. If the vertical approach to difference can be complemented by the horizontal approach to difference, then a truly incarnational aesthetics might result. Scotus, however, is not the key to such a project; Charles Sanders Peirce and Josiah Royce, however, are. Peirce working from Scotus' foundation, developed a logic based on the metaphysics of relations rather than the metaphysics of substance. Josiah Royce working from Peirce's foundation introduced the notion of value into the metaphysics of relations. In their mature reflections, Peirce and Royce introduce a new way to understand the transcendentals. The transcendentals amount to a community of value, a cosmic community of signs.

The rest of this chapter shall develop Peirce's understanding of the new metaphysics of signs and how it might be conceived as the Community of the True. The next chapter discusses Royce's introduction of value into the notion of Being and how, coupled with an expanded understanding of Peirce's logic of signs, becomes the community of the

---

[17]It is well known that Scotus did not believe in the real distinction. Many Scotian scholars, however, agree that Scotus' formal distinction is not a direct challenge to Aquinas' real distinction but, rather, a parallel. I do not have space to get into the intricacies of the parallels. I mention it to demonstrate the possibility of Scotian affinity with von Balthasar's aesthetics even if Scotus started with a completely different starting point. See, e.g., the discussion in Grajewski, op. cit.

Good. The final chapters, then, proceed to bring all these threads of thought together into the conceiving of the third transcendental, the community of the beautiful.

THE LOGIC OF SIGNS

Peirce, like Scotus, was interested in logic.[18] Logic for Peirce, however, meant a logic not only found in the mystery of human thought but also found in the world of Nature. Indeed, Peirce's deepest conviction was that both Nature and Mind had been artificially separated and that their necessary connection could be found again in a reexamination of the nature of Being. Peirce approached the question of Being with the conviction that Being is intrinsically logical. As he put it:

> The conception of *being* arises upon the formation of a proposition. A proposition always has, besides a term to express the substance, another to express the quality of that substance: and the function of the conception of being is to unite the quality to the substance. Quality, therefore, in its very widest sense, is the first conception in order in passing from being to substance.[19]

[18]The interested reader might consult the following for an introduction to the thought of Charles Sanders Peirce: Charles Sanders Peirce, *Collected Papers* (Cambridge, Mass.: Harvard University Press, 1931–1958); Robert S. Corrrington, *An Introduction to C. S. Peirce* (Lanham: Rowman & Littlefield, 1993); Christopher Hookway, *Peirce, The arguments of the philosophers* (London: Routledge, 1985); Karl-Otto Apel, *Charles S. Peirce: From Pragmatism to Pragmaticism,* originally published in German as *Der Denkweg von Charles S. Peirce: Eine Einführung in den amerikanischen Pragmatismus* by Suhrkamp Verlag, Frankfurt am Main, trans. John Michael Krois, reprint, 1967 (Atlantic Highlands, N.J.: Humanities Press International, 1995); Murray G. Murphey, *The Development of Peirce's Philosophy,* reprint, 1961 (Indianapolis and Cambridge: Hackett Publishing Company, 1993); James Feibleman, *An Introduction to Peirce's Philosophy: Interpreted as a System,* foreword by Bertrand Russell (New York and London: Harper & Brothers Publishing, 1946).

[19]Charles Sanders Peirce, "On a List of New Categories," in *Peirce on Signs: Writings on Semiotic by Charles Sanders Peirce,* James Hoopes, ed. (Chapel Hill and London: University of North Carolina Press, 1991) 26. It is traditional to refer to citations of Peirce's works in terms of the volume number and page number of the *Collected Works of Charles Peirce,* Charles Hartsthorne, ed. For example, 1.234 stands for a reference found in vol 1, p. 234. I prefer, however, to refer to the actual article by name in the belief that a reader might be able to use other more readily accessible anthologies to find the same material. Thus, I will use the article's name and the anthology in which I have found it. If existing anthologies do not have the work in question, I shall return to the traditional method to refer to Peirce's works.

Note here an important subtlety. Quality is a conception and not an impression. Thus, the formation of a proposition cannot result from some intuitive grasp of substance through the immediacy of that substance's quality. If quality is not immediately intuited, then the formation of a proposition must solely rely in comparing the alternatives to immediate intuition, two conceptions, namely substance and quality. Such comparison becomes mediated through another conception, the conception of being, and a proposition is formed. Thus, the key to Peirce's logic is his understanding of Being. Being as intrinsically logical means that the act of Being is the act of forming a proposition, and the forming of a proposition depends upon the elementary act of comparison or contrast. Being brings into relation what can be compared or contrasted. Being, in other words, is intrinsically relational.

Peirce pinned logic's most elementary act in the very nature of Being. It is the act of comparison or contrast. In that, he follows the great logician Augustus De Morgan.[20] The comparison between two individuals involves a complete act of thought which relates the two individuals together. De Morgan put it:

> Any two objects of thought brought together by the mind, and thought together in one act of thought, are *in relation*. Should anyone deny this by producing two notions of which he defies me to state the relation, I tell him that he has stated it himself; he has made me think the notions in the relation of *alleged impossibility of relation*; and has made his own objection commit suicide. Two thoughts cannot be brought together in thought except by a thought: which last thought contains their relation.[21]

In other words, the elementary logical act of comparison is only possible because of a "third" which relates the two individuals being compared. Peirce recognized in De Morgan's thought the issue around which the ancient scholastic debate between Ockham and Scotus revolved:

---

[20]De Morgan had questioned logic's most stalwart axioms: the relations of identity, non-contradiction, and exluded middle. He believed that logic had unnecessarily narrowed the number of relations and there existed more. All these relations have, in common, the act of including or excluding some individual from a collection of individuals. De Morgan asked if, in comparing two individuals, a different relation besides inclusion or exclusion from a class exists. He suggested that there was and it formed a new type of logic, the logic of relations. His findings can be found in Augustus De Morgan, "On the Syllogism of No. IV and on the Logic of Relations," *Cambridge Philosophical Transactions* X:331–58. Peirce refers to this work in many of his writings.

[21]De Morgan, op. cit., 339 quoted in John E. Smith, *Royce's Social Infinite: The Community of Interpretation* (New York: The Liberal Arts Press, 1950) 93.

Scotus sees several questions confounded together under the usual *utrum universale est aliquid in rebus*. . . . The whole difficulty is with the actually indeterminate universal, that which not only is not necessarily *this*, but which, being one single object of thought, is predicable of many things. In regard to this, it may be asked, first, is it necessary to its existence that it should be in the mind: and, second, does it exist *in re*? There are two ways in which a thing may be in the mind,—*habitualiter* and *actualiter*. A notion is in the mind *actualiter* when it is actually conceived; it is in the mind *habitualiter* when it can directly produce a conception. It is by virtue of mental association (we moderns should say), that things are in the mind *habitualiter*. In the Aristotelian philosophy, the intellect is regarded as being to the soul what the eye is to the body. The mind *perceives* likenesses and other relations in the objects of sense, and thus just as sense affords sensible images of things, so the intellect affords intelligible images of them. It is as such a *species intelligibilis* that Scotus supposes that a conception exists which is in the mind *habitualiter*, not *actualiter*.[22]

The significance between conceptions seen either as *actualiter* or *habitualiter* may be demonstrated in terms of our previous discussion over whether a work of art can be copied. Conceptions *actualiter* affirms that ideas are mere copies of the sense-image. The original individual "outside" the mind becomes "copied" inside the mind. Thus, the mind guarantees the reality of the individual by acting like a material hologram.

Unfortunately, since universals "exist" in the difference between individuals, such a view of conceptions destroys any hope for the reality of the universal. In other words, Raphael would be unable to copy Michelangelo's *David* in an original way. Raphael's vision of the *David* would be purely passive. A conception *habitualiter,* on the other hand, recognizes an activity to the mind akin to vision. Though, like vision, it registers the reality of that which is "seen," it does so in a productive, i.e., active way. The eyes of the intellect, in other words, produces the idea much like Raphael "conceives" Michelangelo's *David* in a faithful yet strikingly original way. That Raphael's *David* cannot be mistaken for Michelangelo's *David* guarantees the reality of the original individual. That Raphael's *David,* however, is an original in its own right guarantees the reality of a common vision shared by both Raphael and Michelangelo. Raphael's *David* affirms in its faithfulness and originality both the reality of the individual and the reality of a universal grasped

[22]Charles Sanders Peirce, "*Fraser's* the Works of George Berkeley," in *The Essential Peirce: Selected Philosophical Writings*, reprint, 1871 (Bloomington and Indianapolis: Indiana University Press, 1992) 92.

by the genius of both Michelangelo and Raphael. That Raphael's copy has as much value as Michelangelo's original reveals the stakes present in the choice between nominalism (the idea *actualiter*) and Scotus' proposal (the idea *habitualiter*).[23]

Peirce saw the significance right away. He quickly moved to translate Scotus' insight into a logical system. To translate Scotus' conviction of the reality of the universal into a logical system, Peirce realized that a new type of logic was required. This new logic would have to deal less with substances than with relationships. Scotus' metaphysical reality became for Peirce the reality of relation. Relations were a third reality along with the physical and the mental. Peirce's third reality, like Scotus', is thought-like but independent of the knowing mind. Peirce had a name for it, the *interpretant*. He put it this way:

> Suppose we wish to compare the letters *p* and *b*. We may imagine one of them to be turned over on the line of writing as an axis, then laid upon the other, and finally to become transparent so that the other can be seen through it. In this way we shall form a new image which mediates between the images of the two letters, inasmuch as it represents one of them to be (when turned over) the likeness of the other.[24]

This image making, the mind *habitualiter,* is a representation that also is a mediation of that which relates the two letters. In other words, it is akin to interpretation; it is an interpretant. These three elements together as a whole, this production, constitutes the idea but not the idea as in the image a camera makes but a new notion of idea, the sign.

A sign compares two individuals, that which is represented (the signified) and that which represents it (the signifier). Nominalism stops there. Signs are purely conventional. A signifier is arbitrarily assigned to the signified. Peirce's sign knows no such arbitrariness. The two individuals being compared (the signifier and the signified) are related by an interpretant which enables their comparison. Together, the signifier, the signified, and the interpretant constitutes a sign which is Peirce's

[23]In the interest of being accurate, I must mention that Peirce considered Scotus as, even too nominalist. In his review of Berkeley's thought, Peirce says of Scotus' thought as "separated from nominalism only by the division of a hair." Peirce, "*Fraser's* the Works of George Berkeley," 87. Peirce's main objection to Scotus was the doctrine that the universal "contracts" in the individual. In other words, the individual contracts within itself the entire universal. Peirce thought that compromised the reality of the universal. Nonetheless, others have pointed out that Peirce did not so much reject the doctrine as transform it through modern conceptions. See, e.g. the discussion in Boler, op. cit., 151ff.
[24]Peirce, "On a List of New Categories," 27.

understanding of the "idea." As such, the idea as sign is not something that remains invisible, "hidden" in the mysteries of the human mind. Signs make visible the invisible. Another way of saying the same thing is to say that we experience more than we sense.[25]

Peirce described sign in many different ways. The following description, however, brings out the intrinsic dimension of sign as making visible the invisible:

> We see that the action of reason and the will, that is, by the action of a sign, matter becomes determined to a Form; and we infer that wherever Matter becomes determined to a form it is through a sign. Much that happens certainly happens according to Natural Law; and what is this Law but something whose being consists in its determining Matter to Form in a certain way? Many metaphysicians will answer that Law does not make Matter to become determined to Form but only recognizes in a general way, that which happens quite independently. But do these men mean to say that it is mostly by chance that all stones allowed to drop have hitherto fallen? If so, there is no reason to suppose that it will be so with the next stone we may let loose. To say that would be to paralyze reason. But if it is not mere chance then evidently it has some cause or reasons. To say that this is a sign is merely to say that it has its being in producing the union of Form and Matter. Why suppose it has any further being, especially since in order to do so, you must evolve a conception that the human mind has never possessed? You might talk of such a thing, but think it you could not. Nor does anybody propose that. Those who hate to admit that anything of the nature of a sign can act upon matter imagine that they can express the phenomena with less, and do not dream of insisting upon more.[26]

With this argument, Peirce was attacking the nominalist notion that the sign simply exists, invisibly, in the mind; it has no visible physical ramifications. Peirce's sign, unlike the nominalist sign and like Scotus' real universal, has both a visible and an invisible dimension. Indeed, Peirce's sign brings about a determination of matter and form. Signs make possible the shape of the universe. If Von Balthasar's aesthetics is a matter of "seeing the form," then Peirce's logic is a matter of seeing the invisible universal in the visible sign. Thus, Peirce's interpretation of the mind *habitualiter* into the logic of signs reveals thought as intrinsically visible. In other words, thought as the production of signs has a

---

[25]I am in debt for this additional insight to Professor Don Gelpi.

[26]Charles Sanders Peirce, *Sketch on Dichotomic Mathematics*, unpublished manuscript found in the Charles Sanders Peirce Collection, housed at Houghton Library, Harvard University, 1973.

dimension that is "outside" the mind and, thus, intrinsically visible yet, through the logic of signs, it is perceivable inferentially, indeed intuitively. If Ockham had made mind subjective, Peirce made mind objective. For this reason, Peirce's philosophy of signs is sometimes known as objective idealism. Indeed, because thought is objective, the universe is thought-like. As such, the world consists of a universe of signs. Such a view of mind has ramifications for the understanding of the true.

An ancient understanding of truth was phrased by the scholastics as *adequatio rei ad intellectum*, i.e., truth concerns the correspondence of an object to our understanding of it. Kant would have phrased it as the "conformity of a representation to its object."[27] Peirce's understanding of sign transforms this ancient definition in an important way. Since sign involves interpretation rather than representation, the correspondence theory of truth becomes transformed. Peirce's sign contains the necessary element of interpretation as a third type of knowing beyond the knowing of the senses (percepts) and the knowing of reason (concepts). Peirce, however, had a much broader understanding of interpretation than we have today. The following passage from an unpublished manuscript is worth quoting in full:

> Let us examine this operation of interpretation. . . . Let us take first the example of a very perfect sign, say, a demonstration of Euclid, for the entire demonstration is a sign. What is it to interpret this? Probably the first attempt at an answer will be that it is the immediate feelings of the force of the demonstration. But no; we ought to take the whole effect of the sign, or at least the whole of the essential part of it, to be the interpretation, so long as we have used the word interpretation to mean that effect the causing of which constitutes the being of the sign. Now it is not in any feeling or even in any particular act of thought that that effect consists but in the *belief,* with all that the belief essentially effects. Belief does not principally consist in any particular act of thought, but in a *habit* of thought and conduct. A man does not necessarily believe what he thinks he believes. He only believes what he deliberately adopts and is ready to make a habit of conduct. It would thus be plain enough that a sign, as a sign, produces physical effects, even if there were any other way than that for one mind to communicate with another, and even if the action of the will were not the most important fact in the world.[28]

The power that brings about the determination of matter by form, the power that gives shape to the universe involves belief on the part of the

[27]Hookway, op. cit., 45.
[28]Peirce, *Sketch on Dichotomic Mathematics.*

human creature. It is not that belief enables signification but that sig-nification involves belief. That smoke signifies fire does not depend on our belief that it is so, but if we see smoke rising from the basement of our house, we will rush to the basement in the belief that there is a fire. In other words, Peirce makes the point that whatever we believe, we be-lieve to be true. Thus, the goal of searching for "truth" makes little sense. We do not find truth in searching for it as one would seek some object but in, as Peirce put it, "the fixation of belief."

Peirce proposed there are four major ways to "fix" belief. One way to "fix" belief is the way of "tenacity," i.e., holding to one's belief inde-pendently of any reason that calls for change in such belief. This is the way of the rugged individualist. It is eminently unsatisfying for "unless we make ourselves hermits, we shall necessarily influence other's opin-ions; so that the problem becomes how to fix belief, not in the individ-ual merely, but in the community."[29] Thus, another way to "fix" belief in a community context is the way of "authority." This has been the "chief means" by which belief has been "fixed" throughout history. It is morally and mentally superior to that of "tenacity," but, such a method can "regulate opinions upon every subject. Only the most important ones can be attended to, and on the rest men's minds must be left to the action of natural causes." Thus, the "willfull adherence to a belief, and the arbitrary forcing of it upon others, must, therefore, both be given up, and a new method of settling opinions must be adopted, which shall not only produce an impulse to believe, but shall also decide what proposition it is which is to be believed."[30] This is the *a priori* method of traditional philosophy. Unfortunately, as Peirce notes, such a method produces a harmony of opinion that resembles more the "de-velopment of taste" encouraging following the latest "fashion" than the discovery of the true. Thus, a new method must be found "by which our beliefs may be caused by nothing human, but by some external per-manency—by something upon which our thinking has no effect."[31] Peirce called this new method pragmatism.[32]

---

[29]Charles Sanders Peirce, "The Fixation of Belief," in *The Essential Peirce: Selected Philosophical Writings*, Nathan Houser and Christian Kloesel, eds. (Bloomington and Indianapolis: Indiana University Press, 1992) 117.

[30]Ibid., 119.

[31]Ibid., 120.

[32]Peirce later changed the name of the method to pragmaticism to distinguish it from the pragmatism of William James and others who, he felt, had thoroughly mis-understood the nature of this proposed method.

Peirce described this new method in a review he made of *The World and the Individual* written by the "American Plato," his soon-to-become greatest disciple, Josiah Royce.

> A certain writer [Peirce himself] has suggested that reality, the fact that there is such a thing as a true answer to a question, consists in this: that human inquiries,—human reasoning and observation,—tend toward the settlement of disputes and ultimate agreement in definite conclusions which are independent of the particular standpoints from which the different inquirers may have set out; so that the real is that which any man would believe in, and be ready to act upon, if his investigations were to be pushed sufficiently far.[33]

This new way to "fix" belief is difficult to grasp in all the subtlety that a method built upon a logic of relations or signs has over a method built upon a logic based on a substantial view of mind and matter. If its subtleties are not appreciated, then misunderstandings such as those of William James might occur.

One of the subtleties that may be mentioned is that Peirce's new proposal, first and foremost, is a proposal for a method to "fix" belief rather than a description of how belief comes about. William James, e.g., made the mistake to take Peirce's pragmatism as a psychological description of belief. Belief, according to this interpretation, equates our practical actions to our mental conceptions. Such an interpretation is totally dyadic and missing the third element of Peirce's logic of sign. Belief, in such an interpretation, functions as the material hologram of previous discussion. Belief makes a perfect "copy" of a conceptions into a practical act. Peirce's logic of sign, however, excludes this possibility. Peirce's pragmatic method makes a true whole of the physical and the psychical elements of reality that is the sign. In other words, belief mediates a psycho-physical reality into a whole, the sign. Belief leads to conceptions and practical acts into a whole whose reality, like Raphael's *David,* can at the same time signify another's reality yet stand on its own. Such a method "fixes" belief by taking seriously the "otherness" of reality which, paradoxically, can challenge previously "fixed" beliefs. By being receptive to that which is "other," Peirce's pragmatism allows a community to incorporate the "other" into its beliefs without destroying the "otherness" that prompted such belief in the first place.

Another subtlety of Peirce's pragmatism that often goes unappreciated is its foundation on a logic of relations. Relations, or signs, are

---

[33]Peirce, "*Fraser's* the Works of George Berkeley," 230.

notoriously subtle notions. Relations are, intrinsically, invisible. Try to imagine, for example, a "pure" relation, i.e., a relation that has no fundament (signified) or terminus (signifier). It is impossible. It is, as Meister Eckhart once suggested for mystical vision, trying to see the eye with the eye itself. Indeed, relations become visible only when they are "caught" in the act of relating a fundament to a terminus. Peirce's pragmatic method builds upon this "invisible" nature of relations to "fix" belief in the community. A pragmatic community overcomes doubt and gains belief when it becomes convinced of the existence of a real relation. How does this happen? A real relation corresponds to the real universal. It is intrinsically invisible. Yet because real universals become manifest through particular individuals, all real universals carry the possibility of becoming visible. It is this possibility that is demonstrated in the pragmatic method and NOT either the visibility alone or invisibility alone of the real universal. In other words, the pragmatic method "fixes" belief when it can demonstrate that such belief carries the possibility of making visible the invisible. How can such a demonstration occur?

Peirce answers the question with the notion of the "would-be." In other words, if a community believes that a diamond possesses "hardness," then it such belief ought to be able to answer a "would-be" question. What would happen, for example, if a diamond is rubbed against a piece of quartz? A valid belief in the "hardness" of the diamond could and would answer this question through the performance of the experiment. Such a community might even go on to create a society in which tools of exceptional "hardness" are used based on the belief that diamonds are exceptionally "hard." The subtlety enters in when one becomes aware that it is not this practical consequence of belief that constitutes pragmatism. All that pragmatism calls for as a sufficient and necessary demonstration of valid belief is the possibility of answering the "would-be" of what is held as true. The basis for this assertion lies in the "would-be" as a sign. The "would-be," in a sense, refers to the missing terminus (signifier) of a real relation that has its fundament (the signified) in the present belief of a pragmatic community. If the present belief is valid, then such belief will hold true for a future "would-be." In other words, if the relation constituting the present belief of a community is real, then it is capable of relating the future (the "would-be") to the present. Whether this "would-be" has "practical" consequences is irrelevant to the validity of the community's belief. What is essential is that such belief makes possible the future of a community.

Peirce's logic of signs incarnated in the community of pragmatic belief reveals a dimension of logic that has often been ignored. "Logic is rooted in the social principle."[34] As such, Peirce has, in a sense, described what might be thought as the pragmatic equivalent of the transcendental true. The community exercising the pragmatic method to "fix" belief, i.e., the community of inquirers, is also the Community of the True. Indeed, the pragmatic method creates a community organically rooted in the reality of the true. Such a community is not identical with the true but faith in the "would-be's" of its logic of signs leads to the firm hope that someday that identity may be theirs. That such hope is assured follows because the Community of the True is charitably disposed to that which is "other" with a willingness to sacrifice previously held beliefs when "otherness" calls them into question. Thus, Peirce would write:

> It may seem strange that I should put forward three sentiments, namely, interest in an indefinite community, recognition of the possibility of this interest being made supreme, and hope in the unlimited continuance of intellectual activity, as indispensable requirements of logic. Yet when we consider that logic depends on a mere struggle to escape doubt, which, as it terminates in action, must begin in emotion, and that, furthermore, the only cause of our planting ourselves on reason is that other methods of escaping doubt fail on account of the social impulse, why should we wonder to find social sentiment presupposed in reasoning? As for the other two sentiments which I find posed in reasoning? As for the other two sentiments which I find necessary, they are only as supports and accessories of that. It interests me to notice that these three sentiments seem to be pretty much the same as that famous trio of Charity, Faith, and Hope, which, in the estimation of St. Paul, are the finest and greatest of spiritual gifts. Neither Old nor New Testament is a textbook of the logic of science, but the latter is certainly the highest existing authority in regard to the dispositions of heart which a man ought to have.[35]

Thus, Peirce inaugurates a new vision of logic. Moreover, I would say that Peirce also inaugurates a new vision of what is meant by the transcendental of the true. If so, then this Community of the True like the traditional transcendental must lead us as well into the other transcendentals, the good and the beautiful. That this is so is evident in all of

---

[34]Charles Sanders Peirce, "The Doctrine of Chances," in *The Essential Peirce: Selected Philosophical Writings*, Nathan Houser and Christian Kloesel, eds. (Bloomington and Indianapolis: Indiana University Press, 1992) 149.

[35]Ibid., 14–15.

Peirce's writings. The above, for example, suggests that while Peirce recognizes that the "dispositions of the heart" are not identical with logic neither are they mutually exclusive; one includes the others. As such, Peirce's logic of relations opens up the tantalizing possibility of developing new visions of the other two transcendentals. One who took this seriously was Josiah Royce.

PEIRCE'S AESTHETICS

In his Gifford Lectures published as *The World and the Individual,* Josiah Royce proposed a new type of "idealism." Our ideas of the world necessarily involve a judgment of value about the world. Our ideas embody purposeful meaning. As such, Being itself is intrinsically valuable. Whether Royce succeeded in demonstrating his case may be argued. Peirce, to his credit, was the first (in a sense, even before Royce himself) to discern the significance of Royce's struggle with the relation of value and Being. The lack of the notion of values in the logic of signs left a void in Peirce's pragmatism that others soon began to fill with undesirable results. William James, for example, filled the void of the intuition in Peirce's pragmatism by interpreting the "fixing" of belief in a thoroughly psychological way. Alarmed by such "distortion" of his thought, Peirce became more and more concerned on the issue of intuition, judgement and motivation and how it might be clarified in his pragmatism. As Karl-Otto Apel put it:

> It was therefore all the more urgent for Peirce to answer the question how the *summum bonum* or the final goal of all action in general can be made the object of an idea that is explicable as practically meaningful. Asked differently, how can the vision of a final goal . . . . be justified as a *meaningful* hypothesis by means of normative, semiotic logic?[36]

The operative word here is "normative." Peirce's logic of signs had given a satisfying answer to the question of how the true becomes discovered but left open the implicit question of what inspires such discovery in the first place! In other words, the Community of the True has some genesis. It is not an spontaneous gathering of individuals set on discovering the true. Something must account for initiating such a pursuit. Moreover, something must also provide for guiding such a pursuit once it gets started.

Thus, the proposal for a Community of the True left a wide gap in its understanding. The issue of initiation (or motivation) and the issue

[36]Apel, op. cit., 92.

of guidance remained yet to be resolved. These twin issues, fortunately, can be addressed in terms of the issue of value, the normative value of the good, and the aesthetic (and normative) value of the beautiful. As such, these twin issues correspond to the other two transcendentals. When guidance is given to the Community of the True, it reveals itself to be the Community of the Good as well. When inspiration generates the Community of the True and the Good, then the Community of the Beautiful is revealed as well. Peirce came to this conclusion in reviewing Royce's *The World and the Individual*. Peirce's reading of Royce set him on a new appreciation of the good and the beautiful that would culminate as his proposal for the "normative sciences." As Peirce put it in a letter to William James dated November 25, 1902,

> My own view in 1877 was crude. Even when I gave my Cambridge lectures I had not really got to the bottom of it or seen the unity of the whole thing. It was not until after that that I obtained the proof that logic must be founded on ethics, of which it is a higher development. Even then, I was for some time so stupid as not to see that ethics rests in the same manner on a foundation of esthetics—by which it is needless to say, I don't mean milk and water and sugar (8.255).

In Royce's work, Peirce realized that the "fixation" of belief, "the true nature of pragmatism" cannot "as I seem to have thought at first, take Reaction as the be-all, but it takes the end-all as the be-all, and the End is something that gives its sanction to action" (8.256). Actions, to be logical, must be guided, indeed initiated, by ends.

AESTHETICS: A NORMATIVE SCIENCE

Thus, Peirce began a renewed exploration in the relationship between logic, ethics, and (what he called) "esthetics."[37] In his work of 1902, *Minute Logic,* Peirce tells us that he recently come to realize the importance of "esthetics" in logic and that he is not sure of the matter himself. Peirce makes a stab at locating "esthetics" within logical theory. "Esthetics," Peirce theorizes, must be explored as part of "the logic of the normative sciences, of which logic itself is only the third, being preceded by Esthetics and Ethics" (2.197). By normative science, Peirce means "the study of what ought to be" (1.281). It sets up values or

---

[37]Peirce preferred to refer to aesthetics as "esthetics" because of his view of it as a normative science. He did not want his "esthetics" to be associated with any study which might involve the admission of a psychology of appreciation.

norms that need not but ought to be followed (2.156). As such, the "ought" concerns itself with ideals or ends, i.e., with purposes that attract and guide.[38] As such, the normative sciences study the laws that relate the conformity of things to ends. Here Peirce finds a difficulty over which he struggled the rest of his intellectual career. He could understand logic as a normative science, i.e., the theory of controlled thinking, but it was in ethics, the theory of controlled action, that he found the most decisive and clear example of a normative science. In ethics, "the distinctive characters of normative science are most strongly marked" (1.573). What, then, does it mean to say that "esthetics" is a normative science?

Aesthetic qualities, after all, resist being categorized as "good" or "bad." Aesthetic norms frustrate for they obviously present themselves in the beautiful yet as one tries to identify them, they slip past the grip of our understanding. Peirce struggled with this intrinsic nature of aesthetic norms. By the time he gave his lectures on pragmatism, he had made a decisive link between logical truth and falsity and moral goodness and badness, but had not yet realized what the link of logic and ethics to "esthetics" might be.[39] Indeed, Peirce wondered if there was such a science of "esthetics":

> Ethics—the genuine science of normative ethics, as contradistinguished from the branch of anthropology which in our day often passes under the name of ethics—this genuine ethics is the normative science *par excellence,* because an end—the essential of normative science—is germane to a voluntary act in a primary way in which it is germane to nothing else. For that reason I have some lingering doubts as to there being any true normative science of the beautiful (5.130).

Peirce's pessimism arose from his initial attempt to describe the differences between the normative sciences:

> . . . esthetics considers those things whose ends are to embody qualities of feeling, ethics those things whose ends lie in action, and logic those things whose end is to represent something (5.129).[40]

Peirce had made the link between logic and ethics when he realized that logic, like ethics, is a *voluntary* act. Thus, he could distinguish between the two in terms of the different ends or goals of such a voluntary act.

---

[38]Vincent G. Potter, S.J., *Charles S. Peirce: On Norms & Ideals* (Worcester, Mass.: University of Massachusetts Press, 1967) 43–44.

[39]Ibid., 44.

[40]Quoted in Potter, op. cit., 44.

Aesthetics, however, did not fit into this neat scheme. Whether something is ugly or beautiful appears to be independent of any goal, or end, or purpose. Things are beautiful as an end in themselves. Something that is an end unto itself is intrinsically anti-normative. Peirce finds some sort of answer to this dilemma in the meaning of the Greek word *kalos,* the admirable *per se.* As Peirce puts it:

> On the other hand, an ultimate end of action *deliberately* adopted—that is to say, *reasonably* adopted—must be a state of things that *reasonably recommends itself in itself* aside from any ulterior consideration. It must be an *admirable ideal,* having the only kind of goodness that such an ideal can have; namely, esthetic goodness. From this point of view the morally good appears as a particular species of the esthetically good (5.130).

Thus, the admirable *per se* describes a state of affairs which "reasonably recommends itself in itself aside from ulterior consideration." But what can this admirable ideal be in terms of esthetics? What is the esthetically "good"? Peirce answers the question with his equivalent to Von Balthasar's objective affections:

> In the light of the doctrine of categories I should say that an object, to be esthetically good, must have a multitude of parts so related to one another as to impart a positive quality to their totality; and whatever does this is, in so far, esthetically good, no matter what the particular quality of the total may be. If that quality be such as to nauseate us, to scare us, or otherwise disturb us to the point of throwing us out of the mood of esthetic enjoyment . . . then the object remains none the less esthetically good, although people in our condition are incapacitated from a calm esthetic contemplation of it (5.132).[41]

Such a description of the esthetically good has profound implications for a theological aesthetics.

First, the above description of the esthetically good flings the objects of aesthetic appreciation out of the museum into the universal world of experience. Any experience has esthetic quality. On the other hand, Peirce's esthetics allow no such thing as positive esthetic ugliness or, for that matter, esthetic goodness. Things are esthetic as a matter of being. There exist only "innumerable varieties of esthetic qualities but no purely esthetic grade of excellence" (5.132). This is not necessarily a negative perspective for theological aesthetics. That the esthetic good may be found even in the nauseous allows the Christian believer to see

---

[41]Quoted in Potter, op. cit., 46.

God's beauty in the drama that is the Passion of Christ. Peirce pre-
scribes the esthetically good in such a fashion because he realizes that
esthetic quality contains a paradoxical dimension. Esthetic qualities
admit no criticism or control because they relate to the Whole, the ultimate End, the *summum bonum* yet good and bad imply approval or
disapproval. To approve or disapprove of the esthetically good is to approve or disapprove of the ultimate it is intrinsically a part. But how
can one approve or disapprove of an ultimate?

Peirce struggled with this question through the end of his career.
Whether he adequately answered it is a matter of debate. Vincent Potter
argues that the following section from Peirce's 1906 paper, "Basis for
Pragmatism," suggests that he did:

> Every action has a motive; but an ideal only belongs to a line [of] con-
> duct which is deliberate. To say that conduct is deliberate implies that
> each action, or each important action, is reviewed by the actor and the
> judgment is passed upon it, as to whether he wishes his future conduct
> to be like that or not. His ideal is the kind of conduct which attracts him
> upon review. His self-criticism, followed by a more or less conscious
> resolution that in its turn excites a determination of his habit, will, with
> the aid of the sequelae, *modify* a future action; but it will not generally
> be a moving cause to action. It is an almost purely passive liking for a
> way of doing whatever he may be moved to do. Although it affects his
> own conduct, and nobody else's, yet the quality of feeling (for it is
> merely a quality of feeling) is just the same, whether his own conduct or
> that of another person, real or imaginary, is the object of the feeling; or
> whether it be connected with the thought of any action or not. If con-
> duct is to be thoroughly deliberate, the ideal must be a habit of feeling
> which has grown up under the influence of a course of self-criticisms
> and of hetero-criticisms; and the theory of the deliberate formation of
> such habits of feeling is what ought to be meant by *esthetics* (1.574).[42]

If Potter is right, then Peirce solves the issue of critical adoption of the
esthetically good by shifting the question from one of adopting the
ideal itself to the question of why an agent might adopt such an ideal
in the first place. "Thus Peirce has shifted the emphasis from the admirable *per se* to a consideration of the habit of feeling in the agent in the
presence of certain ends proposed as ideals."[43] It is the ideals one adopts
that are subject to criticism and control, not the ideals in themselves.

Potter's interpretation of Peirce's aesthetics appears reasonable but,
I believe, unsatisfying. One is still left with the lingering doubt whether

[42]Quoted in Potter, op. cit., 50.
[43]Potter, op. cit., 50.

Peirce actually pinned down the nature of the aesthetic norm. Indeed, one is left wondering, like Peirce, whether such a norm exists! There is something about the beautiful that reveals its normative character by paradoxically breaking through its own normative sense. The logic of the beautiful appears to be like the logic of the divine names. As soon, as one tries to "name" God, the reality of God shatters the very grasp of the name towards its reference. As such, the problem, I feel, is not with Peirce's logic of signs. It is, I believe, a problem that requires a theological presupposition so that the philosophical may find its completion. The dynamic nature of the aesthetic norm reveals a theological presupposition, the symptom of divinity making itself manifest in the world of reason. Aesthetics, by its very nature, appears to present a rare intersection between philosophy and theology where both benefit in a mutual interaction. It this very intersection that I intend to explore in the last presentation of the transcendental, the Community of the Beautiful.

In that chapter the semiotic aesthetics of Jan Mukarovsky will be presented. Mukarovsky's brilliant analysis of the role of foregrounding in poetic language squarely faces Peirce's dilemma of an aesthetic normative science. The nature of an aesthetic norm is its dynamic contingency. It makes itself present by violating its own norm. As such, it is less an inviolable norm than a "regulative energetic principle." Foregrounding charges, like Hopkins "Pied Beauty," poetic language with directed energy revealing a reality beyond itself. Mukarovsky's notion of foregrounding, in a sense, corresponds to the biblical notion of the *yetzer,* the good and evil inclinations of the heart. In the *yetzer,* I believe, the "missing link" Peirce sought between ethics and esthetics may be found. It corresponds to a non-traditional notion of the imagination as being less a psychology than a cosmology. It is what I call the "anagogical" imagination. The "anagogical" imagination is the "third" type of knowing that "shapes" the heart. As such, the "anagogical" imagination "lights the fuse" which movitates the ethical search after the Good and the logical inquiry into the True. Before we can enter into that conversation, however, we must continue the semiotic transformation of the transcendentals as signifying communities by exploring Royce's proposal for the Community of the Good.

5

The Community of the Good

Charles Sanders Peirce envisioned for us the Community of the True. Having discovered Being as relational, Peirce develops his logic of signs. A logic of signs, in turn, suggests a rethinking of the transcendentals of Being. They too are relational. Moreover, they are relational in a concrete, practical way. The transcendentals, in a logic of signs, reveal themselves as Communities of the True, the Good, and the Beautiful. Such a presentation of the transcendentals represents a Kuhnian "paradigm shift" in the understanding of an ancient and traditional concept. Yet Peirce through his logic of signs successfully demonstrates how such a shift can take place. In a world where Being is relational, a Community of the True discovers the real by interpreting the meaning of difference. What about, however, the other two transcendentals? What about the Good and, especially, the Beautiful? Can Peirce's logic of signs, his semiotics, help us make the "paradigm shift" towards the Community of the Good and the Community of the Beautiful?

The answer, I am arguing, is yes, but not without the help of his disciple, Josiah Royce. Born in 1855 in the mining town of Grass Valley, California, Royce graduated from the University of California at Berkeley in 1875. After studies in Germany and the John Hopkins, he returned for a brief period to teach in his old alma mater. In 1882, William James invited the young Royce into Harvard's philosophy department. Royce spent a total of thirty-four years at Harvard (1882–1916) becoming, as Peirce named him, the "American Plato," that is, America's foremost exponent of philosophical idealism. Royce brilliantly exposed his idealism in *The World and the Individual*. He did so, as will be explained later in the chapter, in the context of the "knowledge of good and evil." As such, Royce's exploration into the nature of reality led him towards an ethical approach in his understanding of Being. During this time he became acquainted with Peirce and admired him as a logician. Peirce, in turn, suggested to Royce that he study logic. Such suggestion led Royce into a thirteen-year study of logic. This study culminated in *The Problem of Christianity*, his masterpiece of 1913. The *Problem* transformed Royce from philosophical idealism to logical realism, namely the pragmatic logic of signs. I shall argue that it also led Royce to describe the Community of the Good.

Both Peirce and Royce illuminate our understanding of the transcendentals by a subtle but revolutionary understanding of Being. Peirce shifted the notion of Being from a substance ontology to a relational metaphysics. Being, Peirce proposed, is relational and, as such, it is logical. Relational Being, moreover, manifests itself through the logic of signs. Such a notion of Being makes Peirce's approach to the issue of difference comparably different from von Balthasar's approach. If von Balthasar's notion of Being depended on the insuperable but analogical difference between Creator and creature, Peirce's notion of Being depended on the relational but logical difference between creatures. If von Balthasar's God was reached through the analogy of Being, then Peirce's God was reached through the logical relationality of Being. These comparably different approaches to the meaning of difference result in different but similar understandings of that crux of theological aesthetics, the *capax Dei*. Von Balthasar's theological aesthetics suggests an extremely personal experience, the humble creature perceiving the awesome Creator. Peirce, on the other hand, suggests a thoroughly relational *capax Dei* based on the communal experience of the real universal.

As such, an imprecise but, perhaps, helpful comparison may be proposed. Von Balthasar emphasizes the "vertical" dimension of the *capax Dei*, while Peirce emphasizes, in a sense, its "horizontal" dimension. This simple comparison between Peirce and von Balthasar alerts us to the fact that a full theological aesthetics must account for both dimensions. Such accounting is nothing more than being faithful to the Love commandment, i.e., to love God with all our heart and the neighbor as oneself. Love, in its fullness, bridges both the "vertical" difference between Creator and creature and the "horizontal" difference between creature and creature. Indeed, the meaning of difference contains as well both dimensions. If von Balthasar raised the issue of a theological aesthetics with his profound study on the meaning of "vertical" difference, then Peirce alerts the von Balthasar fan that a crucial dimension is yet to be explored. It is Royce, I will suggest, who begins to cross the bridge between the "vertical" and the "horizontal."

The bridge to be crossed involves asking the question of the Good rather than the True. Indeed, Royce took Aristotle's ancient thesis *Omne Ens est bonum,* "All Being is Good," as a point of departure. In brief, Royce reasoned that since a person recognizes that "to be" is better than "not to be," lived experience integrates fact and value. The experience of being does not allow dichotomizing the "is" from the "ought."[1] In other words, recognizing our being is to value it. Being has ethical value! Royce brings this insight home in *The World and the Individual* and impresses Peirce who, nonetheless, is disappointed. He notices a definite lack of relational thinking in Royce's metaphysics. After looking at his gift copy of *The World and the Individual,* Peirce wrote Royce a thank you letter where he chided, "when I read you, I do wish that you would study logic. You need it so much."[2] Surprisingly, Royce took him seriously. The next twelve years found Royce sharpening his understanding of logic.

This incursion into logic gave rise to a new maturity in Royce's thought. In 1912, he publishes *Principles of Logic* revealing a revolutionary approach to logical systems of order. As will be explained later in the chapter, Royce develops a logical system ordered not according to abstract algebraic law but as amenably aesthetic geometrical form. Relating form to logic allows Royce to expand Peirce's logical triadic sign into signs having polyadic relations. This new polyadic logic of signs makes a decisive turn from the sterility of the razor simple to the richness of the complex subtle. Such subtle logic corresponds much better to the complexities of knowing in the garden of good and evil. Indeed, Royce's new principle of logic which he calls the "epsilon" principle and, later, becomes the mature logical system sigma, becomes the foundation for the exquisitely nuanced *Problem of Christianity* which, in essence, describes what I call the "Community of the Good." In brief, Royce, with the help of Peirce, recognizes the significance of that dimension of Being which corresponds to the second transcendental, the Good, and gives it philosophical substance through a newly conceived logic of signs. In doing so, Royce transforms the second transcendental of Being into the Community of the Good.

[1]This is, in fact, a critique of Hume's "fact-value" dichotomy. By making so sharp a distinction between fact and value, Hume left the realm of lived experience, Frank M. Oppenheim, *Royce's Mature Ethics* (Notre Dame, Ind. University of Notre Dame Press, 1993) 121.

[2]Quoted in Frank M. Oppenheim, *Royce's Mature Philosophy of Religion* (Notre Dame, Ind.: University of Notre Dame Press, 1987) 43. Royce mentioned the letter in his *Problem of Christianity* (2:117).

Does Royce have a theological aesthetics? Not directly but hidden in his newly conceived logic lies a potentially viable aesthetics. In a wonderful article on Negation written for Hasting's *Encyclopedia*, Royce describes the nature of "negative" theology, the theology of mystical experience. The aim of negative theology, Royce explains, is the sense of a "higher and lower." This sense occurs when a symmetric pair, each the negative of each other, exists in a world filled with complex polyadic relationships. Such complexity draws out of the symmetric negative pair an implicit asymmetry of value, the sense of a "higher and lower." "Higher and lower," however, describes what I consider the fundamental aesthetic experience, the semiotic aesthetics known as "foregrounding." I shall use this aesthetic insight of Royce to describe, in the next chapter, the third transcendental of Being, the Beautiful.

FROM THE TRUE TO THE GOOD

Royce always concerned himself with knowing the True under the conditions of evil. In his day, the philosophical discussion over knowing the True centered on the relationship between the "facts" of perceptible experience and the "ideas" we make of that experience. Royce changed the nature of that debate by adding the condition that the relation between "fact" and "idea" always takes place in the knowledge of good and evil. This condition leads him into an ever deeper inquiry into the nature of Truth. Eventually this inquiry (with some help from Peirce) allows him to make an original and striking contribution on the relationship between the True and the Good. I shall try to describe this intellectual journey by exposing his thought on Being as found in *The World and the Individual*.[3] Royce struggles with the relation between

---

[3]*The World and the Individual*, the informed reader may know, represents Royce's earlier metaphysics. By 1915–1916, Royce gave a series of lectures at Harvard known as the *Metaphysics 1915–1916*. The difference between the earlier and later metaphysics is substantial. Royce's understanding of the thoroughly social nature of Being and, thus, of knowledge becomes crystal clear in the later metaphysics thanks, in no small part, to the influence of Charles Sanders Peirce. From the social nature of Being and knowledge, Royce worked out the inescapable social nature of the Individual. Royce's *Metaphysics 1915–1916*, however, at the time of this writing, exists, as far as I know, in manuscript form and is difficult to get. Fortunately, thanks to the unflagging efforts of one of the leading scholars of Royce's works, Fr. Frank Oppenheim, S.J., Royce's *Metaphysics 1915–1916* should be published by the time this book comes out in print (Josiah Royce, *Metaphysics 1915-1916*, Frank Oppenheim, S.J., and Richard Hocking, eds. [New York: SUNY Press, 1998]). Though I received a pre-final copy of Royce's *Metaphysics 1915-1916*, thanks to the generosity of Father Oppenheim, it came at the time of my final revising of this chapter. Thus, they were not incorporated in the fol-

Fact and Idea bringing to light that three conceptions of Being describe such a relation in the history of philosophy. Royce, then, proposes his own Fourth Conception of Being by examining the difference between Truth as Judgement and Truth as Correspondence. Royce discovers that Truth as Correspondence leads to a view of Being as Individual.

Royce's Fourth Conception of Being, however, exhibits properties of a logic of signs but Royce does not seem to notice. Peirce fortunately does. He encourages Royce to study logic which eventually culminates in a new logic of signs. Royce now begins his own paradigm shift as he explores what a logic of signs implies when knowing takes place in a world that bears the weight of sin. Interpreting signs in the context of a sinful world is best described as interpreting when one "crosses a boundary" into a foreign country. Interpreting signs under the conditions of "crossing a boundary" involves interpreting a mind different from one's own to a third mind. Such interpretation of signs involves a "Will to Interpret," that is, the will to be receptive to that mind which is other than mine and then to make a faithful interpretation of that mind's thought to another mind. Such interpreting reveals the ethical logic Royce calls "loyalty."

"Loyalty," however, creates committed community, a Community of Interpretation. This loyal evergrowing Community of Interpretation Royce identifies as the body of Christ. The Logos-Spirit guides and inspires the Beloved Community by being both its Interpreter and its Will to Interpret. The Beloved Community guided and inspired by the Logos-Spirit calls all individuals to an act of "at-one-ment" with the community. Such "at-one-ment" results in the salvation of the individual. Thus, interpreting signs, in Royce's vision, becomes an act of redemption. Such redemption takes place as the Beloved Community interprets a past tragic Passion to a future salvific Kingdom creating a Community of the present. As such, the Beloved Community is in pilgrimage. It pilgrims towards the future, interpreting the signs of redemption, atoning for evil and thus embodying the second transcen-

---

lowing presentation. Nonetheless, I believe that the basic aims of this chapter to present Royce's thought as the Community of the Good and the suggestion of a potential aesthetics has not been compromised. I do ask the reader to beware, however, that Royce had developed a later metaphysics which built upon *The World and the Individual* and brought his thought much closer to Peirce's own. There exist also in Royce's later metaphysics some explicit references to aesthetics which I do not mention. These references, however, only add to the argument that Royce's thought had aesthetic potential even if not fully developed by this great thinker explicitly.

dental of Being as the Community of the Good. In summary, Royce's thought will be exposed in this section as an ever-deepening exploration into the relationship between Fact and Idea done in the context of the knowledge of good and evil. This leads Royce to envision a new relationship between the True and the Good and, thus, between the Community of the True and the Community of the Good.

BETWEEN FACT AND IDEA

The "World as Fact," Royce tells us, surprises us with its variety of contrasts, its bewildering diversity of different beings. Such a baffling World of facts gives rise to the conviction that there is a "higher" vision or consciousness that allows the Individual to make sense of the facts. This "higher" vision, known as the "Idea," has had two major formulations in the history of philosophy. The Idea has either been seen as an image of "outer sense impressions," or an "ultimate and inexplicable power" to cognize facts external to themselves. Plato would explain this power as the presence of an Ideal World. There is, however, another way to understand this power.

Such understanding depends on recognizing the right relationship between the intellect and the will. "The difference between merely seeing your friend, or hearing his voice, and consciously or actively regarding him as your friend, and behaving towards him in a friendly way, is a difference obvious to consciousness, whatever your theory of the sources of mental activity."[4] This difference, the mere imaging of sense impressions (the intellect) and the active attitude towards these sense impressions (the will), goes beyond the difference between the intellect and the will. "For, as a fact, the intellectual life is as much bound up with our consciousness of our acts as is the will. There is no purely intellectual life, just as there is no purely voluntary life." Indeed, "your intelligent ideas of things never consist of mere images of the things, but always involve a consciousness of how you propose to act towards the things of which you have ideas."[5]

Thus, Royce proposes his definition of idea as "any state of consciousness, whether simple or complex, which, when present, is then and there viewed as at least the partial expression or embodiment of a single conscious purpose."[6] Such definition has definite implications. A

---

[4] Josiah Royce, *The World and the Individual*, introduction by John E. Smith, reprint, 1900 (New York: Dover Publications, Inc., 1959) 21.

[5] Ibid., 22.

[6] Ibid., 22–23.

color simply seen is no idea nor is a sound merely heard. "But a melody, when sung, a picture, when in its wholeness appreciated, or the inner memory of your friend, now in your mind, is an idea. For each of these latter states means something to you at the instant when you get it present to consciousness."[7] Royce's genius begins to show in these brief definitions. Ideas are more than passive intellectual concepts or active inventions of the will. Our will and our intellect, together, subtly relate us to the external World impinging upon us. We do not merely respond to the World; we appreciate it. In terms of the theory of knowledge, Royce says that to understand the World is to appreciate it. Appreciation and understanding together constitute our ideas about the World. This supposition carries an important corollary. Appreciation, like the example of the melody, involves a grasp of the wholeness of a reality. Our understanding, however, can only represent it. Thus, we can appreciate more than we understand. As such, our ideas of the World are never fulfilled. We appreciate, through our ideas, more than we can know.

Royce, thus, points to the "internal" and "external" meaning of an idea. The "internal" meaning, its embodiment of purpose, its representation of an appreciation of a wholeness bigger than the individual, leaves unfulfilled the total grasp of the wholeness of the actual reality, the "external" meaning of the idea. It is the relation between the "internal" and "external" meaning of the idea that ties the "world-knot" of fact and idea. This world-knot, the relation between "internal" and "external," reveals the tension of previous theories of knowledge. If we psychologize the "internal" meaning of the idea, we lose its necessary connection to the wholeness of reality, i.e., the Individual Whole, the "World." If we absolutize the "external" meaning of the Idea, we lose the essential role of the individual. Indeed, the "world-knot" consists in keeping the relation between the World and the Individual in necessary tension. This relationship depends, however, on our conception of Being.

According to Royce, three conceptions of Being present themselves throughout the history of philosophy. All three conceptions of Being relate essence and existence and, thus, conception and perception, in some unique way. The First Conception of Being, for example, sharply separates essence from existence and perception from conception. The Second Conception of Being does the opposite. It radically dissolves the

---

[7]Ibid., 24.

difference between essence and existence towards pure existence and pure perception. The Third Conception of Being errs on the essentialist side. The real is purely essential and, thus, purely conceptual. Royce's strategy, then, appears clear. He will offer a Fourth Conception of Being that avoids these extremes. Essence and existence and perception and conception are distinct but related. The nature of this relation will lead him to affirm with Aristotle, "All Being is Good." Royce's Fourth Conception of Being is comparable to von Balthasar's analogy of Being. Both affirm that in the real distinction of Being a significant relation holds. The conviction of a real relation between essence and existence and perception and conception led von Balthasar to a theological aesthetics. For Royce, this conviction will lead him to a sacred ethics.

The First Conception of Being

Royce denotes the First Conception of Being as Realism. It makes a sharp distinction between the "what," i.e., essence, and the "that," i.e., existence, of Being. Royce, of course, refers to the real distinction of Being but in its extreme form. This extreme distinction between essence and existence corresponds, in turn, to the epistemological conviction that perception and conception have little in common. Perception is one thing; conception another. As such, conception encounters perception dyadically in order to produce the mind's knowledge of the real. Such dyadic encounter results in making reality completely independent of the action of the mind. Only perception may "touch" the real. Conception must conceive the real indirectly on its own. As such, Royce describes, essentially, Ockham's razor. Royce's description of the "realist" position reveals another dimension of nominalist thought. Ockham's razor slices away the role that feeling plays in the understanding of reality. This consequence follows in the way Realism, or, rather, nominalism, defines the difference between real and unreal thoughts.

Since ideas and reality are sharply distinct, real thoughts can be distinguished from fictitious ideas only in the way they refer to emotion or feeling. A real thought corresponds to the *what* of an external reality, an essence unmoved by passion or feeling. Fictitious thoughts, on the other hand, depend "wholly upon ideas, the hopes, dreams, and fancies which conceive them." Because ideas are unsubstantial, they can be formed by irrational processes. Fictitious thoughts exist because feeling, emotion, and dreams have the power to shape, indeed, conjure unsubstantial ideas. A fictitious thought, in other words, is a reality that is purely *that*, i.e., mere existence without essence.[8] Such a position has implications in the understanding of "difference." The "realist" position sacrifices the *that*, i.e., the "difference," of beings, to the determination of the *what*, i.e., the "identity," of beings. Thus, reason proceeds from essence to existence as a judgment of identity.[9] This has the unfortunate effect of subordinating the meaning of difference to the identity of essence. It also denies a role to feeling or emotion in determining reality. Indeed, any idea whose source can be traced to feeling, emotion, or fancy is fiction. The negative implications of such a conception of Being for a theological aesthetics seem evident enough.

The Second Conception of Being

The Second Conception of Being, Mysticism, asserts "that to be means, simply and wholly, to be *immediate*."[10] Royce sees this approach as a pure empiricism. Indeed, he maintains "that the mystics are the only thoroughgoing empiricists in the history of philosophy."[11] Experience, mystics assert, shows explicit human ideas as fleeting, partial, disconnected and contradictory. This happens because we do not go deeper into the interior of experience itself. We seek to go beyond the pure immediacy of experience by making ideas of the experience. If we would go deeper and deeper into experience, the mystics say, a place will be found from which there is no beyond, the peace of the pure immediate. "Only in the immediate that has no beyond, is such peace. Now that is the Reality, that is the Soul. Or, to repeat the Hindoo phrase: "That art Thou. That is the World. That is the Absolute." Thus, for the Mystic, Reality involves the quieting of thought. "Reality is that which you immediately feel when, thought satisfied, you cease to think." Thus, "Mysticism defines Real Being as wholly within Immediate Feeling."[12]

As such, mysticism concentrates entirely on existence at the expense of essence. This position accentuates the role of perception denigrating the role of conception. Indeed, it is anti-conceptualist. This has the salutary effect of emphasizing the differences of existents, but it does so at the expense of their identity. The net effect, unfortunately, is to lose the meaning of the difference between existents. Difference, in

---

[8]Ibid., 62.
[9]Oppenheim, *Royce's Mature Ethics*, 106.
[10]Royce, *The World and the Individual*, 80.
[11]Ibid., 81.
[12]Ibid., 82.

this conception of Being, has no "teeth." Since there is no real identity, there is no real difference. Every existent merges with another in a postmodern-like world of arbitrary meaning. In other words, the individual becomes absorbed into the world of existence as, some mystics have proposed, a drop of water becomes absorbed in the ocean. Thus, Royce finds fault with Mysticism (or, at least, extreme empiricism). He rails against a conception of Being as "ineffable immediate fact which quenches ideas."[13]

The Third Conception of Being

The Third Conception of Being may be put this way. "What is, gives warrant to ideas, makes them true, and enables us to define determinate, or valid, possible experiences."[14] In other words, ideas must "conform" to reality. "To be real now means, primarily, to be valid, to be true, to be in essence the standard for ideas."[15] This notion of Being has as inspiration the Being of mathematical forms.

The mathematical creations of the human imagination have "all the variety, the stubbornnesss, and the frequently unexpected characters which, in the ordinary world, are said to belong to real beings."[16] It is a free creation of the mathematician's mind, but a creation accomplished by the laws of validity. The world of mathematics, however, may be the world of validity but is it the world of reality as well? What complicates the question is that the world of validity appears to have a rigid and objective nature. The constructive imagination manages to unite freedom with consciousness, will and intellect. Nonetheless, it is still a world where the senses are absent, and only concepts exist. As such, Critical Rationalism is predominantly conceptual. It is less the world of the senses than it is the world of concepts.[17]

---

[13]Royce, however, does not rail against all mysticism. The reader is guided towards his study of Meister Eckhart, namely Josiah Royce, "Meister Eckhart," in *Studies of Good and Evil: A Series of Essays Upon Problems of Philosophy and Life* (New York: D. Appleton and Company, 1898) 268. Moreover, Royce's philosophy has often been identified as containing a type of metaphysical mysticism. Frank Oppenheim, for example, identifies Royce's study of Spinoza as well as his essay on "Moral Insight" in the *Religious Aspect* as examples of metaphysical mysticism. See Oppenheim, *Royce's Mature Ethics*, 57.

[14]Royce, *The World and the Individual*, 266.

[15]Ibid., 202.

[16]Ibid., 226.

[17]Ibid.

As predominantly conceptual, the world of validity, that is, the world of Critical Rationalism, depends on judgment. The reality of a concept can not be "proved" through empirical evidence. The senses do not exist in that world. The conceptual equivalent of the scientist's laboratory is the human capacity for judgment. Judgment, however, has both a subjective and an objective dimension. Subjectively, judgment weaves already present ideas into a larger more meaningful idea. Judgment synthezises. Objectively, judgment combines ideas that have an external meaning, i.e., possess a meaning which is "at once Other than themselves, and, in significance, something above themselves." Judgment, then, involves both a Truth no longer independent of our ideas but also not defined by them.

Thus, "To judge is to judge about the Real. It is to consider internal meanings with reference to external meanings. It is to bring the *what* into relation with the *that*."[18] The *that*, however, exists as an individual while the *what* is a universal. Thus our judgments paradoxically make Reality more and more indeterminate. The more we judge, the more we enter the world of abstraction. Reality, in this view of Being, paradoxically becomes more and more ghostly the harder we try to conceptualize it. As such, Scotus' concern for the individual presents itself again to critique this notion of Being. Both the individual and the universal are realities in their own right. In judging the validity of an idea, we may grasp the universal but we leave the individual far behind.

The Key to Truth

The individual, however, is the key to Truth. Consider what uniqueness involves. An individual determines his or her uniqueness not only by including various identifying characteristics but also by excluding many others. Indeed, an individual gains identity more by what it isn't than what it is. This has certain implications for an understanding of Truth. If the unique, determinate individual represents Truth, then Truth "is a step from vague possibilities, and towards determinateness of idea and of experience. . . . Being, then, viewed as Truth, is to be in any case something determinate, that excludes as well as includes."[19] Thus, when judgment consults experience it is to give ideas a more determinate character, to limit themselves "to this content and no other."

Yet human experience never reaches such determination. It remains for us "the object of love and of hope, of desire and of will, of

[18]Ibid., 271–73.
[19]Ibid., 206.

faith and of work, but never of present finding."[20] Nonetheless, Individual Determination reveals the very nature of the Real, an ideal "towards which we endlessly aim." The Third Conception of Being, however, fails to grasp the "Real as the finally determinate that permits no other." In this failure, Critical Rationalism loses the insight that the internal and external meaning of ideas have profound connections. "Their linkage is the deepest fact about the universe."[21] Indeed, at the heart of their linkage lies the nature of the meaning of difference. It becomes, for Royce, the guiding principle behind his proposal for a Fourth Conception of Being.

The Fourth Conception of Being

The problem with Critical Rationalism is a one-sided concern with Truth "as that about which we judge." There is, however, another understanding of Truth which also must be taken into account. Truth has an ancient definition as the "correspondence between our ideas and our objects." Both understandings are needed in an understanding of Being.[22] This assertion may be illustrated by referring to the previous dialogue between Albertus and Sophia with the material hologram corresponding to the aesthetic equivalent of Critical Rationalism. Truth as judgment involves the relation of similarity. The internal meaning of an idea must be similar to its external meaning. As such, it is a version of the copy theory that was the subject of Albertus' and Sophia's dialogue. Thus Truth-as-judgment when applied to an aesthetic reality (say Michaelangelo's *David*) functions as a material hologram. If the copy of Michaelangelo's *David* resembles the original *David* itself in every way, then the copy is judged real. Unfortunately, the copy of the *David*, aesthetically, is hardly the same reality as the original. This aesthetic example suggests Truth-as-judgment fails because it destroys, like the material hologram, the meaning of difference and, thus, the meaning of the dynamic relation between the internal and external meaning of the idea. In order to complement and, thus, correct this understanding of Truth, Royce proposed the complementary notion of Truth's correspondence.

Correspondence, unlike, judgment need not require a relation of similarity. A map illustrates the difference. A map consists of symbolic elements depicting some actual terrain. Unlike a photograph, a map's

[20]Ibid., 297.
[21]Ibid., 209.
[22]Ibid., 210.

symbols bear little likeness to the actual terrain depicted. A map reveals that correspondence need not exhibit a relationship of likeness between two objects. Indeed, a squiggle can correspond to an actual river! Thus, Royce asks:

> But what, then, is the test of the truthful correspondence of an idea to its object, if object and idea can differ so widely? The only answer is in terms of Purpose. The idea is true if it possesses the sort of correspondence to its object that the idea itself wants to possess. Unless that kind of identity in inner structure between idea and object can be found which the specific purpose embodied in a given idea demands, the idea is false. On the other hand, if this particular sort of identity is to be found, the idea is just in so far true.[23]

A map, for example, fulfils the definite purpose of transforming relationships of terrain into symbolic relationships on paper. True correspondence occurs if the symbols of the map match its intended purpose, an accurate guide to an actual terrain. Another way of saying this is that "an idea, again, is true, as a chess player is skillful, or an artist is powerful, or a practical man is effective."[24]

Thus, Royce transforms Critical Rationalism by adding the requirement of truth's correspondence to illuminate "the deepest aspect of the universe," the linkage between the internal and external meaning of ideas. As such, this linkage involves both intellectual and volitional elements. As Royce put it:

> Whatever else our ideas are, and however much or little they may be, at any moment, expressed in rich, sensuous imagery, it is certain that they are ideas not because they are masses or series of images, but because they embody present conscious purposes. Every idea is as much a volitional process as it is an intellectual process. It may well or ill represent or correspond to something not itself, but it must, in any case, make more or less clearly articulate its own present purpose. The constructive character of all mathematical ideas, the sense of current control which accompanies all definite thinking processes, the momentary purposes more or less imperfectly fulfilled whenever we conceive anything,— these are evidences of what is essential to processes of ideation. Volition is as manifest in counting objects as in singing tunes, in conceiving physical laws as in directing the destinies of nations, in laboratory productions as in artistic productions, in contemplating as in fighting. The embodied purpose, the internal meaning, of the instant's act, is thus a

---

[23]Ibid., 306.
[24]Ibid., 310.

conditio sine qua non for all external meaning and for all truth. **What we are now inquiring is simply how an internal meaning can be linked to an external meaning, how a volition can also possess truth, how the purpose of the instant can express the nature of an object other than the instant's purpose** [emphasis mine].[25]

The lengthy quote with the added emphasis underlines the motive for Royce's Fourth Conception of Being. Royce sees Being as having intrinsic ethical value. Being is not only true. Being is also good. Because Being is not only true but also good, Royce can ask when does will possess the truth. The will's truth corresponds to rather than judges the real. As such, there is a yes and no to our willed convictions. Royce's Fourth Conception of Being, then, reveals a dimension of Being, i.e., Moral Being, implicit in the second transcendental, the Good, but rarely made explicit.[26]

A NEW DIRECTION

Royce's Fourth Conception of Being emerged from his struggle to understand the relation between Fact and Idea. That relation presents itself as Truth. Royce, like Scotus, realized, however, that the individual was the key to Truth. This means that Being as Individual becomes the key to the relation between perception and conception. Being as individual, however, requires Truth to be less a judgment than a correspondence. Truth as correspondence reveals the role the will plays in the intellectual search for the True. Thus, in that extremely significant relation that connects Fact to Idea both the intellect and the will is to be found. Moreover, it is in that significant relation that the connection between the True and the Good is also to be found. What Royce failed to notice, however, was the sign-like nature of that relation. Truth as

[25]Ibid., 311.

[26]Much is left unsaid about the significance of Royce's Fourth Conception of Being due to the twin demands of a forced brevity of presentation and disciplined focus on the aesthetic implications of Royce's thought. Royce scholars would, justifiably, find this description of one of Royce's greatest insights rather "thin." They would (indeed, they have!) point out that Royce's Fourth Conception of Being shows its genius in revealing the "social" nature of true individuality which, in turn, is founded on the affective love of an individual to a neighbor. I can only respond with acknowledging their justifiable complaint and after my deep regrets that the "social" nature of interpreting signs could not have been developed further. My only defense is my own judgement that Royce's rich thought cannot be fully exposed in one chapter and such development needs to be sacrificed for the greater whole, namely, the aesthetic project I have called the Community of the Beautiful.

Correspondence, like symbols on a map, is intrinsically sign-like. Peirce immediately recognized the potential semiotics in Royce's Fourth Conception of Being and chided him to study the logic of signs. It is not often that a teasing remark results in a productive outcome. Peirce's chiding, however, led Royce to a study which culminated in the *Principles of Logic*.[27] Royce, emerging from this intense study, now begins his most mature work, *The Problem of Christianity*, which he models after the new logic. The role of the will in the search for the True now begins to shape, as well, a Community of the Good.

THE COMMUNITY OF INTERPRETATION

Can signs be redemptive? Traditional theological doctrine, of course, identifies certain signs, the sacraments, as redemptive. Hispanic theologians further see in the signs of popular religion a redemptive dimension. Royce, however, constructs an entire philosophical system around the redemptive nature of signs. This philosophical system he calls the Community of Interpretation. The next section attempts to expose the intricacies of Royce's redemptive Community of Interpretation. Royce took Peirce's logic of signs and applied it to his own preoccupation with the problem of evil. These two major sources of motivation produces a philosophical system that may be seen to start as the problem of interpreting signs in the presence and confrontation with evil. Guided by the logic of signs, Royce adds new nuances to Peirce's triadic logic which leads him to the ethical notion of "loyalty."

Loyalty concerns the will to interpret a mind other than one's own to another mind. Such interpreting results in community, i.e., a community of interpretation. Done in the context of the knowledge of good and evil, such interpretation amounts to a reconciliation of an individual to a community of interpretation. It is, in a sense, an "at-one-ing," i.e., drawing into and becoming "one" with a community, which heals the tragic consequences of evil. Royce identifies such a redemptive community in the community known as the body of Christ. The body of Christ becomes manifest in the unifying activity of interpreting individuals guided and inspired by the "Logos-Spirit" that acts as the Interpreter for the community. It is a community in pilgrimage to a future end whose fruits shall be full reconciliation. This brief

---

[27]My copy comes from Josiah Royce, "Principles of Logic," in *Royce's Logical Essays: Collected Logical Essays of Josiah Royce*, Daniel S. Robinson, ed., reprint, 1914 (Dubuque: Wm. C. Brown Company, 1951) 310–78.

sketch, then, describes the next major section of this chapter. It aims to demonstrate Royce's transformation of the second transcendental of Being into the Community of the Good.

Interpreting Signs in the Garden of Good and Evil

Hispanic theologians ought to find a kindred intellectual spirit in Josiah Royce. Rarely has a modern philosopher (before the Holocaust) confronted the problem of evil as persistently and consistently as Royce. Indeed, Royce felt the problem of evil to be one of the most important issues pressing the philosophy of his day. Indeed, the problem of evil may be said to have been his chief inspiration motivating all his works.[28] Like Hispanic and Latin American theology, Royce affirms the fact that all intellectual inquiry takes place in a confrontation with evil. Royce, however, also has another insight to offer Hispanic theology. As mentioned earlier, the early missionaries in the Americas came preaching redemption while the native religions preached cosmic order. Royce, in his reflections on evil, offers a way of reconciling Christian Redemption and Cosmic Order. Royce saw all evil as a "disteleology," that is, as irrevocable events whose effects continue long after the event to work against a future end. Evil disteleology includes "death, error, sin, misunderstandings, misfortunes, and so forth."[29] In other words, evil introduces dynamic disorder and chaos into the world which serve to place in doubt the future.[30]

What does Christian redemption mean in the context of the cosmic disorder that is evil disteleology? It means interpreting signs in the garden of good and evil. As Royce put it:

> If the being of the world involves interpretation, then the interpretation of evil will not amount to showing that it is only an apparent evil. It will involve that which for the person who suffers the evil would appear as a reconciling element in his life.[31]

In brief, interpreting signs in the knowledge of good and evil involves redemptive suffering whose product is reconciling the disorder and chaos

---

[28]Oppenheim, *Royce's Mature Ethics*, 152.

[29]Ibid.

[30]The early missionaries to the Americas found the Indian's concern with "evil spirits" rather disconcerting and difficult to reconcile with the doctrine and dogma they so faithfully tried to transmit to their new converts. Royce's notion of "disteleology" would, I believe, have been of great help here.

[31]From Royce's Last Lectures in Metaphysics 1/15 quoted in Oppenheim, *Royce's Mature Ethics*, 153.

evil introduces into the world. Christian redemptive suffering reconciles the world's ends to the chaos produced by the presence of evil. The details of this compact statement will now occupy our attention.

The Knowledge of Good and Evil

Perhaps the most motivating issue for Royce's philosophy lies in the nature of the relationship between intellectual inquiry and the experience of evil. As he himself put it, "To what extent does an experience of evil add to our intellectual ability?"[32] Royce realized that the answer to that question means confronting a paradoxical situation. Can one do good without knowing evil? A moral choice, after all, is a conscious choice which involves "a knowing of something *against* which one chooses, as well as something in favor of which one decides."[33] As such,

> the consciousness of every moment of moral choice involves, also, a consciousness—a confession, if you will—of the presence in the chooser of that which he himself regards as evil. He not only coldly knows, he includes, he possesses, he is beset with some evil motive; and, nevertheless, he conquers it. This is involved in the very formal definition of a moral act.[34]

Thus, Royce is saying, doing good involves more than resisting the temptation to sin. Moral choice involves the very presence of sin in our consciousness. We do not simply decide for the good against the bad as a simple act of the will. The very presence of sin in our consciousness also means the consciousness of both good and evil. Doing good, then, involves not simply an act of will but also an act of knowing. Thus, "the knowledge and presence of evil form, in very manifold and complex ways, a moment in the consciousness and in the life of goodness."[35]

The place of the knowledge of good and evil in the willing of the good leads to a certain cooperation between the will and the intellect:

> The man who has sinned may gain inspiration for reform from coolly considering the very heart and the essence of his sin, that he may find in

---

[32]Josiah Royce, "The Knowledge of Good and Evil," in *Studies of Good and Evil: A Series of Essays Upon Problems of Philosophy and Life* (New York: D. Appleton and Company, 1898) 90. The mature Royce answered this question in a more penetrating ay in his masterpiece, *The Problem of Christianity*. There he describes what he calls the "three attitudes of will" showing only one as right. Frank Oppenheim considers Royce's analysis of will the "turning point in *The Problem of Christianity*."

[33]Ibid., 99.

[34]Ibid.

[35]Ibid., 112.

its fruits the seeds of coming virtue. The man who has the temptation, by facing it, and so by knowing its secret, may win control over it, and may thereby use his opportunity for holiness. When in progress I abandon one knowledge for another, I do so because the other is more of a knowledge.[36]

Thus, doing the good does not so much undo the sin but, rather, reconciles us to it. It does so "in the sense that it can make us feel that on the whole the sin was better done than not done."[37] In other words, doing the good in the knowledge of good and evil is less the undoing of evil (the traditional doctrine of atonement) but a *felix culpa* which leads us to the knowledge that "we should rather have had the sin and its atoning act, than neither."[38]

This unique view of atonement is one of Royce's most striking and original contributions. Though its orthodoxy can be called into doubt, it, nonetheless, contains a very traditional idea. The knowledge of good and evil calls all individuals to atone for the reconciliation of sin. Such atonement is not the traditional atonement, i.e., the payment of a debt or the sacrifice of a scapegoat, but rather atonement as *felix culpa* which inspires and guides heroic virtue, the defining characteristic of saints.[39] As Royce's thought matured, this atonement theory became an "at-one-ment" theory, a theory of building community through the interpretation of signs. Such "at-one-ment" begins when the boundary of a mind other than my own is crossed.

CROSSING THE BOUNDARY

Royce, in *The World and the Individual*, still framed his Fourth Conception of Being as a relation between these two terms, i.e., the World and the Individual. As such, Royce kept having difficulties with articulating the inspiring vision his ethics of loyalty demanded. Royce, however, finally saw in Peirce's logic of signs a fresh inspiration. The crucial issue, Royce realized, is not so much knowing an object external

[36]Ibid., 124.
[37]Elizabeth Flower and Murray G. Murphey, *A History of Philosophy in America*, vol. 1 (New York: Capricorn, 1977) 754.
[38]Ibid.
[39]Indeed, the process of canonization in the Roman Catholic Church is an inquiry into the heroic virtue of the would-be saint. For details and bibliography, see Alex García-Rivera, *St. Martin de Porres: The "Little Stories" and the Semiotics of Culture*, foreword by Robert Schreiter and, Virgilio Elizondo, Faith and Cultures (Maryknoll, N.Y.: Orbis Books, 1995).

to my mind but, rather, knowing a mind truly different from my own! Royce, apparently leaning on his Californian background, suggests a brilliant example:

> If a traveller arrives at a boundary provided with (A) Gold coins (perceptions) and (B) bank notes (conceptions), he may discover that while both A and B are good on one side (that is, on the side *from which* he travels) neither A nor B are good on the other (that is, the side *to which* he travels); A is not legal tender in the country q to which he goes, and although B is convertible into A, A is not legal tender in q. The difficulty can only be overcome only if a process which is neither the presentation of A, nor the attempted conversion of B into A is introduced. The process C of *interpreting* A in terms of whatever it is that corresponds to A in q, is exactly the process required.[40]

The crossing of a national frontier, perhaps the border between Mexico and California, amounts to the encounter of a mind truly different from my own. Thus, if I cross the Mexican border with American silver dollars and my checkbook from Wells Fargo and try to buy a souvenir, or even a meal, I may be out of luck. I could have exchanged my silver dollars for Mexican pesos at the border, but then I would be left with a useless checkbook (i.e., conceptions). Similarly, I might have written a check at the nearest Wells Fargo bank to the border and gotten more silver dollars. In crossing the border, however, I would now have useless dollars (i.e., perceptions) and no checkbook (conceptions) at all!

Perceptions and conceptions show their inadequacy when a boundary is crossed, when a stranger is encountered. Perceptions and conceptions fail to grasp the truly other. As such interpreting knows in a different way than conceiving or perceiving. Interpreting knows across differences. Interpreting grasps the meaning of difference. For this reason it is, as well, communal. In truly knowing a mind different from my own, the interpreter, myself, and the other have become a small community.

Royce, however, adds another element which Peirce had already developed. Signs are not made in a temporal vacuum. Signs are made in the context of signs already made. Signs have a history! Because signs are historical, they also have a future. Signs are addressed to future selves or individuals. Triadic interpretation, then, involves a temporal dimension. "The *present* interprets the *past* to the *future*."[41] Royce's

---

[40]Josiah Royce, *The Problem of Christianity* (New York: The MacMillan Company, 1914) I:130ff.

[41]John E. Smith, *Royce's Social Infinite: The Community of Interpretation* (New York: The Liberal Arts Press, 1950) 84.

logic of signs results in communities with a past and headed for the future. Thus, interpretation is knowledge that is infinitely richer than either perception or conception alone. Perception, or conception are self-limiting process. Once their actions are done, their significance ends. Interpretation, on the other hand, in its infinite conversation with present, past, and future minds is capable of leading "to what neither one of these can produce alone, namely, a view of God, the universe and man's place in it."[42]

Royce's use of Peirce's logic of signs into a temporal process of interpreting which creates community adds a new nuance to the community of inquiry. We interpret as in a mirror darkly. The historical reality of signs reveals present experience as fragmentary and dispersed. We interpret but we do so as pilgrims of experience. Yet such an act of interpreting also joins us to a common future. As Smith so well put it:

> For Royce the elementary processes of comparison and the more complex processes of interpretation represent, above all, our attempts at unification and the creation of community. Ultimately, interpretation aims at self-knowledge through a unification and clarification of both our ideas about ourselves and our ideas about the world of which we are a part. . . . Unification of what was previously dispersed and fragmentary is achieved precisely through the "third" of comparison and interpretation, and such unification is of the essence of the type of growth characterizing human beings.[43]

The elementary act of comparing or constrasting difference is not only an elementary act of knowing but also an elementary act of union. Signs unify as they interpret![44]

LOYALTY

Interpreting a mind truly different from my own involves a certain attitude of will. Royce recognizes, like Hispanic theology, that the encounter with human difference involves conflict. That encounter, however, can become an opportunity for creating community. The encounter with a mind truly different from my own might make me realize my own narrow and estranged perspective. I have crossed a

---

[42]Ibid., 85.

[43]Ibid., 95.

[44]This is, in essence, Royce's famous "epsilon" principle which forms the backbone of his logic of signs. I have decided not to develop it here but refer the interested reader to Frank Oppenheim's fine exposition in *Royce's Mature Philosophy of Religion*, op. cit.

boundary and now I stand either with impoverished but familiar riches or I can convert my universe of discourse into a new, unfamiliar but truly rich experience. This essential moment of crossing boundaries, of encountering that which is other, is also a moment of decision. Will I or will I not decide to interpret? This moment is also Hispanic theology's moment. It is the moment when Iberian missionary meets the Mexican priest. It is the moment when an Irish bishop encounters Hispanic popular religion. It is the moment that decides between hell or redemption. It is the moment when one wills to interpret.

The will to interpret, as Royce puts it, involves the decision to attain

> a luminous vision of your ideas, of my own, and of the ideas of the one to whom I interpret you. This vision would look down, as it were, from above. In the light of it, we, the selves now sundered by the chasms of the social world, should indeed not interpenetrate. For our functions as the mind interpreted, the mind to whom the other is interpreted, and the interpreter, would remain as distinct as now they are. There would be no melting together, no blending, no mystic blur, and no lapse into mere intuition. But for me the vision of the successful interpretation would simply be the attainment of my own goal as interpreter. This attainment would as little confound our persons as it would divide our substance. We should remain, for me, many, even when viewed in this unity.[45]

This unity, surprisingly, is both an ideal event—"the spiritual unity of our community"—and an empirical event—"I have compared pairs of ideas . . . and discovered their mediating third idea."[46] Indeed, Royce goes on to his famous formulation, "all, we three,—you, my neighbor, whose mind I would fain interpret, —you, my kindly listener, to whom I am to address my interpretation,—we three constitute a Community . . . a Community of Interpretation."[47]

This has the striking corollary that community may be treated as one would treat an individual:

> A community is not a mere collection of individuals. It is a sort of live unit, that has organs, as the body of an individual has organs. A com-

[45]Royce, *The Problem of Christianity*, II:210. Royce's description of interpretation must move the Hispanic theologian. It raises a haunting question. What would the Latin American Church have looked like if the process above had taken place? And then, the Hispanic theologian realizes that it did take place. Interpretation is the reason why there is a Latin American Church. Mary of Guadalupe became the interpreter who interpreted the indigenous mind to an Iberian mind. Royce has, in a sense, described, in part, the role popular religion plays in the Latin American and Hispanic Church!

[46]Royce, *The Problem of Christianity*, II:215.

[47]Ibid., II:211.

munity grows or decays, is healthy or diseased, is young or aged, much as any individual member of the community possesses such characters. Each of the two, the community or the individual member, is as much a live creature as is the other. Not only does the community live, it has a mind of its own, —a mind whose psychology is not the same as the psychology of an individual human being. The social mind displays its psychological traits in its characteristic products,—in languages, in customs, in religions,—products which an individual human mind, or even a collection of such minds, when they are not somehow organized into a genuine community, cannot produce. Yet language, custom, religion are all of them genuinely mental products.[48]

That a community can be treated as an individual is one of Royce's greatest ethical insights. It envisions a type of ethics that is more than the ethics of how an individual ought to act as morally autonomous agent but rather the ethics of how an individual ought to act as member of a community (and, of course, how a community ought to act towards a member individual).

Such an ethics describes a certain type of act which is difficult to name. It concerns the "very human motives for behaving towards his community as if it not only were an unit, but a very precious and worthy being."[49] It is the act of "his own heart's desire."[50] Such an act of devotion is hard to describe. Royce, however, ventures forth a name. "I know of no better name for such a spirit of active devotion to the community . . . than the excellent old word 'Loyalty.'"[51] Loyalty is

> the willing and thoroughgoing devotion of a self to a cause, when the cause is something which unites many selves in one, and which is therefore the interest of a community. For a loyal human being the interest of the community to which he belongs is superior to every merely individual interest of his own. He actively devotes himself to this cause.[52]

But what, exactly does devotion to a cause mean? It means, Royce says, devotion to a community, a Community of Interpretation. The Community of Interpretation, then, describes Royce's meaning of loy-

---

[48]Ibid., I:62.

[49]Ibid., I:66.

[50]Royce, *The Problem of Christianity*, I:67. Note here the aesthetic implications. If theological aesthetics may be defined as "that which moves the human heart," then Royce's ethics as "the act of the heart's desire" describes the ethical response to an aesthetic experience.

[51]Royce, *The Problem of Christianity*, I:68.

[52]Ibid.

alty. Loyalty is dedication to interpreting an ideal in such a way that it results in the loving union of individuals.[53]

Royce's Community of Interpretation begins when an individual "crosses a boundary," i.e., encounters a mind different from one's own. This encounter with difference may or may not result in the inspired choice to truly understand this different mind. If the will to interpret is there, then interpretation takes place and a community happens. It is no ordinary community. For in the will to interpret, the interpreter surrenders his own understanding towards understanding an other's mind. As such, it amounts to discovering a foreign land. On such a discovery, interpretation occurs and all three minds form a loving union of individuals. But what type of community takes place? It is here where Royce introduces his understanding of Christianity.

Royce asserts that the creed of Christianity consists in three fundamental doctrines: the Beloved Community, sin, and atonement.[54] In describing the Beloved Community, Royce took the Pauline notion of the body of Christ to heart:

> This new being is a corporate entity,—the body of Christ, or the body of which the now divinely exalted Christ is the head. Of this body the exalted Christ is also, for Paul, the spirit and also, in some new sense, the lover. This corporate entity is the Christian community itself.[55]

In other words, the Beloved Community is now a super-organic person who is the *whole* Christ himself. This community is also a Community of Interpretation with a historical past (Jesus of Nazareth) in pilgrimage to the future (the Kingdom of God). Though the historical Jesus is now no longer present, Jesus left us the "Logos-Spirit" in order to guide and inspire the Community in interpreting its past to the future for the present and will lead us into all truth.

Christianity, then, is less a community begun by Jesus Christ as it is a community interpreting Jesus Christ through the guidance and inspiration of the Holy Spirit in pilgrimage to the here but not-yet Kingdom of God. As such, the Community of Interpretation takes on redemptive dimensions. Individuals do not interpret in an ethical vacuum. Indeed, interpretation takes place in the garden of the knowledge of good and evil.

---

[53]The reader ought not to miss the universal implications in Royce's notion of "loyalty." Loyalty as loving union of individuals is, in a sense, loyalty to a "universal" loyalty, i.e., a deep commitment to the practical growth of genuine loyalty in *every* human being whether friend or foe.

[54]Ibid., I:35ff.

[55]Ibid., II:425.

As discussed above, Royce realizes that a logic of interpretation which accounts for the will must also account for the knowledge of good and evil. The knowledge of good and evil, acquired in the Garden of Eden, begins not as "resisted temptation but from actual sin."[56] As such, interpretation can not be an "innocent" logic. Interpretation carries "the essential penalty of sin."[57] As such, interpretation either leads us towards life or death, towards a living community of love or a deadly community of hate.

Interpretation, thus, leads to life as an "at-one-ment."[58] Interpretation is an "at-one-ing" act "which elevates the morally detached individual to the superhuman life of the divinely loyal community."[59] This divinely loyal community, however, knits itself together through the action of the Interpreter-Spirit, or, as Royce calls it, the Logos-Spirit. The Logos-Spirit corresponds to the unity of the Incarnate Word and the Holy Spirit of Christian doctrine. When the individual interprets with the Community, the result is an atonement, i.e., an "at-one-ment," a becoming one with the Community. Such atonement is essentially a decision for love in the context of knowing evil. Thus when an individual wills to interpret under the inspiration of the Logos-Spirit who also is the Will-to-Interpret, such interpreting becomes as well a moment of salvation. In his reading of Christianity, Royce transforms the Community of Interpretation into a Community of Salvation through his brilliant appropriation of Peirce's logic of signs. As such, the Community of Interpretation inspired by the Will-to-Interpret is a community making a decision towards the Good. Under such conditions, the Community of Interpretation becomes, as well, the Community of the Good!

THE COMMUNITY OF THE GOOD

Thus, under Royce's exposition, the search for the True in the garden of good and evil becomes a Community of Interpretation hero-

---

[56]Royce, "The Knowledge of Good and Evil," 117.

[57]From a Note appended to the fifth draft of *The Problem of Christianity* quoted in Oppenheim, *Royce's Mature Philosophy of Religion*, 51.

[58]I spelled atonement this way to signify the special emphasis Royce gives to atonement. It is not the atonement most theologians associate with Anselm. Royce's atonement is based more on the Pauline vision of communion in community, an "at-one-ment" of the repentant individual into the body of Christ. See, specifically, Royce's interpretation of Paul's vision of community in Royce, *The Problem of Christianity*, lecture 2.

[59]Oppenheim, *Royce's Mature Philosophy of Religion*, 52. A traditional theologian might substitute the word "superhuman" for the theological term "supernatural."

ically interpreting the signs of their own redemption. In doing so, the Community of Interpretation becomes a Community of the Good. The perceptive reader may ask, however, where is grace to be found in this salvific community? Is not grace a defining characteristic of the Beloved Community? Indeed, implicit in the entire discussion of the Community of the Good is the problem of grace. For Royce, "The problem of grace is the problem of the origin of loyalty."[60] One cannot merely choose a cause at random and then decide to become loyal. This is even more so in the case of the Beloved Community. The cause itself must be compelling. It must somehow elicit one's love. Only then can one become loyal. As Royce himself put it:

> It [loyalty] will always be to you the finding of an object that comes to you from without and above, as divine grace has always been said to come. . . . The cause is a religious object. It finds you in your need. It points out to you the way of salvation. Its presence in your world is to you a free gift from the realm of the spirit—a gift that you have not of yourself, but through the willingness of the world to manifest to you the way of salvation. This free gift first compels your love. Then you freely give yourself in return.[61]

The role of grace as the origin of loyalty lifts up the issue of Beauty in Royce's thought. Loyalty cannot be forced. It must be elicited. This, however, corresponds not only to grace but also to Beauty. Grace, like Beauty, calls and compels. It moves one's heart. Thus, Royce, though silent about Beauty and the beautiful, implicitly alludes to these in his doctrine of grace. Indeed, Royce rarely mentions Beauty or the beautiful but all throughout his work there are many insights that suggests a "hidden" Roycean aesthetics. The next section examines Royce's work for signs of such a "hidden" aesthetics.

ROYCE'S HIDDEN AESTHETICS

Richard Clarke Cabot once wrote Royce why he had omitted Beauty as one of the sources in *Sources of Religious Insight*. In a letter dated June 25, 1912, Royce admits to Cabot that

> Yes, beauty is a "source" that my list ought to have contained. . . . My omission of that source is a defect, and needs a simple confession as

---

[60]Royce, *The Problem of Christianity*, I:191.

[61]Josiah Royce, *The Sources of Religious Insight* (New York: Charles Scribner's Sons, 1912) 206.

such, although I believe that I have never heretofore told you what I suppose to be the nature and source of this defect in my view of such things. Personally, I have *some* access to beauty especially in *two* realms, viz.; music, and nature-beauty; together with a fairly warm, but, as you know, limited access to poetry. As to music and nature-beauty, I am, and must remain, naïve, ignorant,—at best childlike. My own childhood was passed in a mining town, and later in S[an] F[rancisco]. I never saw any beautiful object that man had made until I was twenty years, I left California for Germany. . . . Of beauty, therefore, I must not prophesy. The less I say about beauty, the more sincere will be, and sound, the little that I have any right on occasion to stammer. . . . So here is the defect. It is subjective and insignificant. What beauty I *have* known has meant to me some things that I long to say, if I might, and that have brightened the world for me with a light that I deeply wish to be able to characterize. But it all remains for me, in *this* life, either unutterable, or tragic, or sacred. . . . Read me then, always subject to this defect, which you, or anybody, must condemn, without my being able to defend myself.[62]

Thus Royce confesses to his "defect." He would include beauty as one of the sources of religious insight but his understanding of aesthetics or beauty left much to be desired. Nonetheless, he senses that a familiarity with beauty would allow him to express "some things that I long to say."[63] Indeed, Royce warns Cabot to read his work with the knowledge that he writes with this "defect." In spite of all this confessing, however, a careful review of Royce's works, especially his logic, reveals many hidden aesthetic insights.

Royce's discussion of Moral Being, for example, gives crucial insights into an aesthetics. Truth, for example, as correspondence rather

---

[62]Josiah Royce, *The Letters of Josiah Royce*, John Clendenning, ed. (Chicago and London: University of Chicago Press, 1970) 577–78.

[63]It is interesting to note here a segment of a famous letter Peirce wrote to Royce (June 30, 1913) within a year of Peirce's death:

As for my *Pragmatism*, though it is very well as far as it goes, it chiefly goes to improve the *security* of inference without touching, what is far more important, its *Uberty*. It doesn't for instance seem to have any thing to say as to our exaltation of *beauty*, *duty*, or *truth*. . . . I am going to insist upon the superiority of Uberty over Security in the sense in which *gold* is more useful than *iron* though the latter is more useful in some respects" (printed in *Transactions of the Charles S. Peirce Society*, 26 [1990] 141–43).

By *Uberty*, Peirce meant as Frank Oppenheim notes, "full breasted fecundity." The quote indicates a certain sensitivity by both Peirce and Royce of what I would call the aesthetic roots of reason. The fecundity of reason, in other words, is a manifestation of its orientation to Beauty. These deep thinkers of logic apparently had grasped this neglected dimension of logic or reason.

than judgment helps envision the nature of the aesthetic experience. Going back to Albertus and Sophia's dialogue, we see part of the reason why Raphael's *David* carries aesthetic value while the *David* of the material hologram does not. Raphael's *David* **corresponds to** Michaelangelo's original *David* not simply resembles it. Raphael does not attempt to **copy** Michaelangelo's *David* but rather **embody** Michaelangelo's aesthetic purpose. Part of the difference between the material hologram's and Raphael's copy of *David* is the difference between a **mere copy** and a **good copy**, i.e., good in the moral sense. A good copy does not simply make a successful likeness of the original but, rather, matches successfully the intended purpose of the original creation towards the embodying of an aesthetic ideal. As such, it is a **good** copy. Royce's insight into Moral Being shows striking congeniality with Peirce's late aesthetics. Both support an aesthetics based on the ideal. Note, however, that a **good** copy does not necessarily make it a **beautiful** copy. Royce's insights reveal the dimension of the Good in all Truth, even the Truth of copying an original work of art. To get at the dimension of the beautiful, we must dig a bit deeper.

Nonetheless, an ideal aesthetics raises a significant issue. How does one account for the validity of an aesthetic experience? Are not some aesthetic experiences invalid? The pageantry of one of Albert Speer's Nazi rallies may be aesthetically beautiful but it also corresponds to an aesthetic experience that takes us far, very far, from the Beauty that is God. What Critical Rationalism and Royce's Fourth Conception of Being helps us understand is that if Beauty constitutes reality, then aesthetics must be held accountable for the validity of the reality of that presenting itself as beautiful. Royce's works suggest such validity implies a principle of correspondence. Such correspondence, however, is only possible if one distinguishes Beauty from the beautiful. Beauty, as the real, can then be related to an aesthetic experience, the beautiful. This has the important consequence that Beauty always corresponds with the beautiful but not all that appears beautiful corresponds to real Beauty. This important consequence, then, suggests that one ought to be able to tell the difference between the really beautiful and the beautiful that deceives. This adds a dimension to theological aesthetics that von Balthasar leaves very unclear.

Royce, moreover, adds another tantalizing dimension towards a theological aesthetics. Judgments of Truth which correspond to Reality embody ideas towards determining a reality that is at the same time profoundly individual and profoundly Whole. As such, a vision of Being spreads before us which is

in essence a realm of fact fulfilling purpose, of life embodying idea, of
meaning won by means of the experience of its own content. The now
present but passing form of our human consciousness is fragmentary.
We wait, wonder, pass from fact to fact, from fragment to fragment.
What a study of the concept of Being reveals to us is precisely that the
whole has a meaning, and is real only as a Meaning Embodied.[64]

This grand vision of Being suggests that aesthetics may also be seen as
Beauty fulfilling the beautiful, of life as the embodying of Beauty, and
the beautiful as fragmentary yet meaningful experiences of the greater
Whole, Beauty itself. It suggests the truly beautiful as a Community in
pilgrimage to Beauty. It suggests the Community of the Beautiful. Does
von Balthasar's aesthetics fit within this implicit vision? It is difficult to
say. Von Balthasar's aesthetics lacks the clarity of Royce's or Peirce's
thought. His contribution to our project continues to be the goading
prompt rather than the clear answer towards the reality of a theological
aesthetics. There exists, however, an interesting intersection in Royce's
thought with von Balthasar's. It is found in Royce's logic.

A LIVING LOGIC

The relationship between von Balthasar and Royce lends itself to
further exploration. Von Balthasar's crucial aesthetic insight, "seeing
the form," has an important connection to another element of Royce's
thought, logic. As such, the reader may be experiencing not a little im-
patience with the author. "What does logic have to do with aesthetics or
von Balthasar?" I respond by asking for more of the reader's already
taxed patience and pointing to the clearly implicit yet not-so-obvious
relationship between order and form. "Seeing the form" involves as well
a vision of order. Order, however, reflects the laws of logic. "Seeing the
form," then, in its vision of order also reflects a logic. There is something else to consider, however. While all aesthetic form embodies a system of order, not all systems of order contains aesthetic form. While
von Balthasar makes the former clear, the latter, though implicit, is less
clear. The distinction, however, is crucial if the notion of an aesthetic
validity is to be made. In other words, not all beautiful things are necessarily things of beauty. Royce, in his insight into logical order, makes
clear this distinction and, thus, helps us see a dimension of von
Balthasar's aesthetics, a dimension little developed by the master.

---

[64]Royce, *The World and the Individual*, 368.

Royce in *Principles of Logic* reexamined the role of both intellect and will in logic through the notion of order. Logic, in Royce's time, envisioned order, like Critical Rationalism, as purely conceptual. Order, this view held, consists of numbers. Numbers, however, are less a matter of experience than a matter of the mind. Numbers can be conceived but not experienced. Numbers, however, exhibit ordered behavior, i.e., they follow certain rules, an algebra, which can be "discovered." No wonder, then, that so many mathematicians feel that an algebra (the lawful behavior of numbers) suggests that numbers are "really" real.[65] This identification of the purely conceptual with the "really" real makes numerically ordered systems an Ockhamian festival. Numerical order knows little of lived experience, however. It knows only the logic of Ockham's razor. Such, however, was the logic Royce received before the turn of the century. Through Peirce's influence and the contribution of the logician, A. B. Kempe, Royce conceived a new way to envision logical order. Ten years later, Royce called this new vision of order "system Sigma."

There are other ways, Royce said, to conceive logical order besides the algebra of numbers. Royce built upon the work of the logician, A.B. Kempe. Kempe asked himself what would happen if the points in a finite line segment were conceived as logical entities. Up to now, logical entities had simply been numbers. Kempe, to his amazement, realized that treating these points as newly conceived logical entities forms a logical system of order with a unique property. The position, i.e., order, of one point to the next can always be determined because a point "in-between" these two points can always be found! This happens because of the properties of a line form. Any two points along a line can be subdivided again and again. Thus, a finite line-segment produces an ordered system because "between any two points on a line, there is an intermediate point, so that the points on a line constitute, for geometrical theory, at least a dense series."[66] Points on a line conceived as elements of an ordered set turn out to be perfectly logical. Kempe discovered a connection between geometrical form and a logical system of order!

Royce, upon reading Kempe's work, realized the congeniality of Kempe's new system with a triadic logic of signs. Geometrical form embodies triadicity! Any geometric form can be analyzed in terms of an

---

[65]This philosophical issue continues to be a great problem in contemporary mathematical logic. The interested reader may whet his or her appetite for the interesting controversies this view has caused in Davis, Phillip, and Hersh, Reuben, *The Mathematical Experience* (Boston: Houston, Mifflin Co., 1981). See especially chapter 7, "From Certainty to Fallibility."

[66]Royce, "Principles of Logic," 373.

intermediate, a "third" point which relates two other points on the form. All these points, then, constitute a system ordered less by the laws of algebra than the laws of form! Kempe's proposal astounded many logicians weaned on Ockhamian milk. A "third" that interprets the order between two points smacks of willfull human intervention into the purely conceptual world of Ockhamian logic. Indeed, the principle of a "third" interpretant in the world of logical order means a world where difference "makes a difference." Geometrical form, after all, knows the difference between a circle and a square. A logic of numbers, on the other hand, knows only conceptual form. A logic of numbers "forms" its world ideally. Such a world can not know true difference.

Royce saw in Kempe's system a way to combine the insights gained in *The World and the Individual* and Peirce's triadic logic of signs. A world ordered by the principle of a third "interpretant" whose source is geometrical form requires entities that truly differ one from another. Points on a line must truly differ from one another if they are at all to trace the shape or form of a line! Kempe's system reaffirms the nature of difference in a triadic system. "Thirds" reveal the meaning of difference while "dyadic," i.e., "ideal" order, subordinates the meaning of difference. Royce immediately saw the implications of Kempe's system. There is only one kind of entity that allows true difference to exist, namely, the individual, the key to Truth.

Thus, Royce began to formulate a logic of signs that combines Kempe's and Peirce's insights. Logical order consists not simply as a collection of objects but as a collection of *individual* objects. Such an affirmation makes logicians weaned on Ockham's milk cringe. An individual object, Royce explains, is

> one that we propose to regard at once as recognizable or identifiable throughout some process of investigation, and as unique within the range of that investigation, so that no other instance of any mere kind of object suggested by experience, can take the precise place of any one individual.[67]

In defining the individual object as such Royce demonstrates an affinity with Scotus. To propose treating an object as both recognizable and unique is to treat an object as *this* object, or as Scotus would say a *haeccecity*. Moreover, to treat an object as *this* object and not another requires an attitude of will that can sustain attention upon the object yet is not warranted by the object itself. The will must freely attend its focus on the individual object.

[67]Ibid., 350.

This relationship between will and individual object may be more fully described. As Royce puts it:

> The concept of an individual is thus one whose origin and meaning are due to our will, to our interest, to so-called pragmatic motives. We actively postulate individuals and individuality. We do not merely find them. Yet this does not mean that the motives which guide our will in this postulate are wholly arbitrary, or are of merely relative value. There are some active and voluntary attitudes towards our experience which we cannot refuse to take without depriving ourselves of the power to conceive any order whatever as present in our world . . . to conceive of individual objects is a necessary presupposition of all orderly activity.[68]

Unique individuals, however, throw a monkey wrench into a purely ideal system of order. True difference does not lend itself well to absorption into pure abstraction. Yet abstraction ruled the logic which Royce now challenged. No wonder then some traditional logicians recoiled in horror at Royce's proposal.

A question, however, remains. It is all well and good to postulate the unique individual but what, exactly, constitutes a unique individual? Since the unique individual resists conceptualization, then how can such an entity be described? Royce, of course, had an answer:

> This set of objects may be defined as, "certain possible modes of action that are open to any rational being who can act at all, and who can also reflect upon his own modes of possible action." Such objects as 'the modes of action' have never been regarded heretofore as logical entities in the sense which classes and propositions have been so regarded. But in fact our modes of action are subject to the same general laws to which propositions and classes are subject."[69]

Thus, modes of action replace numbers as logical elements. "Singing," "dancing," and "painting" become valid logical entities forming a well defined system of order.[70] Royce, like Einstein, had combined the logical equivalent of space and time into a new geometric theory of "relativity," i.e., a triadic theory of interpretation relating order and form. As such, Royce's theory allows an ethical formulation.[71]

---

[68]Ibid.

[69]Ibid., 373–74.

[70]The perceptive reader may also appreciate that "seeing the Form" is also a "mode of action."

[71]Royce's new system of order based on geometrical form, i.e., system Sigma, parallels, in my estimation, the proposal made by Einstein of the General Theory of

Royce's new logical entities, the "modes of action," make clear the accounting of both intellect and will in the new logical system. In Royce's logic "concepts unite in a very characteristic way—'creation' and 'discovery,' an element of contingency and an element of absoluteness."[72] Thus, Royce's logic affirms the "discovery" proper to a Realist position while at the same time acknowledging the "creation" activity of mind of a Conceptualist position. A logic whose entities are "modes of action" lends itself well to describing an ethics. Royce's logical system, however, also raises the possibility of a new philosophical aesthetics.

By modeling system Sigma as a geometry of order, Royce, in a sense, gives logic "eyes." Each "third" interpreting order in the system Sigma is also describing an overall geometry. As such, triadic interpretation within system Sigma is also the act of "seeing" geometrical form. Thus, Royce's logic becomes a "seeing logic" which, like von Balthasar's insight, may be said as well to be a "seeing the form." That Royce did not see the aesthetic implications of his system seems hard to explain. Yet it is true that it was the Good not the Beauty of Being that inspired his logic. Nevertheless, Royce through his study of logic brought forth medicine to heal deep wounds caused by Ockham's razor. Intellect and will, the eye's vision and the mind's imagination, numerical order and geometrical form, all found organic unity under Royce's new theory of "relativity." Though Royce did not explicitly see the aesthetic implications of his logic, he did conceive an essentially aesthetic notion, the sense of a "higher and a lower" occurring when negation occurs in a logical system of order when ordered according to geometric form.

The Aesthetics of Negation

Royce observed that Kempe's geometrically ordered system of logic obtains an interesting property. The obverse of Kempe's system results in a logical world of elements all related as the obverse of each other.

Relativity. Einstein, like Royce, geometrized what was considered purely numerical, namely space and time. In Newtonian physics, time and space are conceived numerically. Their reality consists in that they are essentially measurable. A number sufficiently describes an extension in space or a period of time. In other words, space and time are essentially quantitative. On the other hand, when scientists plot these numbers under experimental conditions, say the motion of a baseball from a pitcher's hand to a catcher's glove, form emerges, such as a parabola. Scientists ignored the role of form in Nature until Einstein suggested that motion be thought less as a numerical trajectory in space than a geometry which wove space and time into patterns. Royce did no less than Einstein.

[72]Royce, "Principles of Logic," 363.

The obverse of an element is, in a sense, its "negative." More generally, the obverse is what an element is "not." Thus, "cat" is the negative of "not-cat." They are also obverses of one another. "Cat," however, is also the obverse of "dog." A "cat," after all is not a "dog." "Cat," however, is not the negative of "dog." In other words, all negative pairs are obverses of each other but not all obverses are negatives of each other. More important, however, is the fact that negatives only occur as symmetric pairs whereas obverses occur in unlimited asymmetric relationships. Thus, whereas "cat" and "not-cat" can only exist as a symmetric dyadic pair, "mouse," "cat" and "dog" form an asymmetric obverse relation. A world of obverses, then, constitutes a most interesting world. A world of obverses is a world of unique individuals having nothing in common yet intrinsically related! Moreover, a world of obverses allows for infinitely more complex relationships than a world of negatives. Royce saw in the obverse of Kempe's system the possibility of combining his insight into Being as Individual and Peirce's logic of signs. Royce called such a system an "O-collection."[73]

This did not make Royce's system any less triadic. Indeed, Royce proved that his obverse system functioned triadically. Royce's obverse system, however, now allowed for infinitely more complex logical relations. Triad, tetrad, quintad, sextad, octad, indeed, poly-ad relations flourished in Royce's obverse system of relations. Royce's O-collection could now describe complexity. As such, Royce's logical O-collection becomes the obverse (and antidote) of Ockham's logical razor. Where Ockham's razor slices in two, Royce's O-collection knits into ever more complex patterns. Royce's O-collection becomes, in a sense, form come alive. Indeed, Royce called it a "living logic." Royce's obverse collection, however, has another curious and profoundly aesthetic property.

In a world of simple logical negatives, one cannot make positively affirmative or negative statements:

> From the logical point of view, there are no modes of actions which are essentially positive, and none which are essentially negative. If a man says in answer to the request to work in the vineyard, "I go not," his act is, logically speaking, both affirmative and negative. He negates the request "Go work"; he takes the contradictory, but for that very reason, also distinctly affirmative attitude of positively refusing to work.[74]

[73]The "O" refers to "obverse."

[74]Josiah Royce, "Negation," in *Royce's Logical Essays: Collected Logical Essays of Josiah Royce,* Daniel S. Robinson, ed., reprint, 1914 (Dubuque: Wm. C. Brown Company, 1951) 186.

In other words, to say yes to a proposition is to say no to its negative. Likewise, to say no to the same proposition is to say yes to its negative. "Yet common sense and ordinary experience sharply distinguish purely negative terms or terms that are defined by negation, from terms that are positive."[75] "Rich" is defined as the contradictory of "poor" yet common sense recognizes that one term has positive value and the other negative value. Thus, Royce raises the question: Where does value in ordinary experience come from?

Giving as example Lewis Carrol's *Hunting of the Snark*, Royce inquires into the nature of value in experience. The *Hunting of the Snark* involves a London Barrister dreaming that the Snark is "defending the pig on the charge of deserting his sty." It is a confused legal conundrum in which the valuable pig is held responsible for the business insolvency which his absence causes. The Snark, in the pig's defense, argues "The charge of Insolvency fails, it is clear, if you grant the plea, 'Never indebted.'" What the Snark does is to point that the charge of insolvency involves the negative relation "solvent" to "insolvent." Yet this negative relation takes place in a "limited universe of discourse," that is in a discourse where "solvency" and "insolvency" also refer to "debtors." "Debtors," however, refer to those with the power to pay their debts when due. As such, we no longer have the pure negative relation "solvent" to "insolvent" but, rather, the more complex relation solvent debtors to insolvent debtors. A solvent debtor, however, takes on a positive value for such a debtor always desires to pay his debts. An insolvent debtor takes on a negative value for the opposite reason. Thus, the Snark cleverly brought into the consciousness of the Court that the legality of "solvency" vs. "insolvency" does not hinge on the cold logic of the pure negative but rather involves a "limited universe of discourse" that alters the judgment of "solvency" or not towards the judgment of the value of debt. The pig, never having been in debt, can not then be so judged![76]

Royce's example serves to prove that

> "pure negation" can play no part in our concrete thinking and life, simply because it involves a merely symmetrical and logical relation between objects each of which is the negation of the other, and therefore is in a wholly symmetrical relation with the other, while there is no reason to declare one of the two negations to be the "positive" and "affirmative"

[75]Ibid., 187.

[76]Royce's account may be found in Royce, "Negation," 190–93. The perceptive reader may notice the striking parallel between Royce's notion of a "limited universe of discourse" and the claims of contextual method in theology.

member of the pair. **It is in association with the other relations which
life and experience most significantly present that negation becomes of
concrete importance.** When a man refuses to steal, society and the moral
law are interested, not merely in the purely logical distinction between
stealing and not-stealing, but also in what else the man does who does
not steal [emphasis mine].[77]

My emphasis serves to highlight the important role Royce's O-collection
plays in the matter of negation. Royce makes clear that negation in a system of complex relations, that is, negation contextualized, is the source of
value. Negation, in such a system as Royce's O-collection, results in the
giving "lower" or "higher" value to the two elements being negated.

This observation has an important religious application.[78] Heaven
and hell may be symmetrical negations of one another but they are
asymmetrically related. Heaven holds a "higher" value than "hell."
Indeed, all our religious notions are asymmetrical:

> It is important to see that the logical symmetry of the not-relation is
> needed as the basis of such unsymmetrical relations between good and
> evil, heaven and hell, salvation and perdition. Without negation none of
> these contrasts could be defined, none of these distinctions between the
> lower and the higher could come to clear consciousness at all; hence
> negation is an absolutely essential function of our thought and will.
> Without negation there would be no clearness with regard to values, no
> knowledge of heaven or hell, of good or evil. . . .[79]

This has certain practical implications for our conduct. The values obtained in our negations depend on the asymmetrical relations under
which those negations are made. In other words, the values obtained in
our negations depend on how we limit our "universe of discourse," how
we contextualize our negations. Thus, "the practical moral of all such
instances is that, both in our definition of the not-relations which interest us and in our whole use of negations, we should carefully consider the universe of discourse which we propose to employ as the field
within which to make our logical distinctions, and also the asymmetrical distinctions of value which arise within that universe."[80]

Royce has given us understanding as to how negation and value relate in an O-collection. Negation and value, however, is at the heart of

[77]Royce, "Negation," 269.
[78]The theologian may note the critical use of the notion of a "higher" and "lower" in
Aquinas' fourth way of demonstrating God's existence. *Summa Theologica* I q. 2 art. 3.
[79]Ibid., 199–200.
[80]Ibid., 201.

von Balthasar's theological aesthetics. Indeed, the *capax Dei* of the mystic, Royce says involves "a contrast between 'created being' and 'uncreated being.' Now whatever the relation of creation is, it is obviously viewed by those in question as unsymmetrical." The God of mystical experience is not merely the uncreated God but the God from which the created "emanates," or "descends," or is "produced." Thus,

> It follows that the so-called "negative theology," never tells us anything in terms of 'pure negation.' On the contrary, it very volubly characterizes a set of unsymmetrical distinctions of value, of preciousness, of grades of being, and of processes of emanation, which include various not-relations, but which depend for all their interest upon the fact that the mystic presents to us something of which he can say that it is best known "when most I feel there is a lower and a higher."[81]

It is here, I believe, where Royce comes closest to articulating a theological aesthetics. It is also here, I believe, that Royce comes closest to describing von Balthasar's "seeing the form."

The negative, or apophatic, language of mystical experience is, under the conditions of the O-collection, an aesthetics. In other words, Royce sees negative theology as needing to take place in a "limited universe of discourse." The mystical experience does not escape contextualization, it depends on it! For only in the context of asymmetrical relationships can its intended negation of conceptualization result in the mystical but thoroughly essential experience of a lower and a higher. It is an aesthetics very different, however, than the aesthetics described by the principle of "unity-in-variety." It is an aesthetics grounded in the experience of higher and lower! Such an aesthetics, fortunately, can be described. It is the semiotic aesthetics known as foregrounding and it shall become for us, the basis for the proposal of a community of the beautiful.

[81]Ibid., 203.

6

The Community of the Beautiful

A rich conversation is now drawing to a finish. Hispanic theology prompts the twin questions about the meaning of difference and the relationship between cosmic order and redemption. As such, it urges the theologian to explore the problem of good and evil as the struggle for meaning in the light of human and cosmic difference. In difference, the tragic story of the Latin Church of the Americas has shown, lies hell or redemption. Such struggle, Hispanic theology has come to realize, involves the aesthetics of signs and symbols. Von Balthasar then joins the conversation. Indeed, von Balthasar affirms, aesthetics is the key to such questions but it is not simply a philosophical aesthetics. What is at stake is the *capax Dei*, the human capacity to perceive the unperceivable, the finite capacity to experience the infinite, the naming the unnameable. Such capacity is ours as an intrinsic grace that nevertheless originates outside human subjectivity. It is found in the very structure of Being in the insuperable yet analogous difference between Creator and creature. As such, the *capax Dei* is, in essence, the capacity to experience Beauty, the site of the beautiful. It is, in von Balthasar's words, "seeing the form."

Von Balthasar's "seeing the form," however, raises as many questions as it answers. It identifies a theological approach to Hispanic theology's problem but gives precious little guidance to the philosophical basis of that approach. "Seeing the form" takes on, for us, the guise of the goading prompt which is, as well, a guiding light as we continue the conversation. Von Balthasar's light takes us to a conversation with Charles Peirce, whose logic of signs begins to give flesh to von Balthasar's aesthetic suggestions. Peirce's logic of signs has a cosmological dimension. Being is relational. Being manifests itself as the difference between creatures. The difference between creatures, however, reveals the transcendental dimensions of Being. This takes place in the logic of the sign, i.e., the elementary act of comparison of difference requiring a "third" mediating element, the interpretant. Together, the difference and its "interpretant" reveal the meaning of the difference. Interpreting a sign allows us to perceive more than we can know. As such, the logic of signs suggests the transcendental dimensions of Being—the True, the Good, and the Beautiful—may best be seen as relational realities, i.e., as communities interpreting signs. Indeed, Peirce shows us how Being manifests itself as a community interpreting the signs of reality, i.e., the Community of the True. Peirce, however, leaves only faint suggestions as to the shape of the other two transcendentals, the Good and the Beautiful. Aesthetics, Peirce tells us, is the foundation of the normative sciences—logic, ethics, and aesthetics. The True is built upon the foundation of the Good and the Good, in turn, is built on the foundation of the Beautiful.

At this point Peirce's friend and convert, Josiah Royce enters the conversation. Our intellectual inquiry, Royce reminds us, takes place in the encounter with evil. Royce asks the question of what it means to interpret signs in the knowledge of good and evil. To answer this question, Royce suggests Aristotle's dictum for a philosophy of Being—"All Being is Good"—as part of the logic of signs. Interpreting signs makes manifest Being as Good. The transformation of this ontological presupposition into a logic of signs requires another insight into the nature of Being. Being is fundamentally Individual. This insight allow Royce a redemptive formulation of Peirce's logic of signs. Interpreting signs, indeed, leads to a community of interpretation, but it also involves the transformation of an isolated individual into a member of such a community. The elementary act of comparison is also an elementary act of union. This unitive transformation of interpreting signs involves the ethical notion of "loyalty" to the community. "Loyalty" leads the individual to will-to-interpret a mind different from one's own to another mind. Such sacrifice of long-held assumptions to the receptivity of an other's assumptions results in an act of "at-one-ing" for the evil in the world, i.e., an act of unitive transformation into a community of loving interpretation of one another. When such "loyalty" refers to the Beloved Community of Christianity, the individual finds redemption in an "at-one-ment" with the inspiring and guiding "Logos-Spirit," which acts as the ultimate Interpreter of the community. As such, the "Logos-Spirit" guides the community in pilgrimage to the logical goal of all such interpreting—the Kingdom of God. Royce, then, effectively shows us the Community of the Good.

So far, however, none of our conversations has shown us the "form" of the Community of the Beautiful. Royce, however, did leave us one tantalizing suggestion. Royce expanded Peirce's logic of signs to include complex sign relationships without sacrificing the triadicity of Peirce's elementary sign. Consider, Royce said, a logical system of order that consists solely of unique individuals, i.e., individuals who are uniquely different (obverses) from one another. This logical world of unique individuals, the O-collection, has a unique property. A symmetrical obverse pair, i.e., a negation, becomes asymmetrical in value (one becomes a "higher" and the other a "lower") through the contextual relationships of the other elements in the system. Royce, however, did not see this as an aesthetic insight. I feel, however, that negation in an O-collection can become the key towards visualizing the Community of the Beautiful. Thus, like the characters in the opera "The Marriage of Figaro," Hispanic theology, von Balthasar, Peirce, and Royce have joined in aesthetic conversation towards solving a problem originating in the history and life of the Latin Church of the Americas. It is now time to join them and offer my own voice in this marvelous opera.

I will argue that Being has an intrinsic aesthetic dimension. Being's aesthetics are revealed when the two "differences" of Being—the difference between Creator and creature and the difference between creatures—are taken into account. These two "differences" are implicit in the medieval debate over God's absolute power (*potentia Dei absoluta*) and God's ordained power (*potentia Dei ordinata*). God's absolute power concerned God's ability to create a world other, even better, than this one. It concerns the power of God the Creator. God's ordained power, on the other hand, concerns God's love for *this* world rather than another. It concerns God's love for the difference of *these* creatures. Being, however, involves both of these dimensions of God's power. Being, after all, not only *is* but is *this*. These two dimensions implicit in Being form the equivalent of Royce's negation within an O-collection. God's absolute power in creating the universe gives the cosmos an implicit essentially aesthetic symmetry—to be or not to be. God's ordained power, on the other hand, reveals a love of difference, a love for *this* world. Thus, God's ordained power reveals a cosmos awash in God's love giving the essentially negative symmetry of existence an asymmetric "higher" and "lower" value through the contextualizing relationships ordained among the individual differences of Being's creatures. Being, in other words, is intrinsically aesthetic.

Having developed this notion of Being, I will attempt to locate it in a logic of signs—the semiotic aesthetics of "foregrounding" proposed by the semiotician Jan Mukarovsky. The semiotics of poetry, Mukarovsky suggests, consists of the principle known as "foregrounding," the lifting up of a bit of background and giving it value. The perceptive reader ought to immediately recognize the congeniality of "foregrounding" with Royce's negation within an O-collection. Indeed, "foregrounding" resembles von Balthasar's "seeing the form" and Peirce's "logic of signs." Mukarovsky's semiotic aesthetics prompts my suggestion of Being as Foregrounding, i.e., the "difference that 'difference' makes." As such, Mukarovsky's semiotic aesthetics becomes an auxiliary element in this constructive proposal which, in a sense, "marries" Peirce's and Royce's logic of signs with von Balthasar's insight into "seeing the form."

I then return to the original question asked at the beginning of this book: *what moves the human heart?* The answer is explored through a reappropriation of that long and ancient tradition called the "spiritual senses." The nature of the spiritual senses reveals a pragmatic sense developed by Ignatius of Loyola. This spiritual sense finds resonance in the Rabbinical notion of the *yetzer ha'Ra* and the *yetzer ha'Tov*, the good and evil imagination. Tracing the biblical notion of the "heart" and the "imagination" reveals the *yetzer* as the imagination that moves the human heart. Such a movement is best described in the Magnificat where an example of foregrounding, "lifting up the lowly," is given. Indeed, Mary's Magnificat suggests that what moves the human heart is the foregrounding of what I call the *anagogical* imagination. As such, the imagination corresponds to the "third" type of knowing that forms and shapes the interpreting Community of the Beautiful. Interpreting the signs of imagination reveals the "form," or rather the "heart," of the Community of the Beautiful.

AN AESTHETIC CONCEPTION OF BEING

This section has as main aim the development of an aesthetic conception of Being. The elements for such a development have already been described. Von Balthasar alerted us to the crucial dimension of the third transcendental of Being. Being as beautiful grounds all the others. Peirce developed his logic of signs by postulating Being as Relational. Royce continues our extended reflection through his Fourth Conception of Being—Being as Individual or the Good. Together, Peirce's and Royce's notions of Being suggest what Royce called an O-collection, a world of interrelated unique individuals. All that is needed, then, to develop an aesthetic conception of Being is the notion of Being as "negation," or as, I shall demonstrate, "foregrounding." Being as Relational, Individual, and Foregrounding constitutes Being as intrinsically a negation within an O-collection which gives all Being a sense of a "higher" and "lower." This sense of a "higher" and "lower" in the very nature of Being corresponds, as we shall see, to von Balthasar's *Mysterium Paschale.* Its development begins, however, by a question first posed by Peter Lombardus.

Peter Lombardus in his *Sentences* asked a particularly fecund question. Can God create a better world?[1] The question did not appear out of the blue. It arised out of a long theological tradition concerning the nature of God's omnipotence. The tradition may be traced back to Peter Damiani who wrote a treatise called *De divina omnipotentia* against those who argued, as Aristotle did, that not even God can change the past.[2] Damiani argued that God could have Rome not founded if God so wished. Anselm of Canterbury, however, was shocked. Damiani's argument implied a weak God. An omnipotence without limits means that God can also annihilate himself. God's power, Anselm asserted, must at least be limited by the principle of logical non-contradiction. Lombardus's question lifts out of the middle of this furious debate over God's omnipotence the crux of the issue. At the heart of the debate lies the fundamental Christian belief of the contingency of the world. Because God created the world, the world is radically contingent on God.

A contingent world, however, raises the question of its own necessity. God did not have to create the world *this* way. God could have created a different world if God had willed it so. The most that can be said by a theologian about a contingent world is that God, in creating the world, would not fall in some Self-contradiction. God cannot violate the logical principle of non-contradiction. Thus, the relationship between God and *this* world revolves around the logic of non-contradiction. On the other hand, God did make *this* particular unique world. Contingency also means that the finite order which characterizes this particular unique world is also dependent on God's power. As such, the particularity of *this* world appears to limit God's power beyond the logical principle of noncontradiction. Such a conclusion, however, makes

---

[1]"An Deus possit facere aliquid melius quam facit" found in Book 1, Distinction XLIV of the *Sentences.* Quoted in Steven J. Dick, *Plurality of Worlds: The Origins of the Extraterrestrial Life Debate from Democritus to Kant* (Cambridge: Cambridge University Press, 1982) 31.

[2]Damiani supported Gregory VII in the investiture struggle in the eleventh century.

the created order a necessary manifestation of God's power. Lombardus asked the question of a better world in order to answer this dilemma.

Aquinas answered Lombard's question by sharpening a Scholastic distinction between God's absolute power (*potentia Dei absoluta*) and God's ordained power (*potentia Dei ordinata*).[3] God's absolute power emphasizes the "difference" between Creator and creature. As such, God's absolute power means that God can, indeed, create a better world.[4] God's ordained power, on the other hand, emphasizes the "this-ness" of this world, i.e., the "difference" between creatures. Indeed, God's omnipotence in its two Scholastic distinctions encompasses the two "differences" that have highlighted our conversation up to this point. As such, the two distinctions in God's omnipotence suggest that a full theological aesthetics depends, in great part, in how one relates them. As we have seen, all our conversation partners acknowledged the two "differences," and, thus, the distinctions between God's powers. Nonetheless, each put a different emphasis on one "difference" over the other. Von Balthasar, for example, stressed the "difference" between Creator and creature in his analogy of being in order to understand the "difference" between creatures. Peirce and Royce, on the other hand, stressed the "difference" between creatures in the logic of signs in order to understand the "difference" between Creator and creature.[5] Is there, however, another way to relate the two "differences," and, thus, the two powers? And, if so, what are the implications for a theological aesthetics?

These questions, in a sense, were asked in the fecund theological debates of the eleventh and twelfth centuries. These questions were raised by an important theological consideration. *This* world was cre-

---

[3]Whether, in fact, Aquinas made such a sharp distinction is, of course, debatable. Since I am not an Aquinas' scholar, I am not in a position to debate it. On the one hand, Scotus felt Aquinas did make such a sharp distinction. On the other hand, Scotus' and Aquinas' position differ only by a matter of degree. In any case, my main argument with Aquinas' position on the distinctions in God's power is not the degree of the distinction but the conclusion that the ordained order of *this* world is an arbitrary even if wise choice of God. I believe it is much more than that.

[4]Amos Funkestein, *Theology and the Scientific Imagination*, op. cit., 121.

[5]I do not wish to be misunderstood here. All our conversation partners understood, appreciated, and accounted for both the transcendence and immanence of God in their understanding of Being and reality. I am merely observing that the way they relate these two divine realities reveal a decisive starting point. One reality is used to understand the other in each case. Thus, von Balthasar begins with the transcendence of God in God's absolute difference (and absolute power) to understand the immanence of God. Peirce and Royce begin with the immanence of God in God's ordained difference (and ordained power) to understand the transcendence of God.

ated through God's omnipotence. As such, both distinctions need an accounting in light of a particular, created world. Aquinas, Scotus, and Ockham all took different positions on the proper relationship between God's absolute and ordained power in light of a unique, particular creation. Aquinas, for example, reasoned that in the context of God's absolute power, God's ordained power suggests a certain arbitrariness. God's absolute power means God could have created an infinity of worlds. Nonetheless, God ordained *this* particular world. For Aquinas, this meant an arbitrary even if wise choice by the Creator. That God could be arbitrary in his power, however, deeply troubled Duns Scotus. Aquinas, Scotus felt, had too sharply distinguished between *potentia Dei absoluta* and *potentia Dei ordinata*. These were not two kinds of divine powers but merely different aspects of the same divine omnipotence.

Ockham, contrary to both Aquinas and Scotus, collapsed the distinction. Only God's absolute power may be taken into account as responsible for the contingency of the world. "Every divine act can be analyzed in view of what could have been otherwise—*de potentia Dei absoluta*. . . .[6] If Lombardus had asked the question of a better world, Ockham asked simply "why something and not nothing?" It is Hamlet's question of "to be or not to be" phrased in nominalist terms. By accounting for the contingency of *this* world purely on God's absolute power, Ockham had effectively destroyed a belief in "real" universals. Ockham's nominalist answer to Lombard's question also had the unfortunate effect of excluding theology from one of the most marvelous conversations in Modernity, the natural sciences.

Nowhere is the question of real universals more troublesome than in the natural sciences, especially physics. It is one thing to claim in our day that universals are real. It is another to claim they are natural! On the other hand, nowhere but in the natural sciences is the belief in a real universal a living, practical tradition. If one is to make an effective claim for the reality of universals, then an exploration of how the natural sciences use universals is a necessity. The issue of real universals in terms of the natural sciences may be put in the form of a question.[7]

---

[6]Funkestein, op. cit., 134.

[7]"Natural" real universals, in the seventeenth and eighteenth century, were called "laws of Nature." Though modern physics rarely understands physical Nature in those terms, it nonetheless bases much of its contemporary theoretical foundation on various natural "constants" such as the speed of light, the gravitational constant, and Planck's constant or principles such as the Heisenberg uncertainty principle. If not "laws," physical constants and principles are nevertheless "law-like." As such, the ques-

"Why should we assume that nature is well structured, and hence intelligible?"[8] One, for example, can easily imagine, without logical contradiction, a universe where massive bodies repel, i.e., a universe where gravity makes people fall "upwards" rather than "downwards." In other words, one can imagine a logical "universal" (all massive bodies repel) in an imaginary world that contradicts the physical order of Nature. Natural scientists, on the other hand, have the unmistakable conviction that Nature is, indeed, well-ordered and, thus, intelligible. Intelligibility in Nature, however, implies a real, i.e., "natural," universal. Thus, a dilemma poses itself for the theologian who believes in the contingency of the universe.

The theologian must assert the contingency of the universe. The natural order of things does not necessarily need to be the way it exists in the present. God could have created a better world. On the other hand, the theologian possesses the capacity to assert the necessary intelligibility of *this* universe. Within these two assertions, the contingency and the intelligibility of the universe, lie a series of implications that depend in a large part whether one takes Aquinas', Scotus', or Ockham's position on the relationship between *potentia Dei absoluta* or *potentia Dei ordinata*. Affirming solely the contingency of the universe places the theologian squarely on Ockham's camp. A theologian who feels all that can be asserted about *this* universe is its contingency believes, with Ockham, that the absolute power of God accounts for the entire divine omnipotence. Such a theologian can only focus on the existential dimension (i.e., the "to be or not to be") of the universe and has little to say to those interested in the intelligibility of the universe (such as natural scientists).

The theologian, on the other hand, who, with Aquinas, makes too sharp a distinction between the absolute and the ordained power of God also makes too sharp a distinction between the contingency and intelligibility of the universe. The universe may be understood apart from its intrinsic contingency. Such a position also gives the theologian little to say about the intelligibility of the universe. Scotus' position, however, makes the question of contingency relevant to the question of intelligibility. God's act of creating *this* world was both an act of absolute power and an act of ordaining power. It was an act which like the crucified Seraph reveals the awesome power of God in the weakness,

---

tion of real universals remains alive even in the contemporary physical sciences! Cf. Funkestein, op. cit., 120.

[8]Funkestein, op. cit., 119.

i.e., the limitations, of a particular creation. The theologian who takes Scotus' position finds, then, a common ground (the intelligibility of the universe) yet distinctive approach (the contingency of the universe) in the natural order of *this* world with which to converse with natural scientists. A question remains to be answered, however. How, exactly, can the theologian use the belief in the contingency and the intelligibility of the universe in dialogue with natural scientists whose major premise is simply the intelligibility of the universe?

Natural scientists often come up against rival, even contradictory, scientific theories. Such theories can only be decided by using a peculiar criterion particular to the natural sciences. Which theory is the most elegant? This question weans out competing rival theories by the conviction that Nature's intelligibility also possesses an aesthetic dimension. Nature's intelligibility is not only logical; it is also elegantly beautiful. Though natural scientists may be loath to say the natural universe is contingent, they would most likely agree that it is beautiful. The natural scientist can teach the theologian that if God created *this* world, God did so not simply as an arbitrary choice of possible worlds but because it was elegantly beautiful. The theologian, in turn, may then be inspired to take a new look at the ancient debate over God's omnipotence with a new conviction. The contingency of the world may be said to be a symptom of the Beautiful. Indeed, this conviction may be developed along the lines of Royce's aesthetics of negation.

Royce's aesthetics of negation, as the reader may remember, demonstrated that in a world of interrelated unique individuals, an O-collection, a purely symmetric negative pair becomes asymmetrically charged with value (a "higher" and a "lower") by the contextualizing power of the interrelations. The theologian who takes Scotus' position on the relationship between God's absolute and ordaining powers can make the claim that the world created by such an omnipotent God contains in its very being an aesthetics of negation. God's absolute power, after all, constitutes an intrinsic symmetric negative pair in every creature, namely "to be or not to be." Every contingent creature carries the negative symmetric pair of existence in its being. God's ordaining power, on the other hand, constitutes an interrelated world of unique individuals. Every intelligible creature may be said to be part of an O-collection! Since these two powers are intrinsically the same divine omnipotence, the nature of *this* world created by an omnipotent God consists in its very being an intrinsic negation within an O-collection of creatures. The interaction between the intelligibility of the world as O-collection and the contingency of the world in its existential negative symmetry charges the very being of the world with the sense of a "higher" and a "lower." Being, in other words, is, essentially, aesthetic!

The Poetry of Being

Royce's aesthetics of negation helps one understand Being as aesthetic when one takes into account the distinction between God's absolute and ordained power as different aspects of the same divine omnipotence. As such, it remains merely a remarkable observation. The next task involves the demonstration that such a notion of Being has credence in the logic of signs. If we can show that the aesthetics of negation is indeed a semiotic aesthetics, then the aesthetic conception of Being can be given logical flesh. Towards this end, we now turn our attention to the work of Jan Mukarovsky on the semiotics of poetry.

Jan Mukarovsky founded the special school of philosophical or linguistic aesthetics known as the "Prague School." Mukarovsky's most significant writings took place between the 1920s and the late 1940s. Mukarovsky's aesthetics began with his initial recognition that aesthetics is a "social fact." As Mukarovsky put it:

> There are some theoreticians of art who believe that the theory of art is synonymous with the psychology of art and who in a peculiar methodological twist deal with the psychology of the work of art instead of the (absolutely justifiable) psychology of the artist and his creativity. This is a contradiction in terms, for the work once finished ceases to be a mere expression of its author's psychic state and becomes a *sign*, i.e., a *sui generis* social fact which serves supra individual communication, severed from the subjective psychology of its author.[9]

Mukarovsky's notion of the work of art as an aesthetic "social fact," indeed, a sign, follows the basic intuition of the logic of signs that Peirce and Royce developed. Indeed, Mukarovsky's aesthetic "social fact," or sign, corresponds to the intrinsic aesthetic structure which is a work of art. The aesthetic experience consists of the intrinsic triad of artist, work of art, and audience.[10]

---

[9]"Umêlcova osobnost v zrcadle díla: Nêkolik kritickych poznámek k umênovêdné teorii i praxi" (The artist's personality in the mirror of the work: Some critical remarks on the theory and practice of the study of art) *Cestami* [1931] 145, quoted in Jan Mukarovsky, *Structure, Sign and Function: Selected Essays by Jan Mukarovsky* [New Haven, Conn., and London: Yale University Press, 1978] xvi.

[10]For the evolution of this triad in Mukarovsky's thought see the fine introduction given by John Burbank and Peter Steiner in Mukarovsky, *Structure, Sign and Function: Selected Essays by Jan Mukarovsky.*

As such, Mukarovsky may be said to be a semiotician of the "whole." Though described as a structuralist, Mukarovsky nonetheless describes the "whole" more along the lines of Peirce's logic of signs (practically but not self-consciously) than the lines of structuralism. "Structure," for Mukarovsky, consists of a contradictory collection of elements whose intrinsic contradictions create a dynamic interrelated whole. The perceptive reader will notice that in this description of whole, Mukarovsky describes a very different kind of whole from German Romanticism.[11] Indeed, Mukarovsky describes a whole that integrates the insights of Romanticism with the insights of scientific empiricism.[12] Mukarovsky also describes, in a sense, negation within an O-collection. Mukarovsky's contradictory collection of elements can, I believe, be given this interpretation. Unlike Royce, Mukarovsky's semiotics is self-consciously an aesthetics. As such, Mukarovsky serves to put flesh on the tantalizing suggestions of Royce's "aesthetics" of negation. Mukarovsky presents us with a well-developed semiotic aesthetics that can help tie all the different strands of our long conversation together. This, Mukarovsky does, through his original contribution of the semiotics of foregrounding.

Semiotic Aesthetics

Von Balthasar's analogy of Being has much in common with poetic language. As Mukarovsky observed, poetic language differs from standard language in the "esthetically intentional distortion of the linguistic components of the work, in other words, the intentional violation of the norm of the standard."[13] Just as our hearts are moved towards God when our "names" for God are shattered by the reality of God, so does

---

[11]The perceptive reader might also note the resemblance of Mukarovsky's "whole" to Royce's O-collection.

[12]Josef Habrak puts it:

> Structuralism is neither a theory, nor a method; it is an epistemological point of view. It starts out from the observation that every concept in a given system is determined by all other concepts of that system and has no full significance by itself alone; it becomes unequivocal first by integration into the system, which it has its definite, fixed place. The scientific work of the structuralist is thus a synthesis of the science of romanticism which achieved new cognition by deduction from its philosophic system by which it ex-post classified and evaluated the facts, and of the empirical, positivist point of view which, on the contrary, builds its philosophy from the facts which it has ascertained empirically.

as quoted in Jan Mukarovsky, "The Esthetics of Language," in *The Prague School Reader of Esthetics, Literary Structures, and Style, Selected and Translated from the Original Czech*, Paul L. Garvin, ed. (Washington, D.C.: Washington Linguistic Club, 1955) i.

[13]Mukarovsky, "The Esthetics of Language," 20.

poetry begin when standard language becomes shattered by an aesthetic aim. Indeed, intrinsic to Beauty is the violation of the norm.[14] As we have seen, Peirce recognized this. In his struggle to understand what he called "esthetics," Peirce realized that "esthetics" does not allow one to judge any one "esthetic" work as normative, i.e., as beautiful or ugly in itself. The normative character of "esthetic" works consists in that they themselves are not these norms. Indeed, the futile search for a particular "esthetic" norm reveals the dynamic aesthetic signification of "esthetics." "Esthetics" drives the interpretative inquirer to ultimate value, the *summum bonum*. As such, Peirce's understanding of aesthetics is remarkably similar to von Balthasar, Pseudo-Dionyisius, and, of course, Mukarovsky.

What sort of logic of signs, then, corresponds to this intrinsic violation of norms? What sort of semiotics allow one to "see" the "reasonableness," i.e., the "form," of Beauty? Mukarovsky, in a brilliant analysis of poetic language, allows us a glimpse of such a semiotic aesthetics. Following his observation that the systematic violation of a norm is the essence of poetic language, Mukarovsky considers the nature of the aesthetic. There is, Mukarovsky asserts, an "internal antinomy contained in the aesthetic, the antinomy between freedom and boundedness, between uniqueness and generality, which in the extreme cases lead to almost pure unstructuredness, or conversely, structuredness."[15] The perceptive reader may notice in this description an aesthetic restatement of the problem of the real universal. The relationship between the unique and the universal may be a philosophical problem but it is also the source of the beautiful. The relationship between uniqueness and generality, between freedom and boundedness (in other words, the meaning of difference) is also a relationship of aesthetic tension, a point of focused "energy," or as, Mukarovsky put it, "a regulating energetic principle."[16]

As "regulating," such tension acts as a very special type of norm. It is a norm that "makes its presence felt as a limitation on the freedom of

---

[14]As Mukarovsky put it in the case of poetry: "The violation of the norm of the standard, its systematic violation, is what makes possible the poetic utilization of language; without this possibility there would be no poetry" Mukarovsky, "The Esthetics of Language," 20.

[15]Mukarovsky, "The Esthetics of Language," 53.

[16]Jan Mukarovsky, "The Aesthetic Norm," John Burbank and Peter Steiner, eds. and trans., in *Structure, Sign and Function: Selected Essays by Jan Mukarovsky* (New Haven, Conn., and London: Yale University Press, 1978) 49.

his action."[17] Thus, an aesthetic norm involves an intrinsic dynamism which paradoxically presents itself as pointing beyond its own normative character. Thus,

> To sum up, we can state that the specific character of the aesthetic norm consists in the fact that it tends to be violated rather than to be observed. It has less than any other norm the character of an inviolable law. It is rather a point of orientation serving to make felt the degree of deformation of the aesthetic tradition by new tendencies. The negative application, which in other categories of the norm functions only as a concomitant, often uninvited, phenomenon in its positive application, becomes the normal case for the aesthetic norm.[18]

Here, in Mukarovsky's analysis, we see what Peirce had recognized. There is a dynamic quality to the aesthetic norm which, nonetheless, possesses a normative, i.e., regulative, quality. The aesthetic norm is less an inviolable law than a dynamic principle pointing the experience of the beautiful ever beyond itself. Thus, all conversations converge. The beautiful in its dynamism reveals a contingency which at the same time articulates a loving reasonableness, an awesome ordaining which is ultimate and absolute.

How is such dynamism created, however? What is it about poetic language or a work of art that incarnates such sublime tension? Mukarovsky answers these questions with his aesthetic theory of foregrounding. What is foregrounding? Foregrounding "lifts up" a selected piece of the background and gives it value. Thus, "the unit in the foreground . . . occupies this position by comparison with another unit or units that remain in the background."[19] As such, "Foregrounding is the opposite of automatization, that is, the deautomatization of an act; the more an act is automatized, the less it is consciously executed; the more it is foregrounded, the more completely conscious does it become. Objectively speaking: automatization schematizes an event, foregrounding means the violation of that scheme."[20] Foregrounding, in other words, is a special type of comparison which animates as it compares. Against a background, foregrounding accentuates some elements of that background thus animating the whole. In language foregrounding occurs when elements of the background standard language are accentuated through rhythm or diction or, even, association.

---

[17]Ibid., 50.
[18]Ibid., 52.
[19]Mukarovsky, "The Esthetics of Language," 23.
[20]Ibid., 21.

As such, foregrounding is, essentially, a very special type of comparison:

> The mutual relationships of the components of the work of poetry, both foregrounded and unforegrounded, constitute its structure, a dynamic structure including both convergence and divergence, and one that constitutes an undissociable artistic whole, since each of its components has its value precisely in terms of its relation to the totality.[21]

In other words, foregrounding's comparison gives meaning to the whole by creating a dynamic but bounded tension. This dynamic but bounded tension acts as beacon to something beyond itself. As comparison giving meaning, foregrounding follows the logic of signs. Indeed, foregrounding is the logic of aesthetics. It is a semiotic aesthetics.

As such, foregrounding's semiotic aesthetics reveals a unique dimension of the logic of signs perceptible only in the beautiful. The logic of aesthetics reveals a certain direction to the whole. As Mukarovsky puts it:

> It is . . . enough to disturb the equilibrium of this system at some point and the entire network of relationships is slanted in a certain direction and follows it in its internal organization: tension arises in one portion of this network (by consistent unidirectional foregrounding), while the remaining portions of the network are relaxed (by automatization perceived as an intentionally arranged background).[22]

The act of foregrounding not only involves a certain particular dynamism between foreground and background but introduces a system-wide dynamic orienting the whole towards a particular direction. This double action of foregrounding, the particular accent giving wholistic direction, contributes to our understanding of sign as the interpretation of difference. In other words, foregrounding reveals not only the meaning of some particular "difference," the particular accent, but also the meaning of the entire "difference," i.e., the whole. Indeed, foregrounding is "the difference 'difference' makes." As such, foregrounding allows the theologian to postulate an aesthetic conception of Being which implicitly recognizes God's absolute and ordained power as manifestations of a united omnipotence.

Being as Foregrounding

If Peirce found Being to be intrinsically Relational, and Royce found Being intrinsically Individual, then Mukarovsky's semiotic aes-

[21]Ibid., 25.
[22]Ibid., 24.

thetics suggests an intrinsic corollary to an aesthetic conception of Being: *Being as Foregrounding*. Being as Foregrounding has both theological and philosophical dimensions. Being as Foregrounding accounts for both God's absolute and ordained powers. Indeed, Being as Foregrounding may be interpreted as a wholistic act of divine omnipotence. As such, Being as Foregrounding supports the view that all beings participate in some sort of divinely inspired order. This assertion should not be taken as an argument for cosmic design. The order implied in the act of divine omnipotence which is Being as Foregrounding is less the order of design than it is the order realized by an act of love. Being as Foregrounding urges the theologian not to simply answer the question—"Why something and not nothing?"—but to answer it in conjunction with another necessary question—"Why *this* world and not another?" Being as Foregrounding as wholistic act of divine omnipotence requires that both questions be answered simultaneously. Answering either one without benefit of the other tends to lead to a nominalist (i.e., modern) cosmology and epistemology.

When both questions, however, are raised at the same time and are required to be answered at the same time, only one possible answer is possible. God, who did not have to create any particular beings at all and who could have created a universe different from this one, created *this* one out of love for its own uniqueness. An omnipotent God who creates a particular, unique universe does so out of love for its own unique beauty. This answer reveals a God who loves difference, *this* difference. By loving the universe into being, God ordered the universe not according to the laws of design but by the laws of the "heart." In other words, the universe is ordered less by the laws of design than by the laws of the love of difference. The love of difference orders the world in ways that a machine would never be designed. The order of the universe lies mainly in the poetic aesthetics of foregrounding than in the rational design of some giant clock.

Being as Foregrounding also contains philosophical dimensions. Being as Foregrounding may be interpreted as the "difference that 'difference' makes." In other words, foregrounding grounds the meaning of difference. Foregrounding is a "difference" that allows "difference" to be made. In other words, Foregrounding grounds the meaning of difference by revealing the General Whole, the Real Universal, in other words, the "difference 'difference' makes." As such, Being as Foregrounding serves to ground Hispanic theology's many concerns.

Being as Foregrounding helps the Hispanic theologian understand the meaning of difference without sacrificing either the relative nature of cultural differences nor the normative demands of all that is True or Good. Being as Foregrounding allows the Hispanic theologian to make normative claims from the data of cultural experience. Being as Foregrounding also allows the Hispanic theologian to articulate the initial insight of the Latin Church of the Americas of a redemptive cosmic order. Being as Foregrounding relates cosmic order, the difference of creatures, to redemptive order, the difference between Creator and creature. Moreover, Being as Foregrounding confirms the Hispanic theologian's assertion of the intrinsic aesthetics of all reality as well as the aesthetic nature of signs. As such, Being as Foregrounding comes as this Hispanic theologian's contribution to the marvelous opera so far witnessed on these pages. My hope is that Being as Foregrounding shall be seen as an original contribution of the Latin Church of the Americas emerging from four centuries of unofficial but intensive reflection by many unrecognized or unacknowledged *pensadores* or thinkers. Whether this shall be the case only time will tell. In any case, Being as Foregrounding, indeed the semiotics of foregrounding, in general, serves to unify the many conversations that have taken place.

A THIRD TYPE OF KNOWING

As in the last two communities, the True and the Good, the ontology of Being as Foregrounding has a corresponding epistemology. Like Being as Relational and Individual, Being as Foregrounding suggests a third type of knowing that is neither perception nor cognition. This third type of knowing takes a "middle" place between perception and cognition and it is part of the logic of signs. Indeed, this third type of knowing also follows the logic of signs. Like the previous dimensions of the logic of signs, it "interprets" difference creating other signs (the True) and unitive community (the Good). As part of the Beautiful, however, this "interpreting" of difference, this dimension of the logic of signs, takes on its own unique character.

I will argue that the "third" type of knowing that corresponds to Being as Foregrounding corresponds to the long and ancient tradition of the "spiritual senses." The "interpreting" that the "spiritual senses" do amounts to a pragmatist aesthetics exemplified in Ignatius of Loyola's use of the "application of the senses." This pragmatic aesthetics aims to discover what moves the heart, so that the heart may discern the truly beautiful. Discerning the truly beautiful, however, takes place in the garden of good and evil. As such, a consideration of the Biblical notion of heart reveals the Rabbinic concept of the *yetzer Ha'ra* and the *yetzer*

Ha'tov, the "evil" and "good" inclinations. The "heart" moves according to the inclination of the *yetzer*. The semiotic aesthetics of foregrounding, however, directs our biblical investigation and reveals an aesthetic norm: "lifting up the lowly." A heart moved according to this aesthetic norm will discern the truly beautiful creating, in its wake, the Community of the Beautiful. Our entry into understanding the movement of the heart begins with the examination of the long, and almost forgotten, tradition known as the "spiritual senses."

The Spiritual Senses

The notion of "spiritual senses" is not new to pragmatic thought. Jonathan Edwards, the American philosopher and theologian, developed a semiotic theology of beauty depending on great part on the notion of spiritual sense. Edwards, for example, described the "spiritual sense" as

> Things being thus, it plainly appears, that God's implanting that spiritual supernatural sense which has been spoken of, makes a great change in a man. And were it not for the very imperfect degree, in which this sense is commonly given at first, or the small degree of this glorious light, that first dawns upon the soul; the change made by this spiritual opening of the eyes in conversion, would be much greater and more remarkable every way, than if a man, who had been born blind, and with only the other four senses, should continue so a long time, and then at once should have the sense of seeing imparted to him, in the midst of the clear light of the sun, discovering a world of visible objects. For though sight be more noble than any of the other external senses, yet this spiritual sense which has been spoken of, is infinitely more noble than that, or any other principle of discerning that a man naturally has, and the object of this sense infinitely greater and more important.[23]

It was Origen, however, who "invented" the spiritual senses. He derived the doctrine that there exists "a general sense for the divine" which may be subdivided into "a sense of sight to contemplate supernatural things such as the Cherubim and Seraphim; a sense of hearing which perceives voices that do not resound in the exterior air; a sense of taste that can savour the 'bread that came down from heaven for the life of the world'; a sense of smell that perceives what Paul thus describes: 'We are a fragrance of Christ for God'; and a sense of touch, whereby John says that

---

[23]Jonathan Edwards, *The Religious Affections*, reprint, 1746 (Edinburgh: The Banner of Truth Trust, 1994) 203.

he has 'touched the Word of Life with his hands.'"[24] Thus there are "two kinds of senses in us: the one kind is mortal, corruptible, human; the other kind is immortal, spiritual . . . divine."[25]

Origen, here, is not suggesting two different types of senses for two different types of experience, i.e., ordinary experience and mystical experience. Rather, Origen suggests that in the Fall what had been an "original and richly abundant capacity to perceive God" through the five sensory senses degenerated into a lower, material set of five senses and a higher, but greatly diminished, spiritual set of five senses. Thus, the material and the spiritual senses are not two distinct senses for two distinct types of experiences but different aspects of the same senses for the same kind of experience. This same kind of experience is what von Balthasar referred to earlier in chapter 3 as the common ground between ordinary and mystical experience. Indeed, the decisive object "of the 'spiritual senses' is not the *Deus nudus*, but the whole of the 'upper world' which, in Christ, has descended to earth in the fullness of the cosmos of Sacred Scripture. . . ."[26] This cosmos is the cosmos of "heaven and earth, of all things, visible and invisible." In other words, in a world before the Fall, our natural senses would have been awash in the glory of the spiritual dimension of this world. After the Fall, our natural senses have become divided into material and spiritual senses with the spiritual senses much diminished. As such, we perceive very little of the fullness of this world both in its material and spiritual dimensions. Thus, it becomes necessary to exercise our "spiritual" senses so that they may become more adept in perceiving the spirituality of this world.

What is this "fullness of the cosmos," this "spirituality of this world"? The "fullness of the cosmos," in a sense, stems from the belief stated in the Nicene Creed that God created "all things, visible and invisible." This belief suggests a world consisting of both visible and invisible creatures. If "visible" and "invisible" (together if not individually) correspond to "material" and "spiritual," then the belief in "all things, visible and invisible" suggests a belief, as well, in a world consisting of both a created material and a created spiritual dimension.[27] "Fullness of cosmos," then, refers to a cosmological perspective

---

[24]*Contra Celsum*, 1, 48 quoted in Hans Urs von Balthasar, *Seeing the Form*, op. cit., 368.

[25]*Peri Archon* I,1,9 quoted in von Balthasar, op. cit., 368.

[26]von Balthasar, op. cit., 370.

[27]I have suggested elsewhere that a contemporary approach to the nature of the spiritual might be found in the being of relations. In other words, the "invisible" triadic

that refuses to be reduced by the nominalist dichotomy between the material and the spiritual. Both are part of the created world. The "sensing" of the world, then, involves "sensing" both the material and spiritual dimensions of the world. Such "fullness" of sensing, however, appears as aporia to the empirical orientation of contemporary natural sciences. As Phillip Davis and Reuben Hersch have observed, "the accepted assumptions in science are now, and have been for many years, those of materialism with respect to ontology, and empiricism with respect to epistemology."[28] A material cosmos leaves no room for the spiritual cosmos. An empirical epistemology has no place for the spiritual senses. As such, the cosmos, if it is indeed created with both material and spiritual dimensions, is inevitably reduced by contemporary cosmology. Only when the "fullness" of sensing, i.e., the reunion of the "material" and "spiritual" senses, becomes an intentional "art" shall our vision of the universe be truly expanded to include the mystery of faith.

It was Ignatius of Loyola who saw this most clearly. In his exercises, Ignatius calls on the retreatant to "apply his senses" so as to *sentir*, that is, "feel" the mystery of faith each exercise is designed to demonstrate. Ignatius feels that this *sentir* of the mysteries of faith is the object of the exercises "for it is not much knowledge which fills the soul and satisfies it, but feeling and tasting things from within."[29] Almost everyone who has undertaken Ignatius' spiritual exercises can affirm that in the "application of the senses" something spiritual also takes place. The interpretation of what that "something" is has taken two extreme positions. Some have championed that the experience of the exercises is purely a corporal experience; others that it is purely a mystical experience.[30] Von Balthasar, however, feels (and I agree) that the experience of the exercises is a spiritual experience in the sense of an experience taking place through the spiritual senses. As such, it is neither an "ordinary" nor a "mystical" experience but an experience of the full spirituality and materiality of the creation. Indeed, Ignatian "application of the senses" serves for me as the pragmatic model for the semiotics of "foregrounding."

Ignatian "application of the senses," in a sense, interprets the aesthetics of Being as Foregrounding. It is Vision as "inside and outside looking

---

relationship might be the most elemental unit of spirituality. For this suggestion see, Alex García-Rivera, "Creator of the Visible and the Invisible," op. cit.

[28]Philip J. Davis and Reuben Hersh, *The Mathematical Experience*, with an introduction by Gian-Carlo Rota (Boston: Houghton Mifflin Company, 1981) 328.

[29][2:4] of Spiritual Exercises, Puhl.

[30]von Balthasar, op. cit., 378.

into one another in an encounter which is a struggle, a reciprocal influence. 'We not only look at how the world exists; by seeing it we 'exist it' and are awakened by it to the form of light and of spirit, 'so that man can realize in his very foundations all those possibilities of differentiation that are the expression of his person, and so that he may learn to move this his essential difference over all the things that surround him as an instrument of knowledge. . . ."[31] As such, the Ignatian exercises unleash the dynamic nature of the aesthetic norm in the spiritual "empiricism" of consulting the "fullness" of the senses. The Ignatian exercises reveal most clearly the interpretative nature of "application of the senses."

The "application of the senses" as exemplified in the Ignatian exercises suggests to me a possible explanation for the poverty and reductionism of the cosmos in both the natural and the human sciences. Both operate with impoverished Facts and impoverished Ideas. The "application of the senses" reveals, I believe, the "fullness," i.e., the material and spiritual dimensions, of Facts and Ideas and, sign-like, interprets them through the process of the Exercises. As such, the "interpretant" operating in the logic of the Exercises appears to be the movement of the heart. It is the heart's motion that interprets the relation between the "full" Fact and "full" Idea. As such, the "interpretant" of the Ignatian exercises also reveals a struggle. The "interpretant" of the logic of the Exercises takes place in the garden of good and evil. Where is the garden of good and evil? It is, let me suggest, the place that Bible and Tradition have called the "heart," and I shall call the "Anagogical" Imagination.

WHAT MOVES THE HEART?

I began this book by defining aesthetics as "that which moves the heart." It is my intention to connect the semiotics of foregrounding and this intended aim of a theological aesthetics. Indeed, what moves the heart? By "heart," of course, I don't mean the anatomical organ which pumps blood throughout the body. I mean, rather, the biblical notion known as "heart," the *leb* of the Hebrew Scriptures and the *kardias* of the New Testament. I also mean that philosophical notion described by Robert E. Wood as "that which is closest to the 'I,' . . . that region of felt proclivities and significant presences."[32] It is best described, however, by Paul:

[31]Paul Claudel, "La sensation du Divin," in *Nos sens et Dieu*, vol. XXXIII of *Etudes Carmélitaines* (Bruges) 93, 95 quoted in von Balthasar, op. cit., 404.
[32]The quotes come from Robert Wood's presidential address to the Catholic Philosophical Association. Robert E. Wood, "Recovery of the Aesthetic Center,"

Did the good, then, become death for me? Of course not! Sin, in order that it might be shown to be sin, worked death in me through the good, so that sin might become sinful beyond measure through the commandment. We know that the law is spiritual; but I am carnal, sold into slavery to sin. What I do, I do not understand. For I do not do what I want, but I do what I hate. Now if I do what I do not want, I concur that the law is good. So now it is no longer I who do it, but sin that dwells in me. For I know that good does not dwell in me, that is, in my flesh. The willing is ready at hand, but doing the good is not. For I do not do the good I want, but I do the evil I do not want. Now if I do what I do not want, it is no longer I who do it, but sin that dwells in me. So, then, I discover the principle that when I want to do right, evil is at hand. For I take delight in the law of God, in my inner self. But I see in my members another principle at war with the law of my mind, taking me captive to the law of sin that dwells in my members. Miserable one that I am! Who will deliver me from this mortal body? Thanks be to God through Jesus Christ our Lord. Therefore, I myself, with my mind, serve the law of God but, with my flesh, the law of sin (Rom 7:13-25. NAB).

Paul appears to describe a type of internal war, a battle between two opposed, i.e., obverse, inclinations: good and evil. That place where they place, where good and evil inclinations are "shaped" and "formed," that is the place I call the "heart." This place described by Paul and that I call the "heart" is also the place that Origen refers to in his contrast between the corporal and the spiritual senses.[33] It is also the place of much exegetical debate. At issue is the Rabbinic notion of the *yetzer*.

The Yetzer

The basic meaning of the semitic root *yetzer* is "shape, form." Other meanings include "impulse, inclination, instincts, urge, passion, imagination, prompter, bent, nature, lust, Satan, tempter."[34] Forms derived from this root occur some seventy times in the Old Testament. The word *yetzer*, in the main, denotes forms of craftmanship such as pottery. Those passages, however, rarely describe the potter in an everyday context but theologically. The potter may refer to the Creator. Pottery

---

American Catholic Philosophical Quarterly 69, no. 2 (1995) 10, 2. See also Stephen Strasser, *Phenomenology of Feeling: An Essay on the Phenomena of the Heart*, foreword by Paul Ricoeur, trans. and introduction by Robert E. Wood, Philosophical Series, vol. 34 (Pittsburgh: Duquesne University Press, 1977).

[33]von Balthasar, op. cit., 370.

[34]Cohen G. H. Stuart, *The Struggle in Man Betweeen Good and Evil: An Inquiry into the Origin of the Rabbinic Concept of Yetzer Hara'* (Kampen: Uitgeversmaatschappig J. H. Kok, 1984) 10.

may refer to the act of creation. Such uses of the word refer to the notion found in both Israelite and non-Israelite religions that the human race was formed from clay *like* a potter. Thus *yetzer*, itself, can refer to the creation of the human race. *Yetser*, however, also refers to the Creation of Israel such as in Deutero-Isaiah (Isa 43:1, e.g.) where YHWH is referred to as the "former" or *yotsar* of Israel. Moreover, *yetser* is also used to describe God's shaping of history such as in Jeremiah 18 where YHWH through the image of the potter shapes the destiny of the people of Judah. Such meaning has surprisingly modern connotations when referred to the modern notion of culture. YHWH, e.g., may be seen as the "former" or *yotsar* of the culture that is Israel. Other occurrences of *yetser* also connote the sense of framing a plan. Such occurrences frequently occur in conjunction with *leb* or "heart" which is the Hebraic locus for the seat of thought. As such, *yetser* takes on the meaning of "imagination of the heart," the heart's thoughts and purpose (Gen 8:21). Thus, when *yetser* stands alone, it must be translated as something like "purpose," or following the Rabbinic commentators of the Talmud and Mishnah, the *imagination*.[35]

As the "imagination," *yetzer* indicates a "forming" or "shaping" which apparently takes place in a place called the "heart." Indeed, the great exhortation of Deut 6:5, "you shall love the Lord your God with all your heart and with all your soul and with all your might," has been taken by Rabbinic commentaries as the "shaping" of the heart which the *yetzer* connotes.[36] The earliest Rabbinic interpretation on Deut. 6:5, e.g., is found in the Mishnah, *Berakhot* IX.5. In reference to the phrase "with all your heart," the comment reads: "with your two inclinations, with the good inclination [*yetzer*] and with the evil inclination [*yetzer*]." The comment puzzles until one realizes that ancient Judaic psychology saw the human heart as having two distinct inclinations: one towards evil (the *yetser Ha'ra*) and one towards good (the *yetser Ha'tov*).[37] These two inclinations form the core of an Old Testament doctrine of sin. The Talmud, for example, contains several passages which sees the *yetzer*, or imagination, as the most "primordial drive" of the human being, the gift of God to his most excellent creation, the power to "form" or "shape" as the Creator. This primordial drive, however, can

---

[35]"Yetzer," G. Johannes Botterweck and Helma Ringgren, eds., David Green, trans., in *Theological Dictionary of the Old Testament* (Grand Rapids, Mich.: William B. Eerdmans).

[36]Michael Fishbane, *The Kiss of God: Spiritual and Mystical Death in Judaism* (Seattle and London: University of Washington Press, 1962) 3.

[37]Stuart, op. cit., 10.

either lead to idolatry or can if sublimated and oriented towards the divine way (Talmud), can serve as an indispensable power for attaining the goal of creation: the universal embodiment of God's plan in the Messianic Kingdom of justice and peace. . . . In short if the evil imagination epitomizes the error of history as a monologue of man with himself, the good imagination *(yetser hatov)* opens up history to an I-Thou dialogue between man and his Creator.[38]

Thus the Talmud says: "God created man with two *yetsers*, the good and the evil" *(Berach, 61a)*. Martin Buber's commentary on the Deuteronomic passage is also illuminating:

Evil is lack of direction and that which is done in it and out of it as the grasping, seizing, exploiting, humiliating, torturing, and destroying of what offers itself. Good is direction and what is done in it . . . with the whole soul, so that in fact all the vigour with which evil might have been done is included in it.[39]

Thus, one possible interpretation of the Old Testament understanding of "forming" may be the imagination of the heart which directs human creativity and activity. This human creativity has moral dimensions. Not all uses of the creative imagination lead to divine presence. At the same time, the imagination of the heart is God's gift to the human creature.

In summary, the *yetzer* or inclining imagination, as used in the Old Testament and commented on by the Rabbis, depicts the human as

that creature that unites both inclinations within himself. He has the possibility of following the good as well as the evil inclination. . . . So man is the unique creature that has to live in the tension of two worlds. With regard to the good inclination, he belongs to heaven. With regard to the evil inclination, he belongs to the earth. He has to subdue the evil inclination to the good. If man succeeds in mastering his evil inclination and to make it a servant of the good one, he may achieve a higher merit than the angels.[40]

Through the imagination, we become, in Philip Hefner's words "created co-creators,"[41] able to participate (or not) in divine presence. It is this "imagination," or *yetzer* that many scholars believe Paul referred to in the famous passage from Romans above.

[38]Richard Kearney, *The Wake of Imagination: Toward a Postmodern Culture* (Minneapolis: University of Minnesota Press, 1988) 46.

[39]Martin Buber, *Good and Evil* (New York: Scribner's, 1952) 130–31.

[40]Stuart, op. cit., 24.

[41]Philip Hefner, *The Human Factor* (Fortress Press, 1992) 32.

Porter, for example, writes of how the two inclinations were used to understand "flesh" and "spirit" in Romans 7. Thus, "the good impulse dwells in the inner man *(nous)*; the evil impulse has its seat in the body which consists of a positive power antagonistic to spirit, the evil impulse, or sin as potency."[42] Porter writes how the *"nomos tes hamartias,"* i.e., the "law of the heart," has been identified by other scholars with the evil impulse and the good impulse with *"nomos noos mou,"* or the "law of the mind-spirit" in (Rom 7:23). Porter, however, rejects this parallelism between Paul and Rabbinic teaching because the struggle between Law of the flesh and law of the mind is "widely different" than the rabbinic teaching. Many scholars nonetheless feel Porter's rejection is not warranted. There exists similarity as well as dissimilarity between Paul and the Rabbinic teaching on the two impulses. Perhaps Davies' position is the most balanced. As Davies puts it:

> It is our contention, however, that the Pauline distinction between the [sarx] and [pneuma] is not a replica of Hellenistic dualism, not again simply to be explained from the Old Testament. It is rather the complex product of Paul's Old Testament background and his Rabbinical training. It is indeed the latter that affords us the best clue to much in his thought on the flesh and sin. . . . The juxtaposition of the yetzer hara and the divine remedy that the Torah is, we feel, reproduced in Paul's antithesis of the [sarx] and the [phonema tes sarkos] and the Spirit. . . . It is a likely conjecture . . . that [phonema tes sarkos] almost amounts to a literal translation of the yetzer hara.[43]

Davies position makes sense. Paul was trying to "inculturate" Hebraic concepts into a largely Hellenistic church. Paul's depiction of what moves the "heart," I believe, relies on an "inculturated" understanding of the Hebraic *yetzer*. This might explain why the *yetzer* itself may be hard to identify in the New Testament.

From the Old to the New Testament

Tracing the literal Hellenic equivalent of *yetser* into the New Testament is disappointing. If Romans is an example, it is likely that the Hebraic notion of *yetzer* appears in one or more "inculturated" forms. A more productive approach might be to concentrate on the role the "heart" plays in the New Testament corpus. Such an approach reveals a

[42]F. C. Porter, "The Yetzer Hara, a Study in the Jewish Doctrine of Sin," in *Biblical and Semitic Studies* (New York: p., 1901) 11 quoted in Stuart, op. cit., 115.
[43]W. D. Davies, *Paul and Rabbinic Judaism*, rev. ed., reprint, 1948 (New York: Harper & Row, 1967) 26.

certain continuity with the previous discussion of the role of the *yetser* in the Old Testament. The New Testament appears to continue the Hebraic theme of "forming" or "shaping" but adds the nuance of "beholding." Some have suggested that this takes place through a Hellenic shift of the understanding of the heart, *kardia* from a center of moral deliberation to a center of metaphysical deliberation, i.e., *noeo*.[44] Indeed, in the Septuagint, the heart is the organ or seat of *noeo* which means "to direct one's mind to."[45] *Noeo* is an important New Testament verb occurring (along with its derivatives) rather frequently. *Noeo* also has a rich history of connotations in Greek philosophical thought especially as it applies to metaphysics. It would be a mistake, however, to conclude that the New Testament sense of *noeo* slavishly follows the Hellenic metaphysical sense. The New Testament has its own agenda. The New Testament appears to be appropriating notions from various religious and philosophical traditions towards articulation of a new human reality. This appropriation may be seen in the analysis of three important derivates of *noeo: noús, metanoía,* and *diánoia.*

    Noús, e.g., originally meant an "inner sense directed on an object." As such, it is strikingly suggestive of the spiritual sense. In any case, *noús* definitely suggests a special type of seeing or beholding. *Noús* beholds "mental formations," i.e., *noemata*, objects "invisible" to the eye but visible to the *noús*. Thus, the sense of "forming" and the sense of "making" join together in the New Testament use of *noús*. The objects of *noús* are, at the same time, "formed" by the *noús* as well as "beheld" by it.[46] This double sense of "making" and "beholding" is clear in the other derivative term of *noeo—metanoía. Metanoía* commonly appears in the New Testament, especially in the Synoptics and Acts. *Metanoía* calls for a fundamental change in a human reality through a holistic "change of mind." Indeed, *metanoía* calls for a reshaping or re-"forming" of mental structures which is at the same time a new "form" or "shape" of a human life.[47]

    Another New Testament word relevant to the Old Testament notion of *yetser* is *diànoia*. This common word for "thought" or "imagination" has the nuances of resolve or intention. Thus, *diànoia* appears

---

[44]Kearney, op. cit., 79.

[45]Gerhard Friedrich Kittel, Gerhard, "Noeo," in *Theological Dictionary of the New Testament* (Grand Rapids, Mich.: William B. Eerdmans, 1985).

[46]Gerhard Friedrich Kittel, Gerhard, "Nous," in *Theological Dictionary of the New Testament* (Grand Rapids, Mich.: William B. Eerdmans, 1985).

[47]Gerhard Friedrich Kittel, Gerhard, "Metanoia," in *Theological Dictionary of the New Testament* (Grand Rapids, Mich.: William B. Eerdmans, 1985).

to contain the sense of the evil or good inclination found in the Hebraic notion of *yetser*. Matt 22:37, in fact, uses *diànoia* in a direct reference to Deut 6:5. Furthermore, Col 1:21 uses *diànoia* to refer to the impulses of the will. More interestingly, Ephesians calls *diànoia*, the "eyes of the heart" (1:18), a visual metaphor, which may be "enlightened" or "darkened" depending on the "hardness of the heart" (*porosis kardía*, 4:18), a metaphor of "form." Indeed, Heb 8:10 refers back to Deuteronomy in which God intends to "put my laws in their minds (*diànoia*), and write them on their hearts (*kardía*), and I will be their God, and they shall be my people." Thus, God intends to "form" or "shape" the laws of our hearts so that they will lead us to God. As such, *diànoia* also has the sense of "forming" a people such as the *yetser's* sense of the "forming" of Israel.[48]

Thus, the biblical exploration of "heart" suggests some exciting points of contact between a semiotic aesthetics and the Biblical material. The *yetzer*, e.g., serves to describe the "heart" whose "motion" a semiotic aesthetics attempts to describe. Furthermore, the double notion of "making" and "beholding" as found in derivatives of *noús* is particularly exciting for discerning a semiotic aesthetics. "Making" and "beholding" describes rather well the general and pragmatic characteristic of the logic of signs. Moreover, the brief exploration of the possible uses of the Rabbinical notion of the *yetzer* into the New Testament suggests a happy connotation of the *yetzer* with the spiritual senses and, more fascinating, the spiritual senses with the imagination. Indeed, the picture the *yetzer* gives us as the "heart" describes a type of "knowing" where the imagination shaped by and having its source in the spiritual senses attempts to discern an inclination, a "being towards," God who is Beauty in the context of a site where both good and evil dwell. In the context of good and evil, then, a question, however, remains to be asked. Is there a norm that can guide the heart towards Beauty? Is there a norm that can distinguish the movement of the heart between the good and evil inclination, i.e., the truly beautiful and the idolatrous? In other words, can an aesthetic norm be found that can ground the aesthetics of foregrounding? If one accepts the unique nature of an aesthetic norm as suggested by Mukarovsky (it reveals its normative character by violating its own norm), then such an aesthetic norm, I believe, is suggested in the beginning passages of the Magnificat.

---

[48]Gerhard Friedrich Kittel, Gerhard, "Dianoia," in *Theological Dictionary of the New Testament* (Grand Rapids, Mich.: William B. Eerdmans, 1985).

Mary's Song

All these senses that the *yetzer* can take in the New Testament, I believe, come together in what I consider the most significant occurrence of the word, the passage in Luke (1:51) which is part of what is known as the Magnificat: "He has shown strength with his arm; he has scattered the proud in the thoughts (*diànoia*) of their hearts. He has brought down the powerful (*kathaireo dunastes*) from their thrones, and lifted up the lowly (*hypsoo tapeinos,* NAB)." God scatters the proud in their evil imagination, the *diànoia* of their hearts, in order to "lift up" (*hypsoo*) the lowly, a creative act of the good imagination. Thus, *diànoia* appears to refer to the Hebrew Scripture sense of the *yetser* and suggests what the evil and good imagination may mean in the New Testament. The evil imagination, e.g., is associated with the pride of the powerful (*hypereephanos*). The good imagination, on the other hand, is associated with "lifting up the lowly." As such, the key verb *hypsoo* resembles the elementary act of aesthesis, i.e., the lifting up of a foreground out of a background and giving the foreground value. Such "lifting ups" are mentioned over and over again in the Scriptures each time giving new sense to what a theological aesthetics might look like. The Septuagint, for example, often uses *hypsoo* to refer to the joyful exaltation of God, an exaltation "which on the presupposition of abasement means glorification."[49] As such, it reminds one of Von Balthasar's major theme of his theological aesthetics, *Herrlichkeit*, or "Glory of the Lord." The New Testament use of *hypsoo,*, however, in connection with *diánoia* means not so much "the glory of the Lord" but the "joyful exaltation of the Lord" especially in the context of abasement, in other words, the "lifting up the lowly."

"Lifting up the lowly" has all the characteristics of Mukarovsky's aesthetic norm. "Lifting up the lowly" suggests the dynamics characterized by Jesus as the "first shall be last, and the last shall be first." "Lifting up the lowly" reveals a paradoxical, perhaps parabolical, dynamics. It reveals its normative, regulative meaning in its own systematic violation! "Lifting up the lowly" reveals an aesthetic direction than an inviolable law. "Lifting up the lowly" is, indeed, exemplary of Mukarovsky's aesthetic norm. Since "lifting up the lowly" takes place in the biblical "heart" where the good and evil *yetzer* must be discerned, it does have strong ethical implications. Nonetheless, "lifting up the lowly" ought not to be confused with an ethical norm. It is, above all, an aesthetic

---

[49]Gerhard Friedrich Kittel, Gerhard, "Hypsoo," in *Theological Dictionary of the New Testament* (Grand Rapids, Mich.: William B. Eerdmans, 1985).

norm, albeit an aesthetic norm forged in the foundry of the garden of good and evil. As such, "lifting up the lowly's" aesthetics are subtle and need to be considered carefully.

THE ANAGOGICAL IMAGINATION

Part of this consideration needs to take into account the implicit suggestion that the logic of the aesthetic interpreting of signs is akin to the imagination. The "yetzerian" imagination, however, is very different from what we commonly call the "imagination."[50] By imagination, we usually have in mind a subjective psychological faculty whose functions lie somewhere between the senses and reason. The "yetzerian" imagination, however, appears to be quite different from this common view. First, this imagination has both an objective and subjective dimension. It "beholds" even as it "makes." Yet it is a "beholding" and a "making" that takes place in the garden of good and evil and thus the "yetzerian" imagination is also a discerning, an act of discovery as much as an act of expression. Its roots in the spiritual senses suggests its immediate discernment is the "fullness" of the cosmos, the spiritual and material dimensions of the universe. As such, the "yetzerian" imagination has much in common with the mythic imagination which Lawrence Sullivan described for us in the beginning chapter.

There Sullivan explained the mythic imagination in terms of a pragmatic living out a mystery, a type of "imaginal existence."[51] In a fairly cryptic phrase, Sullivan describes the mythic imagination as "significations that reveal the nature of significance."[52] Sullivan's key sense of the religious imagination as "significations that reveal the nature of

[50]The notion of the imagination has a long philosophical and scientific history. The reader may be interested in the following works that attempt to describe or define the imagination: Mary Warnock, *Imagination* (Berkeley: University of California Press, 1978); Kearney, op. cit; Eva Brann, *The World of the Imagination: Sum and Substance* (Lanham, Md.: Rowman & Littlefield Publishers, 1991); John McIntyre, *Faith, Theology and Imagination* (Edinburgh: Handsel Press, 1987); Murray Wright Bundy, "The Theory of Imagination in Classical and Mediaeval Thought," *University of Illinois Studies in Language and Literature* XII, no. 2–3 (1927). 7–281; David Tracy, *The Analogical Imagination: Christian Theology and the Culture of Pluralism* (New York: Crossroads, 1981); Alex García-Rivera, "Religious Imagination," in *Perspectivas: Hispanic Ministry*, Allan Figueroa Deck, Timothy M. Matovina, and Yolanda Tarango, eds. (Kansas City: Sheed and Ward, 1995) 94–97.
[51]Lawrence E. Sullivan, *Icanchu's Drum: An Orientationto Meaning in South American Religions* (Chicago: University of Chicago Press, 1988) 22.
[52]Ibid.

significance" is hard to grasp but it expresses Sullivan's conclusion that for the religious imagination "understanding a reality requires that it has a beginning."[53] As Sullivan puts it:

> Fundamental conditions are conceived in terms of the beginning, the first order, the primordium. The basic structures of appearance, hiddenness, inchoateness, differentiation, uniqueness, multiplicity, language, gesture, stasis, and change **provide footholds for the imagination.** By their very presence in the imagination and in the beginning, these principal realities, envisioned in particular symbols, condition all subsequent forms of contingent being. As a foundation for the imagination, the concept of the beginning makes apparent those qualities and images of being that are inescapably determinative and ceaselessly influential. The picture of primordial being delimits what is really possible. Images of the beginning circumscribe what *in principle* (that is, in relation to what is known to be real, to have appeared from the beginning) can be acted upon.[54]

Sullivan describes the imagination as "fully" sensing the different structures of reality through the perception of an "origin of differences." The religious imagination for Sullivan discerns the origins of differences so that the "fullness" of the cosmos may be discerned. As such, the mythic imagination corresponds, in a sense, to the spiritual senses. Like the spiritual senses, the mythic imagination allows the fullness of cosmic reality to be discerned. Sullivan, however, attributes the foundation of such discerning to an "origin of differences." Such "origin of differences," nonetheless, may have a possible analogy in the "yetzerian" heart. The "yetzerian" heart, after all, involves an origins as well, namely the origins of good and evil. If Sullivan's mythic imagination discerns the "origins of differences" so that the perceptible structures of reality may be discerned, the "yetzerian" heart discerns the good and evil inclination towards an imagination that continues as the Community of the True and the Good.

If the imagination of the "yetzerian" heart corresponds, in part, to Sullivan's notion of the mythic or religious imagination, then a new element is added to the pragmatic logic of signs as Peirce and Royce envisioned it. If the norm of the True and the Good involved a thoroughgoing teleology, the aesthetic norm, the norm of the Beautiful involves, in part, an implicit protology. As such, the obvious question becomes whether the semiotic aesthetics of the Beautiful is compatible

---

[53]Ibid., 25.
[54]Ibid., 26.

with the logic of signs that Peirce and Royce developed. In other words, is there room for a semiotics of origins in the pragmatic logic of signs? The answer, I believe, is found in Royce's aesthetics of negation. The question of "higher" and "lower" carries with it an implicit discernment of the origins of difference. Every negation, every obverse, has as ultimate question the nature of its origins. Indeed, "to be or not to be" circumscribe an origins, an "origin of differences." And it is origins, as Sullivan clearly saw, that drives the question of the ultimate.

Sullivan's insight over the function of origins in the religious imagination reveals another dimension of the aesthetic norm. The aesthetic norm in its dynamism engages the mystery of all reality by discerning its ultimate origins. As such, the imagination of the "yetzerian" heart brings ultimacy to Royce's aesthetics of negation by introducing the ultimate negation, the origins of difference. Sullivan's mythic imagination taken without qualification, however, would make semiotic aesthetics a type of Platonism. There is, after all, an intrinsic teleology in aesthetics: the work of art. The work of art is the "goal" or "aim" of any aesthetic appreciation. Any aesthetics that fails to account for the inherent teleology of the Beautiful has failed to understand the nature of the "call" of Beauty. Nonetheless, Sullivan's point about the intrinsic religious nature of "origins" can not be ignored. Theological aesthetics as *capax Dei* also appreciates mystery. A semiotic theological aesthetics must account for the discernment of the "origins of difference" which engages the question of the ultimate. It must also, however, account for the intrinsic teleology that is the work of art.

This double requirement, the "alpha" and the "omega," origins and end, of the Beautiful ought not to surprise us. Mukarovsky began his analysis of the aesthetic norm by pointing out the intrinsic triadic nature of aesthetics, namely the relationship between original artist, finished work of art, and the audience that beholds the work of art. Origins and Ends together with the "audience," the creatures of the Beautiful, weave the fabric of reality that is True, Good, and Beautiful. Thus, Beauty's "call" is revealed to be both a "call" that originates and a "call" that draws one to an intended end. Beauty's "call" both initiates even as it provides for the experience of the Beautiful. Beauty's "call" reveals the ultimate negation of the Beautiful, origins and ends. Like a Möebius strip, this ultimate negation reveals one continuous whole. Peirce's faith in the "continuum" of reality finds its greatest affirmation in the semiotic aesthetics of the Beautiful.

The double requirement of the Beautiful may be ambivalent in a philosophical aesthetics but, in a theological aesthetics, it cannot be ignored. A theological aesthetics involves, in a sense, an ultimate triadicity, the ultimate triadic sign. This ultimate triadic sign consists of the origins of reality (the "artist"), the ends of reality (the finished "work of art"), and the creatures whose experience "makes" and "behold" reality. A semiotic theological aesthetics accounts for the Beautiful as the experience of a community, an "audience," who experiences Beauty in the dynamic "imaginative" interpretation of Being. This dynamic "imaginative" interpretation of Being takes place in the "heart" as a movement of the "heart" towards good or evil. As such, the movement cannot be said to be identical to an ethical choice. Neither can it be said to be identical to a logical choice. What can be said, however, that this movement of the heart is the "spark," the "lighting of the fuse," which inspires and sets in motion the interpretation of the Good and the True.

Like the True and the Good, the semiotic aesthetics of the "heart" finds pragmatic fulfillment in community. It is, however, the entire community of Being that participates in the pragmatism of semiotic aesthetics.[55] The pragmatism of semiotic aesthetics also manifests itself differently from the pragmatism of the Community of the True and the Good. The interpretive act of foregrounding, unlike the interpretive act of comparison of the True or the interpretive act of redemptive inclusion of the Good, is the aesthetic act of praise. The pragmatism of the Community of the Beautiful results in a Community of Praise, or, in more traditional language, a Liturgy. The Community of the Beautiful, in a sense, finds analogy in Pseudo-Dionysius' cosmic assembly of praise. Unlike Pseudo-Dionysius' cosmic liturgy, however, it is a Community of Praise in the context of the garden of good and evil. As such, Pseudo-Dionysius' term *anagogy* takes on a new meaning in the pragmatic Community of the Beautiful.

The interpretive act of the pragmatic Community of the Beautiful, the semiotic aesthetics of "foregrounding," is also an act of the *anagogical* imagination.[56] Like the *anagogy* of Pseudo-Dionysius, it "lifts up" the praising creature giving the aesthetic sense of a "higher" and "lower." Unlike the *anagogy* of Pseudo-Dionysius, it is *anagogy* done in the garden of good and evil and signifies an act of "liberation," an act

---

[55]Peirce and Royce, of course, also reach this conclusion with the Community of the True and the Community of the Good. It is the Community of the Beautiful, however, that the cosmic nature of community becomes the most clear.

[56]Yes, the term *anagogical* imagination is inspired by Tracy's term, the "analogical" imagination. I have been silent about Tracy's "analogical" imagination for a variety of reasons. I have found Tracy's "analogical" imagination profoundly nominalistic and too optimistic on the power of evil. I have given my reasons publicly (Alex García-Rivera,

of breaking the chains of an evil imagination. *Anagogy* in the garden of good and evil involves more than a passive response to Beauty. It is as well an active response whose redemptive dimensions are described, in part, by Latin American and Hispanic theology's notion of "liberation." Liberation, in the context of the *anagogical* imagination, consists not so much in concretely overthrowing a reigning system of abusive power, but, rather, subverting the foundations of the imagination of such power which perpetuates its "pseudo-existence."[57] Liberation, in the context of the *anagogical* imagination, also means discerning and orienting the heart towards the Good and the True. The *anagogical* imagination liberates both in the aesthetic sense of the subversive nature of the aesthetic norm and in the sense of discerning and orienting the heart towards the source of the truly beautiful, Beauty itself, which founds, in turn, an orienting towards the True and the Good. If the evil imagination "moves" the heart towards the not-really-beautiful, the introduction of the aesthetic norm subverts that movement in its dynamism. The aesthetic norm keeps introducing the question of the relation between ultimate origins and ordained ends. Such a norm is "deadly" to the evil imagination.

The *anagogical* imagination, then, introduces the theological aesthetic norm of "lifting up the lowly" and demonstrates the intrinsic connection between cosmic order and redemption. As such, it shows the continuity of the universal Tradition of the Church with the particular tradition of the Latin American and Hispanic Church. Symbols and cosmic order, popular devotion and cosmic liturgy, faith and liberation— all these themes of both the entire Church and the American Church intertwine and find continuity in the Community of the True, the Good, and the Beautiful. Thus, we have come near the end of our long conversation, our long "opera." Such an "opera," however, needs a final "act." I have given the bare outlines for a Community of the Beautiful. It would seem quite improper to end without a concrete vision of such a community. That will be the purpose of the next chapter.

"Towards a Theology of the Imagination," presentation of June 4, 1996, at San Diego, California, Catholic Theological Society of America Conference, and in "A Matter of Presence," *Journal of Hispanic/Latino Theology* 5, no. 2:22–53). Nonetheless, I believe Tracy's "analogical" imagination is a great contribution to American theology, which continues to inspire generations of American theologians. I have been one of them.

[57]By pseudo-existence, I mean, in the language of Being, existence without essence, which, as such, is an interpretation of the ancient approach to evil known as the "privation of being." This interpretation of evil, I believe, accounts for the "evil" imagination, a "making" which, essentially, "beholds" nothing. Thus, a pseudo-existence.

7

Lifting Up the Lowly

Bless the Lord, all you works of the Lord.
Praise and exalt him above all forever.
Angels of the Lord, bless the Lord.
You heavens, bless the Lord.
All you waters above the heavens, bless the Lord.
All you hosts of the Lord, bless the Lord.
Sun and moon, bless the Lord.
Stars of heaven, bless the Lord.

Every shower and dew, bless the Lord.
All you winds, bless the Lord.
Fire and heat, bless the Lord.
Cold and chill, bless the Lord.
Dew and rain, bless the Lord.
Frost and chill, bless the Lord.
Ice and snow, bless the Lord.
Nights and days, bless the Lord.
Light and darkness, bless the Lord.
Lightnings and clouds, bless the Lord.

Let the earth bless the Lord.
Praise and exalt him above all forever.
Mountains and hills, bless the Lord.
Everything growing from the earth, bless the Lord.
You springs, bless the Lord.
Seas and rivers, bless the Lord.
You dolphins and all water creatures, bless the Lord.
All you birds of the air, bless the Lord.
All you beasts, wild and tame, bless the Lord.

O Israel, bless the Lord.
Praise and exalt him above all forever.
Priests of the Lord, bless the Lord.
Servants of the Lord, bless the Lord.
Spirits and souls of the just, bless the Lord.
Holy men of humble heart, bless the Lord.
Hananiah, Azariah, Mishael, bless the Lord.
Praise and exalt him above all forever.
Let us bless the Father, and the Son, and the Holy Spirit
Let us praise and exalt him forever.
Blessed are you, Lord, in the firmament of heaven.
Praiseworthy and glorious and exalted above all forever.

Canticle of the Three Youth in the Furnace. (Dan 3:57-88, 56 from Sunday Morning Prayer of Week I of the Liturgy of the Hours.)

The Canticle of the Three Youth in the Furnace gives a vivid example of what I call the Community of the Beautiful. In the canticle, the themes of the aesthetic norm, the anagogic imagination, interpreting in the garden of good and evil and the discerning Community of the Beautiful all find vivid expression. As such, this canticle serves to introduce this last chapter.

The above, a canticle rather than a poem, forms part of the Church's Liturgy of the Hours. The Liturgy of the Hours, also known as the Divine Office, attempts a semi-continuous liturgy consisting of hymns, canticles, psalms, and prayers. Its psalter consists of a four week cycle of psalms and canticles. The above finds its place as the first canticle of the psalter. It is a highly revered position. The psalms and canticles of the first day (Sunday) of the first week of the psalter are also the psalms and canticles for the Church's most solemn feasts. As such, the Church reveals its high appreciation for the Canticle of the Three Youth by its very position in the psalter. The Canticle of the Three Youth, however, is part of a larger story within the Bible, i.e., the Three Youths in the Furnace.

Shadrach, Meshach, and Abednego were exiled Jews who were appointed as administrators in Nebuchadnezzar's Babylonia. When King Nebuchadnezzar had a "golden statue" made and ordered all to worship it, these three (among many others) refused. When Nebuchadnezzar heard of their refusal, he had them brought before his court. "Be ready now to fall down and worship the statue I had made," he ordered them, "whenever you hear the sound of the trumpet, flute, lyre, harp, psaltery, bagpipe, and all the other musical instruments; otherwise, you shall be instantly cast into the white-hot furnace; and who is the God that can deliver you out of my hands? (Dan 3:15, NAB)." They refused and, of course, were thrown into the furnace which had been heated "seven times more than usual (Dan 3:19 NAB)." Indeed, the furnace was so hot that "the flames devoured the men who threw Shadrach, Meshach, and Abednego into it, (Dan 3:22, NAB)." Amazingly, however, the king heard singing coming from inside the furnace. Shadrach, Meshach, and Abednego were singing the canticle above. When Nebuchadnezzar came to investigate, he was dumbfounded. "Did we not cast three men bound into the fire (Dan 3:91, NAB)," he asked. Yes, his servants answered. Then, he said, why do "I see four men unfettered and unhurt, walking in the fire, and the fourth looks like a son of God? (Dan 3:92, NAB)."

The story of the three youths in the furnace lends itself, like Peirce's elementary logic of sign, to contrast and comparison. One can contrast, for example, Nebuchadnezzar's call for praise versus the three youth's call for praise, the music and song coming from within Nebuchadnezzar's royal court against the music and song from within the furnace. Royal court versus furnace correspond to quite different "backgrounds" in an aesthetics of "foregrounding." Such comparison reveals Royce's inclusion principle at work. Nebuchadnezzar's call for praise would include the three youth into the community of the royal court. The youths' call for praise, on the other hand, addresses the community of the furnace. That community, however, is much larger than the three youth themselves.

Indeed, the three youth call for "all the works of the Lord" to "praise and exalt him forever." All these works include the invisible creatures (the angels), the visible creatures of the heavens (sun, moon, and stars but also dew, rain, frost, ice and snow), the visible creatures of the earth (mountains, hills, seas, rivers, birds, wild and tame indeed all beasts, even dolphins!), and then those creatures with one foot in the visible and the other in the invisible creation. These include cultural creatures (Israel), the dead (souls and spirits of the just), and the creatures of the good imagination (the "Holy of humble heart"). Thus, the entire creation, the fullness of the cosmos, the visible and the invisible, the "natural" and the cultural, Nature and Plow, all comprise the community addressed by the three youths. The interpreting community of aesthetic discernment is a cosmic community. It is also the community of the furnace.

There is another member of the community we have not mentioned, Nebuchadnezzar himself. It is he, in a sense, that reveals the aesthetic norm of the anagogical imagination. It is he that the aesthetic norm addresses. To Nebuchadnezzar's surprise, the youth are not consumed by the furnace. Indeed, the hotter the furnace, the cooler the youth appear to be. A norm beyond Nebuchadnezzar's control reveals itself in this violation of physical laws. The violation of physical laws, however, is not the aim of the revealed norm. Its aim lies elsewhere. Indeed, the subversive nature of the aesthetic norm begins its anagogic work on Nebuchadnezzar, and he sees a fourth form walking with the three youths. The anagogical imagination reveals itself, and Nebuchadnezzar "sees the form" and interprets correctly: "Blessed be the God of Shadrach, Meshack, and Abednego, who sent his angel to deliver the servants that trusted in him; they disobeyed the royal command and yielded their bodies rather than serve or worship any god except their own God. Therefore I decree for nations and peoples of every language that whoever blasphemes the God of Shadrach, Meshack, and Abednego shall be cut to pieces and his house destroyed. For there is no other God who can rescue like this (Dan 3:95-6, NAB)." The "lowly," indeed, have been "lifted up."

The Canticle of the Three Youth in the Furnace demonstrates how von Balthasar's "seeing the form" emerges out of the Community of the Beautiful. In the interpreting of the aesthetic sign, the Community of the Beautiful becomes itself an aesthetic sign which invites, or rather, "calls," the "other," the "outsider," to interpret. Its "call" manifests itself through the subversive aesthetic norm which gives witness to that original place of mystery in order to create a cosmic community of praise. As such, the aesthetic sign through its norm functions as emerging from an origins but also drawn to an ends. The aesthetic sign finds analogy in the *exitus* and *reditus* of Dionysius' and Aquinas' system. The aesthetic sign's *exitus* and *reditus*, however, takes place in the garden of good and evil. The aesthetic sign "calls" the heart to discern original Beauty so that it may orient itself towards a Beautiful end.

It does this through the anagogical imagination which foregrounds or "lifts up" the discerning heart from the "lowly" Beautiful (God's humbling of absolute power) to its loving origins in Beauty (the full glory of God's absolute power). As such, the anagogical imagination finds an exquisite environment in the garden of good and evil. For the anagogical imagination is the pragmatic discernment of divine power. The anagogical imagination finds analogy in Being's manifestation of God's absolute power lovingly limited towards ordaining a humble but loved for creation. Indeed, the anagogical imagination is an exercise of power. It is discerning power, however. It is the power of the logic of the sensual. Such power requires the full use of our senses in all its material and spiritual dimensions. For it is the power to move the human heart as God "moved" his own heart. Thus, the Community of the Beautiful is also a community of power. The Community of the Beautiful uses its striking powers of sense to discern the "where from" and the "where to" of its powerful sensuality.

Such sensuality, however, begins in difference. It is the contrast or foregrounding that initiates the discerning of the sensual. As such, the Community of the Beautiful discerns the meaning of difference. The meaning of difference, in essence, is the "logic" of the senses. The Community of the Beautiful, in other words, is not simply the "audience" of the Beautiful. It is, as in all triadic logic, a community of interpretation, but it is interpretation of the "application of the senses" in a manner like Ignatius. Thus, the Community of the Beautiful completes the triad of transcendentals and reveals the fullness of the logic of signs which Peirce recovered from Scotus. It is von Balthasar, however, who provides the motivation and the vision towards completing the third transcendental. Von Balthasar's "seeing the form" provided the guiding vision towards completing the aesthetic component of Peirce's and Royce's pragmatic logic of signs. "Seeing the form" eventually led us to consider Mukarovsky's semiotic aesthetics of "foregrounding" and the subversive nature of the aesthetic norm. Indeed Mukarovsky's aesthetic norm is strikingly similar to von Balthasar's analogy of Being. As such, Mukarovsky's analysis leads us from von Balthasar's "seeing the form" to a more semiotic "seeing the sign."

This is the experience of the popular Latin Church of the Americas, which manifests itself in an aesthetics of signs and symbols. Like the community of the Three Youth in the Furnace, this Church has had to discern between royal court and furnace. Indeed, the Latin Church of the Americas has had to walk within a fiery furnace the past five hundred years. Like the Three Youth in the Furnace, this Church recognizes its cosmic dimensions. The cosmic plays a role in almost all its popular practices. Moreover, those who look carefully at this Church's pilgrimage will also see a "fourth" form walking alongside—Mary of the Americas, specifically, Mary of Guadalupe.[1]

[1] I use Mary of the Americas to include all the Marys of Latin and North America, not only Mary of Guadalupe but my own Mary of Cuba, Our Lady of Charity. I do plan to concentrate on Mary of Guadalupe, however, as she has been the most studied and prominent in Hispanic theology. I am also aware that Hispanic theologians such as Orlando Espín warn against calling Our Lady of Guadalupe, Mary of Guadalupe. Dr. Espín prudently warns that Our Lady of Guadalupe may not be identical to the Mary of the Bible. Although I agree with Dr. Espín that Our Lady of Guadalupe contains elements that may not be found in mariological tradition and may function sociologically in non-mariological ways, I do believe that there is a theological connection to Mary of Nazareth and tradition that I will develop in the following pages.

MARY OF GUADALUPE AND THE MARY OF FAITH

The role of the cosmic in the popular religion of the Latin Church of the Americas finds exquisite expression in Mary of Guadalupe. She appears embraced by the sun, standing on the moon, and wrapped in a mantilla of stars. Furthermore, Mary of Guadalupe is, as well, a sign of redemption. She carries the Redeemer in her womb. Thus, cosmic order and redemption intertwine in this "form" which continues to walk with the Latin Church of the Americas in its fiery pilgrimage to the Kingdom of God. As such, Mary of Guadalupe suggests a further dimension to the aesthetic logic of signs. The aesthetics of signs is the place where Faith and Reason meet. This suggestion may best be explored by contrasting the universal Mary of Faith with the particular Mary of Guadalupe.

SOPHIA AND BEATRICE

Murray Wright Bundy in his now classic and definitive work *The Theory of Imagination in Classical and Medieval Thought* describes Dante's view of the imagination as "the culmination of the thought of the Middle Ages.[2] It is, in a sense, a theory of vision which has both Augustinian and Thomistic elements. Dante's theory of vision finds incarnation in his *Divine Comedy* in the character of Beatrice. Dante's theory of vision is also a theory of poetry. In the *Divine Comedy* Dante exposes the philosophical problems a true aesthetic sensitivity brings to the poet. Indeed, Dante is one of the most philosophical of all poets.[3] These philosophical problems are exposed through the metaphor of a journey of a hierarchy of visions. Dante travels through the *Inferno* of corporal vision, the *Purgatorio* of spiritual vision, and, finally, to the glorious *Paradiso* of intellectual vision.[4] The journey for Dante appears to be the struggle of properly discerning the ultimate vision of the earthly Paradise. Each level of vision practices his imagination towards the vision of Paradise.[5] As such, Dante appears to offer a strikingly pragmatic-like account of aesthetic vision.

The journey, however, also reveals the role that Faith and Reason play in a theological aesthetics. Dante is accompanied by Virgil (a type of

---

[2]Murray Wright Bundy, "The Theory of Imagination in Classical and Mediaeval Thought," *University of Illinois Studies in Language and Literature* XII, no. 2–3 (1927) 225.

[3]Ibid., 229.

[4]Ibid., 233.

[5]Ibid., 241.

Reason) through the *Inferno* of corporal vision into the lower levels of *Purgatorio*. There *Dante* meets Beatrice (a type of Faith) which now takes over for Virgil (Reason) and guides Dante through the level of spiritual vision *(Purgatorio)* to the glorious level of intellectual vision *(Paradiso)*. Dante, then, sees distinctive roles for Faith and Reason. Virgil (Reason) can guide Dante from corporal vision to spiritual vision, but Beatrice must then take over and guide Dante from spiritual vision to intellectual vision. Thus, Dante exposes the medieval understanding of the distinctive but complementary role between Faith and Reason. The theological aesthetics of the anagogical imagination corresponds to this understanding but makes the complementary role between Faith and Reason a much more integral role. Nowhere is this closer role more explicitly made in the classical tradition than in Boethius' *Consolation of Philosophy*.

Indeed, Dante's *Divine Comedy* may be seen as "a great elaboration of Boethius's concept of the ascent of the soul to the contemplation the mind of God and its return home to its true home or *patria* in the scheme of the universe."[6] Anicius Manlius Severinus Boethius (c. A.D. 480–524) found himself on the wrong side of the once barbaric and now Arian emperor, Theodoric. Theodoric, rightly or wrongly (it is a matter of controversy), suspected Boethius, who had been his official philosopher of writing against Arianism. Thus, Theodoric arrested Boethius and condemned him to death. There Boethius wrote his *Consolation of Philosophy* which affected the great Medieval tradition in no small way.

The *Consolation of Philosophy* consists of a very special type of dialogue with Sophia, i.e., Wisdom. As such, it falls under the genre of a Wisdom dialogue such as in the second book of Esdras. It is, however, a Wisdom dialogue taking place in the garden of good and evil and, thus, could be also classified as a theodicy. As such, it is a striking example of an earlier Christianity's confidence in the redemptive dimensions of the cosmic order. Most modern writers, however, fail to understand it as such. V. E. Watts, for example, writes in his Introduction to the *Consolation*: "[The *Consolation*] celebrates in verse the truth that has just been proclaimed, God's benevolent government of the universe, for the question of the presence of evil in the world has its solution in the vision of divine peace."[7] Yet Watts wonders, as many modern (not medieval) writers have, why Boethius would write about reason rather than grace. "It seems strange, nevertheless, that writing in the presence of

---

[6]Boethius, *The Consolation of Philosophy,* trans. and introd. by Richard Green, The Library of Liberal Arts (Indianapolis: Bobbs-Merrill, 1962) 8.

[7]Ibid., 24.

death Boethius still prefers reason to faith, and makes no mention of what must be the only fully meaningful consolation for a Christian, the Incarnation of Christ and the doctrine of grace."[5] Watts, I believe, fails to see the gracious roots of the cosmic order that Boethius and, indeed, much of the medieval tradition took for granted. Indeed, Watts would have us pit Dante's Beatrice against Boethius' Sophia.

As such, Watts reveals the symptoms of an iconoclastic Modernity that has lost its sense of Beauty. In Beauty, Beatrice and Sophia, Faith and Reason, Grace and Cosmic Order, Incarnation and Redemption, all find a common ground as the Community of the Beautiful. Watts, apparently, does not recognize this. The Latin Church of the Americas, however, does. Like St. Francis' experience of the crucified seraph, the Latin Church of the Americas experiences Beauty as both joy and sorrow, ecstasy and consolation. Indeed, the community gathered by Mary of Guadalupe exemplifies this ancient Christian understanding.

Mary of Guadalupe represents both Beatrice and Sophia. Mary of Guadalupe, as Beatrice and Sophia, is both the Mary of Faith, Mother of God and Jesus of Nazareth, as well as the Mary of Wisdom, the brown Mother of Mexico embraced by the sun and wrapped by the stars. As such, Mary of Guadalupe reveals yet another dimension of a theological aesthetics. Like Boethius' Sophia, Mary of Guadalupe consoles. Indeed, a theological aesthetics that recognizes the roles of both Beatrice and Sophia is an aesthetics of both ecstasy and consolation. Thus, Mary of Guadalupe creates the Community of the Beautiful as both a community of consolation as well as ecstasy.

Consolation, then, is part of the theological aesthetic moment. Given the aesthetic principle above, "lifting up the lowly," this ought not to surprise us. Consolation is, above all, an act of humility which implies the other theological aesthetic moment, ecstasy. Consolation allows us to ask the ultimate question of reason as asked from within the garden of good and evil, **Why?** This question, the question of theodicy and suffering, is also the question of the relation between origins and ends. Such relation cannot be conceived by a logic that knows little of the beautiful. Indeed, the question of evil in our day has been asked either from the perspective of the True or the perspective of the Good. How can a good and all-powerful God allow innocent suffering? Suffering Christians in the Latin Church of the Americas, however, have asked the question from a different perspective. Such Christians have asked the question of their own suffering from the perspective of the beautiful. Thus, they have discerned a beautiful woman that gives a hint as to the nature of the relation between our origins and our ends. In this beautiful woman, cosmic order and redemption, origins and ends, are shown their profound unity. Such unity, however, could only be seen through the eyes of a Juan Diego who was walking towards home and, surprisingly, subversively, even beautifully was shown a home he never expected. Suffering Christians in the Latin church of the Americas, like Juan Diego, humble their reason in order that their reason be raised by the subversive call of Beauty. In their suffering, they ask to be consoled by the wisdom of Sophia in order to be lifted up towards the higher vision of Beatrice. As such, consolation and ecstasy constitute a "social" act, a discernment of signs which begins in consolation and ends in praise. This "social act," however, belongs, at the same time, to one of the transcendentals. As such, consolation and ecstasy reveal another "social act," the praxis of the Good, a community where the mighty are cast down in a thirst for justice. This "social act," in turn, reveals yet another "social act," the vision of the True, where the soul of the human creature magnifies the Lord.

Thus, we reach, at long last, the end of our reflection's circumference. Hopkins' Pied Beauty and America's Different Beauty converge in the aesthetic principle, "lifting up the lowly." The Glory of the Lord returns as praise and thanksgiving because the Glory of the Lord is a community that has caught sight of a marvelous vision, a universe of justice emerging from a community's experience of divine Beauty, the "lifting up the lowly." Such a community counts as members the sun and stars, the dead and the living, the angels and the animals, and, of course, the marvelous yet lowly human creature. Together, in their splendid differences, these individuals give witness of God's power not only to give life but also to ordain it, not only to grant existence but also to order it. As such, these individuals also give witness to the reality of certain relationships, realities held in common, realities that know little of the subject-object split that plagues our understanding today. These realities, whose commonality has its source in God's ordaining power, eschew what has become in our day an iconoclastic view of redemption. Redemption, in light of God's ordaining power, is less a state of mere existence or an invisible inner reality than an ordained existence, a common reality in the midst of marvelous differences, a community where the invisible becomes visible by the power of a bold and daring spiritual imagination which makes manifest communities of Truth, Goodness, and, above all, the Beautiful.

Having come to the end of this reflection, I now realize the poverty of my own understanding. Attempting to interpret the movement of my heart as I have experienced it through the Latin Church of the Americas, I have barely begun to sketch what I had hoped would be a vision of the Community of the Beautiful. I am consoled only that such a result is consonant with this vision of a theological aesthetics. In exploring the Glory of the Lord, my intellect has been humbled. I lie in wait, for the interpretation that is to follow. May such interpretation be lifted up towards the One who is Beauty and may it result in the enlargement of the Community of the Beautiful.

Bibliography

Anderson, Perry. *Passages from Antiquity to Feudalism.* London: Verso Editions, 1978.

_____. "Art." In *New Catholic Encyclopedia,* William J. McDonald, ed. New York: McGraw Hill Co., 1967.

_____. "Yetzer." G. Johannes Botterweck, and Helma Ringgren, eds., David Green, trans. In *Theological Dictionary of the Old Testament.* Grand Rapids, Michigan: William B. Eerdmans.

Apel, Karl-Otto. *Charles S. Peirce: From Pragmatism to Pragmaticism.* Originally published in German as *Der Denkweg von Charles S. Peirce: Eine Einführung in den amerikanischen Pragmatismus* by Suhrkamp Verlag, Frankfurt am Main, Germany. John Michael Krois, trans., 1967. Atlantic Highlands, N.J.: Humanities Press International, 1995.

Aquino, Maria Pilar. *Our Cry for Life: Feminist Theology from Latin America.* Maryknoll, N.Y.: Orbis Books, 1993.

Arenal, Electa, and Stacey Schlau. *Untold Stories: Hispanic Nuns in Their Own Words.* Amanda Powell, trans. Albuquerque: University of New Mexico Press, 1989.

Augustine. *The Confessions of St. Augustine.* Oak Harbor, Wash.: Logos Research Systems, Inc., 1995. CD. Logos Library System.

Augustine, Aurelius. *The Works of Saint Augustine: A Translation for the 21st Century,* vol. 1, *The Confessions.* A project of the Augustinian Heritage Institute. John E. Rotelle, O.S.A., ed. Maria Boulding, O.S.B., trans. Hyde Park, N.Y.: New City Press, 1997.

_____. *Confessions.* R. S. Pine-Coffin, trans. Hammondsworth: Penguin Classics, 1961.

Baudet, Henri. *Paradise on Earth: Some Thoughts on European Images of Non-European Man.* Middletown, Conn.: Wesleyan University Press, 1988.

Baumgarten, Alexander G. *Meditationes Philosophicae de Nonnullis Ad Poema Pertinentibus,* 1735.

Bettoni, Efram. *Duns Scotus: The Basic Principles of His Philosophy.* B. Bonansea, trans. Washington, D.C.: The Catholic University of America, 1961.

Blondel, Maurice. *Action: Essay on a Critique of Life and a Science of Practice.* Translation of *L'Action,* original work published: Presses Universitaires de France, 1950 <1893>. Olive Blanchette, trans. Notre Dame, Ind.: University of Notre Dame Press, 1984. xxx + 446 pp.

Boler, John F. *Charles Peirce and Scholastic Realism: A Study of Peirce's Relation to John Duns Scotus.* Seattle: University of Washington Press, 1963.

Bonaventure. "The Life of St. Francis." In *Bonaventure,* Ewert Cousins, trans. Preface by Ignatius Brady, O.F.M. The Classics of Western Spirituality. New York: Paulist Press, 1978.

Bonino, Jose Miguez. *Doing Theology in a Revolutionary Situation.* William H. Lazareth, ed. Confrontation Books. Philadelphia: Fortress Press, 1975.

Bosanquet, Bernard. *A History of Aesthetic.* Cleveland: World Publishing, Meridian, 1957.

Brann, Eva. "Ancient Writers." In *The World of the Imagination: Sum and Substance,* 35–56. Lanham, Maryland: Rowman & Littlefield Publishers, 1991.

_____. *The World of the Imagination: Sum and Substance.* Lanham, Md.: Rowman & Littlefield Publishers, 1991.

Buber, Martin. *Good and Evil.* New York: Scribner's, 1952.

Bump, Jerome. *Gerard Manley Hopkins.* Boston: Twayne Publishers, 1982.

Bundy, Murray Wright. "The Theory of Imagination in Classical and Mediaeval Thought." *University of Illinois Studies in Language and Literature* XII, no. 2–3 (1927) 7–281.

Candelaria, Michael R. *Popular Religion and Liberation: The Dilemma of Liberation Theology.* Albany: State University of New York Press, 1990.

Casarella, Peter J. "The Expression and Form of the Word: Trinitarian Hermeneutics and the Sacramentality of Language in Hans Urs von Balthasar's Theology." *Renascence* 48, no. 2 (Winter 1996) 111–35.

Cassirer, Ernst. "Art." In *Critical Theory Since Plato,* Hazard Adams, ed. 926–43. New York: Harcourt Brace Jovanovich College Publishers, 1992.

Chenu, M. D. "The Symbolist Mentality." In *Nature, Man and Society in the Twelfth Century: Essays on New Theological Perspectives in the Latin West.* Translation of *La théologie au douzième siècle.* Original work published: 1957. Preface by Etienne Gilson, Jerome Taylor and Lester K. Little, trans. Chicago: University of Chicago Press, 1968.

Clark, Ronald W. *Einstein: The Life and Times.* New York: Avon Books, 1971.

Claudel, Paul. "La sensation du Divin." In *Etudes Carmélitaines,* vol. XXXIII, *Nos sens et Dieu,* 54–60. Bruges.

Copleston, Frederick. *A History of Philosophy,* vol. 3, *Ockham to Suárez.* The Bellamine Series, vol. XIV. London: Burns and Oates, 1968.

Corrington, Robert S. *An Introduction to C.S. Peirce.* Lanham, Md.: Rowman & Littlefield, 1993.

Cotter, James Finn. *Inscape: The Christology and Poetry of Gerard Manley Hopkins.* Pittsburgh: University of Pennsylvania Press, 1965.

Croce, Bendetto. *Aesthetic: As Science of Expression and General Linguistic,* rev. ed. Douglas Ainslie, trans. New York: Noonday Press, 1922.

Crumley, Bruce. "Archaeology: Cave Art in France." *Time Magazine* 145, no. 5 (1995).

Daigler, Matthew A. "Heidegger and von Balthasar: A Lovers' Quarrel Over Beauty and Divinity." *American Catholic Philosophical Quarterly* 69, no. 2 (1995) 375–94.

Davies, W. D. *Paul and Rabbinic Judaism,* rev. ed. 1948. New York: Harper & Row, 1967.

Davis, Philip J., and Reuben Hersh. *The Mathematical Experience.* Introduction by Gian-Carlo Rota. Boston: Houghton Mifflin Company, 1981.

de Acosta, Jose. *Historia Natural y Moral de las Indias,* critical ed. Gorman O, E. 1590–1608. Mexico City: N.p., 1940.

de Chardin, Pierre Teilhard. *The Divine Milieu.* Translation of *Le Milieu Divin.* Original work published: Paris: Éditions du Seuil, 1957. New York: Harper and Row, Harper Torchbooks/ Library, 1960.

de las Casas, Bartolomé. *Obras Completas.* vol. 9, *Apologiae Adversus Genesium Sepulvedam.* Angel Losada, ed. 1550. Madrid: Alianza Editorial, 1988.

_____. *Historia de las Indias,* 3 vols. 2nd ed. Agustín Millares Carlo, ed. Prepared by Lewis Hanke. Cronistas de Indias por la Biblioteca Americana. Mexico, D.F.: Fondo de Cultura Economica, 1965–86.

De Morgan, Augustus. "On the Syllogism of No. IV and on the Logic of Relations." *Cambridge Philosophical Transactions* X: 331–58.

de Oviedo, Fernandez. *De la Natural Hystoria de las Indias,* facsimile ed. 1526. Chapel Hill, N.C.: University of North Carolina Press, 1969.

de Sahagún, Bernardino. *Histoire générale des choses de la Nouvelle-Espagne.* D. Jourdanet and Remí Siméon, trans. Paris, 1880.

_____. *Historia general de las cosas de Nueva España.* Angel Maria Garibay K., ed. 1956. Mexico: Editorial Porrúa, 1981. 4 vols.

Dick, Steven J. *Plurality of Worlds: The Origins of the Extraterrestrial Life Debate from Democritus to Kant.* Cambridge: Cambridge University Press, 1982.

Donovan, Mary Ann. "Alive to the Glory of God: A Key Insight in St. Irenaeus." *Theological Studies* 49, no. 2 (1988) 283–98.

Dressel, E. "De Isidori Originum Fontibus." *Rivista di Filologia e di Instruzione Classica 3* (1875) 207–68.

Dulles, Avery. "Mystery (in Theology)." In *New Catholic Encyclopedia,* William J. McDonald, ed. New York: McGraw Hill Co., 1967.

Dupré, Louis. "Hans Urs von Balthasar's Theology of Aesthetic Form." *Theological Studies* 49, no. 2 (June 1988) 299–318.

Eco, Umberto. *Art and Beauty in the Middle Ages.* Hugh Bredin. New Haven, Conn.: Yale University Press, 1986.

_____. *Semiotics and the Philosophy of Language.* Advances in Semiotics. Bloomington, Ind.: Indiana University Press, 1984. 242 pp.

Edwards, Jonathan. *The Religious Affections.* 1746. Edinburgh: The Banner of Truth Trust, 1994.

Elizondo, Virgilio. *The Future Is Mestizo: Life Where Cultures Meet.* Bloomington, Ind.: Meyer-Stone Books, 1988.

_____. "Our Lady of Guadalupe as a Cultural Symbol." In *Liturgy and Cultural Traditions,* Herman Power and David Schmidt, eds. 25–33. New York: Seabury Press, 1977.

Espín, Orlando O. *The Faith of the People: Theological Reflections on Popular Catholicism.* Roberto Goizueta. Maryknoll, N. Y.: Orbis Books, 1997.

Fairweather, Eugene R., ed. and trans. *A Scholastic Miscellany: Anselm to Ockham.* The Library of Christian Classics, vol. X. Philadelphia: Westminster Press, 1956. p.

Feibleman, James. *An Introduction to Peirce's Philosophy: Interpreted as a System.* Foreword by Bertrand Russell. New York and London: Harper & Brothers Publishing, 1946.

Fishbane, Michael. *The Kiss of God: Spiritual and Mystical Death in Judaism.* Seattle and London: University of Washington Press, 1962.

Flower, Elizabeth, and Murray G. Murphey. *A History of Philosophy in America,* vol. 1. New York: Capricorn, 1977.

Freddoso, Alfred J., trans. and introd. by Henry Schurrman, trans. *The Summa Logicae,* vol. 2, *Ockham's Theory of Proportions.* Notre Dame, Ind.: University of Notre Dame Press, 1980.

Funkestein, Amos. *Theology and the Scientific Imagination: From the Middle Ages to the Seventeenth Century.* Princeton, N.J.: Princeton University Press, 1986.

Galileo, Galilei. *Dialogues Concerning Two New Sciences.* Translated by Henry Crew and Alfonso de Salvio, trans. introduction by Antonio Favaro. 1914. New York: Dover, 1954.

García-Rivera, Alex. "A Matter of Presence." *Journal of Hispanic/Latino Theology* 5, no. 2 (1994) 22–53.

_____. "Towards a Theology of the Imagination." Conference presentation given June 4, 1996, San Diego, Calif. to the Catholic Theological Society of America.

_____. "The Whole and the Love of Difference: Latino Metaphysics as Cosmology." In *Towards a New Systematics,* Orland Espín and Miguel Díaz. eds. Maryknoll, N.Y.: Orbis Books, forthcoming.

_____. "Artificial Intelligence, 1992, and Las Casas: A 1492 Resonance." *Zygon* 28, no. 4 (1993) 543–50.

_____. "Creator of the Visible and the Invisible: Liberation Theology, Postmodernism, and the Spiritual." *Journal of Hispanic/Latino* Theology 3, no. 4 (1996) 35–56.

_____. "Religious Imagination." In *Perspectivas: Hispanic Ministry,* Allan Figueroa Deck, Timothy M. Matovina, and Yolanda Tarango, eds. 94–97. Kansas City: Sheed and Ward, 1995.

_____. *St. Martin de Porres: The "Little Stories" and the Semiotics of Culture.* Foreword by Robert Schreiter and Virgilio Elizondo. Faith and Cultures. Maryknoll, N.Y.: Orbis Books, 1995.

Geertz, Clifford. *The Interpretation of Cultures.* New York: Basic Books, Inc, 1973.

Gerard Manley Hopkins. "The May Magnificat." In *Gerard Manley Hopkins, Poems and Prose.* Penguin Classics. London: Penguin Books, 1985.

Gerbi, Antonello. *The Dispute of the New World: The History of a Polemic, 1750–1900.* Translation of *La disputa del Nuovo Mono: Storia di una polemica, 1750–1900,* original work published: Italy: 1955. Trans. and revised by Jeremy Moyle, Pittsburgh: University of Pittsburgh Press, 1973.

Gilbert, Katharine Everett, and Helmut Kuhn. *A History of Esthetics.* New York: MacMillan, 1939.

Gilson, Etienne. *History of Christian Philosophy in the Middle Ages.* New York: Random House, 1955.

_____. *Jean Duns Scot: introduction à ses positions fondamentales.* Paris: J. Vrin, 1952.

_____. *The Spirit of Medieval Philosophy.* A.H.C. Downes, trans. New York: Scribner's, 1940.

Glacken, Clarence J. *Traces on the Rhodian Shore: Nature and Culture in Western Thought from Ancient Times to the End of the Eighteenth Century.* Berkeley: University of California Press, 1967.

Goizueta, Roberto S. *Caminemos con Jesús: Toward a Hispanic/Latino Theology of Accompaniment.* Maryknoll, N.Y.: Orbis Books, 1995.

Grajewski, Maurice J., O.F.M. *The Formal Distinction of Duns Scotus: A Study in Metaphysics.* Ph.D. diss. Washington, D.C.: The Catholic University of America Press, 1944.

Guerrero, Andrés. *A Chicano Theology.* Maryknoll, N.Y.: Orbis Books, 1987.

Guerrero, Jose Luis. *El Nican Mopohua: Un intento de exégesis.* Mexico, D.F.: Universidad Pontificia de Mexico, A.C., 1996.

Gutiérrez, Gustavo. *Las Casas: In Search of the Poor of Jesus Christ.* Robert Barr, trans. Maryknoll, N.Y.: Orbis Books, 1993.

_____. *Teología de la liberación,* 7th ed. New introduction, "Mirar Lejos." 1968. Lima: Centro de Estudios y Publicaciones, 1990.

Harris, C.R.S. *Duns Scotus.* Oxford: Clarendon Press, 1927. 2 vols.

Harrison, Carol. *Beauty and Revelation in the Thought of St. Augustine.* Oxford Theological Monographs. Clarendon Press: Oxford, 1992.

Hefner, Philip. *The Human Factor.* Unpublished manuscript. N.p., 1992.

Hennelly, S.J., Alfred T. *Liberation Theologies: The Global Pursuit of Justice.* Mystic, Conn.: Twenty-Third Publications, 1995.

Holmes, Urban T., III. *A History of Christian Spirituality: An Analytical Introduction.* New York: Seabury Press, 1980.

Hookway, Christopher. *Peirce.* The arguments of the philosophers. London: Routledge, 1985.

Irenaeus. *Adversus Haereses Find Rest of Cite.*

Isasi-Diaz, Ada Maria. *En la Lucha/In the Struggle: An Hispanic Women's Liberation Theology.* Minneapolis: Fortress Press, 1993.

Kearney, Richard. *The Wake of Imagination: Toward a Postmodern Culture.* Minneapolis: University of Minnesota Press, 1988.

Keen, Benjamin. *The Aztec Image in Western Thought.* New Brunswick, N.J.: Rutgers University Press, 1990.

Kittel, Gerhard. "Dianoia." In *Theological Dictionary of the New Testament.* Grand Rapids, Mich.: William B. Eerdmans, 1985.

_____. "Hypsoo." In *Theological Dictionary of the New Testament.* Grand Rapids, Mich.: William B. Eerdmans, 1985.

_____. "Metanoia." In *Theological Dictionary of the New Testament.* Grand Rapids, Mich.: William Eerdmans, 1985.

_____. "Noeo." In *Theological Dictionary of the New Testament.* Grand Rapids, Mich.: William B. Eerdmans, 1985.

_____. "Nous." *In Theological Dictionary of the New Testament.* Grand Rapids, Mich.: William B. Eerdmans, 1985.

Kretzmann, Norman, Anthony Kenny, and Jan Pinborg, eds. *The Cambridge History of Later Medieval Philosophy.* Cambridge: Cambridge University Press, 1982.

Lawlor, Leonard. *Imagination and Chance: The Difference Between the Thought of Ricoeur and Derrida.* Intersections: Philosophy and Critical Theory. New York: State University of New York Press, 1992.

Leff, Gordon. *The Dissolution of the Medieval Outlook: An Essay on the Intellectual and Spiritual Change in the Fourteenth Century.* New York: Harper & Row, Harper Torchbooks, 1976.

León-Portilla, Miguel. *Aztec Thought and Culture.* Norman, Okla.: Oklahoma University Press, 1963.

Lotz, Johannes Baptist. "Transcendentals." In *Sacramentum Mundi,* Karl Rahner, ed. London: Herder and Herder, 1970.

Loux, Michael J., trans. *The Summa Logicae,* vol. 1, *Ockham's Theory of Terms.* Notre Dame, Ind.: University of Notre Dame Press, 1974.

Marenbon, John. *Later Medieval Philosophy* (1150–1350). London: Routledge & Kegan Paul, 1987.

McIntyre, John. *Faith, Theology and Imagination.* Edinburgh: Handsel Press, 1987.

Milward, Peter, S.J. *Landscape and Inscape: Vision and Inspiration in Hopkin's Poetry.* Grand Rapids, Mich.: William B. Eerdmans, 1975.

Mukarovsky, Jan. "The Aesthetic Norm." John Burbank, and Peter Steiner, ed. and trans. In *Structure, Sign and Function: Selected Essays by Jan Mukarovsky.* New Haven, Conn., and London: Yale University Press, 1978.

_____. "The Esthetics of Language." In *The Prague School Reader of Esthetics, Literary Structures, and Style, Selected and Translated from the Original Czech,* Paul L. Garvin, ed., Washington, D.C.: Washington Linguistic Club, 1955.

_____. *Structure, Sign and Function: Selected Essays by Jan Mukarovsky.* New Haven, Conn. and London: Yale University Press, 1978.

Murphey, Murray G. *The Development of Peirce's Philosophy.* Indianapolis and Cambridge: Hackett Publishing Company, 1993.

Murray, Peter and Linda. "The Immaculate Conception." *1996 The Oxford Companion to Christian Art and Architecture.* Oxford: Oxford University Press.

Nöth, Winfried. *Handbook of Semiotics.* English-language revised and enlarged edition of *Handbuch der Semiotik,* 1985, by J. B. Metzlersche Verlagsbuchhandlung. Advances in Semiotics. Bloomington and Indianapolis: Indiana University Press, 1990.

Oakes, Edward T., S.J. *Pattern of Redemption: The Theology of Hans Urs von Balthasar.* New York: Continuum, 1997.

Oppenheim, Frank M. *Royce's Mature Ethics.* Notre Dame, Ind.: University of Notre Dame Press, 1993.

_____. *Royce's Mature Religion.* Notre Dame, Ind.: University of Notre Dame Press, 1987.

Padgen, Anthony. *The Fall of Natural Man: The American Indian and the Origin of Comparative Ethnology.* Cambridge Iberian and Latin American Studies. Cambridge: Cambridge University Press, 1986.

Peirce, Charles Sanders. *Collected Papers.* Cambridge: Harvard University Press, 1931–1958.

_____. "The Doctrine of Chances." In *The Essential Peirce: Selected Philosophical Writings,* Nathan Houser and Christian Kloesel, ed. Bloomington and Indianapolis: Indiana University Press, 1992.

_____. "The Fixation of Belief." In *The Essential Peirce: Selected Philosophical Writings,* Nathan Houser and Christian Kloesel, eds. Bloomington and Indianapolis: Indiana University Press, 1992.

_____. "Fraser's the Works of George Berkeley." In *The Essential Peirce: Selected Philosophical Writings,* 1871. Bloomington and Indianapolis: Indiana University Press, 1992.

_____. "On a List of New Categories." In *Peirce on Signs: Writings on Semiotic by Charles Sanders Peirce,* James Hoopes, ed. Chapel Hill, N.C., and London: University of North Carolina Press, 1991.

_____. *Sketch on Dichotomic Mathematics.* Unpublished manuscript found in the Charles Sanders Peirce Collection, housed at Houghton Library, Harvard University, 1973.

Phalan, John Letty. *The Millennial Kingdom of the Franciscans in the New World.* Berkeley: University of California Press, 1970.

Porter, F. C. "The Yetzer Hara, a Study in the Jewish Doctrine of Sin." In *Biblical and Semitic Studies,* 93–156. New York: N.p., 1901.

Potter, Vincent G., S.J. *Charles S. Peirce: On Norms & Ideals.* Worcester, Mass.: University of Massachusetts Press, 1967.

Pseudo-Dionysius. *Pseudo-Dionysius: The Complete Works.* John Farina, ed. Classics of Western Spirituality. New York: Paulist Press 1987.

Rahner, Karl. "La doctrine des 'Sens Spirituels' au Moyen-Age." *Revue d'Ascétique et de Mystique* 14, no. 55 (1933) 263–99.

_____. "Mystery." In *Sacramentum Mundi.*

_____. Spirit in the World. William Dych, trans. New York: Herder and Herder, 1968.

Ricard, Robert. *The Spiritual Conquest of Mexico.* Originally published in French as *Conquête Spirituelle de Mexique,* published as volume XX of *Travaux et Mémoires de L'institute d'Ethnologie* by the University of Paris. Lesley Bird Simpson, trans. California Library Reprint. Berkeley: University of California Press, 1966.

Riches, John. "Balthasar and Rahner." In *The Analogy of Beauty: The Theology of Hans Urs von Balthasar,* John Riches, ed. Edingburgh: T. & T. Clark, 1986.

Rorem, Paul. *Biblical and Liturgical Symbols Within the Pseudo-Dionysian Synthesis*. Toronto: Pontical Institute of Medieval Studies, 1984.

Royce, Josiah. "The Knowledge of Good and Evil." In *Studies of Good and Evil: A Series of Essays Upon Problems of Philosophy and Life*, 89–124. New York: D. Appleton, 1898.

_____. *The Letters of Josiah Royce*. John Clendenning, ed. Chicago and London: University of Chicago Press, 1970.

_____. "Meister Eckhart." In *Studies of Good and Evil: A Series of Essays Upon Problems of Philosophy and Life*, 261–97. New York: D. Appleton, 1898.

_____. *Metaphysics 1915–16*. Frank Oppenheim, S.J., and Richard Hocking, eds. New York: SUNY Press, 1998.

_____. "Negation." In *Royce's Logical Essays: Collected Logical Essays of Josiah Royce*, Daniel S. Robinson, ed. 1914, 179–204. Dubuque: Wm. C. Brown, 1951.

_____. "Principles of Logic." In *Royce's Logical Essays: Collected Logical Essays of Josiah Royce*, Daniel S. Robinson, ed., 1914, 310–78. Dubuque, Wm. C. Brown, 1951.

_____. *The Problem of Christianity*. New York: MacMillan, 1914.

_____. *The Sources of Religious Insight*. New York: Charles Scribner's Sons, 1912.

_____. *The World and the Individual*. Introduction by John E. Smith, 1900. New York: Dover, 1959.

Santayana, George. *The Sense of Beauty: Being the Outline of Aesthetic Theory*, 1896. New York: Dover, 1955.

Scannone, Juan Carlos. *Sabiduria Popular, Símbolo y Filosofía: Dialogo Internacional en Torno a una Interpretación Latino Americana*. Buenos Aires: Editorial Guadalupe, 1984.

Schreiter, Robert J. *Constructing Local Theologies*. Maryknoll, N.Y.: Orbis Books, 1985.

Schrödinger, Erwin. *What is Life?* 1944. Cambridge: Cambridge University Press, 1967.

Scola, Angelo. *Hans Urs von Balthasar: A Theological Style*. Originally *Hans Urs von Balthasar: Uno stile teologico*, (Milan: Editoriale Jaca Book) 1991. Ressourcement: Retrieval and Renewal in Catholic thought. Grand Rapids, Mich.: William B. Eerdmans, 1995.

Segundo, Juan Luis. *Faith and Ideologies*. Maryknoll, N.Y.: Orbis Books, 1984.

Smith, John E. *Royce's Social Infinite: The Community of Interpretation*. New York: The Liberal Arts Press, 1950.

Smith, Jonathan Z. "What a Difference a Difference Makes." In *To See Ourselves as Others See Us: Christians, Jews, "Others" in Late Antiquity*, Jacob Neusner and Ernest S. Frerichs, eds. Studies in the Humanities, 3–48. Chico, Calif.: Scholars Press, 1985.

Snow, C. P. *The Two Cultures: And a Second Look.* Cambridge: Cambridge University Press, 1969.

Solís, J. Trinidad Martínez, Pbro. "Piñatas y Colación." In *Las Posadas con lecturas Biblicas.* An educational pamphlet containing *las posadas* for parochial use. Los Angeles: Librería San Pablo, n.d.

Soustelle, Jacques. *Daily Life of the Aztecs: On the Eve of the Spanish Conquest.* Originally published as *La vie quotidienne des aztèques à la veille de la conquête espagnole,* Paris: Hachette. Patrick O'Brien, trans., 1955. Stanford: Stanford University Press, 1961.

Strasser, Stephen. *Phenomenology of Feeling: An Essay on the Phenomena of the Heart.* Foreword by Paul Ricoeur, Robert E. Wood, trans. and introduction, Philosophical Series, vol. 34. Pittsburgh: Duquesne University Press, 1977.

Stuart, Cohen G. H. *The Struggle in Man Betweeen Good and Evil: An Inquiry Into the Origin of the Rabbinic Concept of Yetzer Hara.'* Kampen, The Netherlands: Uitgeversmaatschappig J. H. Kok, 1984.

Sullivan, Lawrence E. *Icanchu's Drum: An Orientationto Meaning in South American Religions.* Chicago: University of Chicago Press, 1988.

Tatarkiewicz, Wladyslaw. "The Great Theory of Beauty & Its Decline." *Journal of Aesthetics and Art Criticism* 31, no. 2 (1972) 165–79.

The Holy See. *Catecismo de la Iglesia Católica.* Washington, D.C.: United States Catholic Conference, 1992.

Todorov, Tzvetan. *The Conquest of America.* Translated by Richard Howard, trans. New York: Harper & Row, 1984.

Tracy, David. *The Analogical Imagination: Christian Theology and the Culture of Pluralism.* New York: Crossroads, 1981.

von Balthasar, Hans Urs. *To Be Noted, but Volume 4.* New York: Crossroads, 1984.

_____. *The Glory of the Lord: A Theological Aesthetics.* Joseph Fessio and John Riches. New York: Crossroads, 1983. 8 vols.

_____. *My Work: In Retrospect.* Originally in German, *Mein Werk—Durchlike.* Freiburg: Johannes Verlag, 1990. Communio Books. San Francisco: Ignatius Press, 1993.

_____. *The Glory of the Lord: A Theological Aesthetics.* vol. 4, *The Realm of Metaphysics in Antiquity.* English trans. of *Herrlichkeit: Eine Theologie Ästhetik,* Band III, I: *Im Raum der Metaphysik,* Teil I: *Alterium* (Einsiedeln). John Riches, ed. Oliver Davies, Andrew Louth, Brian McNeil, C.R.V., and John Saward, Williams. trans. 1967. San Francisco: Ignatius Press, 1989.

_____. *The Glory of the Lord: A Theological Aesthetics,* vol. 1, *Seeing the Form.* Translation of *Herrlichkeit: Eine theologische Ästhetik, I: Schau der*

Gestalt. Joseph Fessio and John Riches, ed. Erasmo Leiva-Merikakis, trans. New York: Crossroads, 1983.

_____. *The Glory of the Lord: A Theological Aesthetics,* vol. 2, *Studies in Theological Style: Clerical Styles.* Translation of *Herrlichkeit: Eine theologische Ästhetik, II: Fächer der Stile, I Klerical Stile.* John Riches, ed. Andrew Louth, McDonagh, and Brian McNeil, trans. New York: Crossroads, 1984.

_____. *The von Balthasar Reader.* Medard Kehland, S.J. and Verner Löser, S.J. eds. Robert J. Daly, S.J., trans. New York: Crossroad, 1997.

Warnock, Mary. *Imagination.* Berkeley: University of California Press, 1978.

William of Ockham. *Philosophical Writings: A Selection.* Philotheus Boehner, trans. and introduction, 1957. The Library of Liberal Arts, founder Oskar Piest. Indianapolis: Bobbs-Merrill, 1964.

Winfield, Richard Dien. "The Dilemmas of Metaphysical and Transcendental Aesthetics." In *Systematic Aesthetics,* 1–58. Gainesville, Fl.: University Press of Florida, 1995.

Wittgenstein, Ludwig. *Tractatus Logico-Philosophicau.* Translation of *Annalen der Naturphilosophie.* Original work published: 1921. D. F. Pears and McGuiness, trans., introduction by Bertrand Russell. 1922. London: Routledge and Kegan Paul, 1974.

Wolter, Allan B., O.F.M. *The Transcendentals and Their Function in the Metaphysics of Duns Scotus.* Philosophy Series. St. Bonaventure, N.Y.: The Franciscan Institute, 1946.

Wood, Robert E. "Recovery of the Aesthetic Center." *American Catholic Philosophical Quarterly 69,* no. 2 (1995) 1–25.

Index

aesthetics, viii, 5, 9–11, 22, 26, 35, 54, 65,
  71, 74, 76, 82, 99, 101, 107, 116–117,
  143, 154–156, 170
  cultural, 60
  linguistic, viii, 164
  philosophical, 12–13, 15, 36, 65,
    69, 72, 82, 150, 155, 164, 184
  semiotic, 35–36, 118, 158, 164–165,
    168, 171, 180, 184–185, 191
  theological, viii, 1, 5, 9–15, 17, 20,
    22, 24–25, 33–35, 40, 49, 54, 61,
    65, 73, 76, 83, 90, 94, 96, 126,
    145, 154, 181, 184–185, 192
aesthetics of negation, 163–164, 184
anagogical imagination, 158, 174, 182,
  186, 189–190
anagogicus excessus, 88
anagogy, 30, 81, 88, 185–186
analogy, 63, 79–82, 190
analogy of being, 78, 80, 82, 102, 120,
  126, 165, 191
apophatic, 23, 25, 27, 31, 72
Appearances, 70, 72
Aquinas, Thomas, 79, 97, 160–162, 190
Aquino, Maria Pilar, 55
Aristotle, vii, 126
ars divina, 16
ars humana, 16
at-one-ment, 123, 136, 142, 156
Augustine, 9, 20, 25, 29–30, 53, 82, 94

Balthasar, Hans Urs von, viii, 8, 15, 19,
  35, 61, 63–65, 73, 75–78, 80, 81–86,
  88–90, 94–96, 102, 107, 116, 120, 126,
  145, 146, 154–155, 157–159, 165, 181,
  190–191
Barth, Karl, 15
Baumgarten, Alexander G., 9–10
Beloved Community, 123, 141, 143
Blondel, Maurice, 77
Bonaventure, 85–88
Bosanquet, Bernard, 13

Cabot, Richard Clarke, 143–144
capax dei, 65, 74, 76, 86, 120, 154–155, 184
Carrol, Lewis, 153
Casarella, Peter, 83, 85
Cassirer, Ernst, 12
Chardin, Pierre Teilhard de, 18
Chenu, Marie-Dominique, 75
Common Nature, 100–101
community
  of interpretation, 133, 139–142
  of signs, 102
  of the beautiful, 3–5, 37, 103,
    118, 119, 145, 154–155, 158,
    170–171, 185–186, 188, 190, 195
  of the good, 34, 103, 114, 118,
    119–121, 123–124, 133, 142–143,
    156, 186
  of the true, 33, 102, 112–113–114,
    119, 124, 185–186
concept, 99, 101, 108, 128
Congar, Yves, 75
cosmology, 70–71, 118

Cotter, James, 18
Council of Trent, 49
Counter-Reformation, 49
Critical Rationalism, 128–131, 145
crucified seraph, 87, 89, 162

Damiani, Peter, 159
Daniélou, Jean, 75
Dante, 90, 192
de Acosta, Jose, 42, 44, 45
de las Casas, Bartolomé, 44, 53
de Lubac, Henri, 75
de Montesinos, Fray Anton, 43–44
de Morgan, Augustus, 104
de Porres, Martin, 3–4
Deck, Alan, S.J., 54–55
difference, 29, 32, 39–40, 42–44, 57, 61,
    65, 72–73, 92–93, 101, 127, 149, 157,
    160, 169, 183–184
Dualism, 70
Dupré, Louis, 75

Eckhart, Meister, 111
Edwards, Jonathan, 171
Elizondo, Virgilio, vii, 54–58, 61
encomendado, 43
epsilon, 121
Espin, Orlando, 59
esthetics, 114–115, 117, 118, 165
extrincism, 77

felix culpa, 136
foregrounding, viii, 35–37, 157–159,
    167–170, 173, 189, 191
form, 26, 61, 70–72, 84, 89, 93, 94,
    107–108, 145, 158, 192
formal distinction, 100
Francis of Assisi, 86–88, 194

Galen of Pergamum, 47–48
Geertz, Clifford, 84
Goizueta, Roberto S., 59
Guadalupe, Our Lady of, 39–40, 57–59,
    61, 191, 192, 194
Gutiérrez, Gustavo, 44, 51

habitualiter, 105–107

Hefner, Philip, 178
Heidegger, Martin, 95
Hispanic theology, vii–viii, 8, 65, 76, 96,
    134, 138–139, 153, 155, 157, 169–170,
    186
Hopkins, Gerard Manley, 7, 12, 15–16,
    18–19, 22, 26–28, 36–37, 94, 118, 195

Idealism, 78, 113
Ignatian exercises, 4, 173–174
Ignatius of Loyola, 9, 158, 170, 173, 191
imagination, 13, 23–25, 118, 177,
    182–183, 185
imitative representation, 69–70
incarnation, 11, 15, 19, 33–34, 39, 73, 82
inculturation, 4
Inquisition, 49
interpretant, 33, 106, 148, 156, 174
interpretation, 57, 123, 137–138, 165, 185
interpretative origination, 69–71
Interpreter, 123
interpretive musement, 8, 12
Irenaeus, 11

James, William, 96, 110, 113, 114, 119

kallos, 20
Kant, Immanuel, 13, 95, 97, 108
katophatic, 21–23, 24, 27, 31, 71–72
Kempe, A. B., 147–148, 150

lifting up the lowly, 8, 37–38, 181, 194–195
liturgy, 16–17, 19–20, 185, 195
logic of signs, 17, 33–34, 103, 110, 112,
    118, 123, 136, 155–158, 160, 168, 183,
    184, 191
Lombardus, Peter, 159–160
loyalty, 123, 133, 140–141, 143, 156

Magnificat, viii, 19, 36, 158, 180
Marion, Jean Luc, 95
Mary, viii, 19, 36–37, 39, 83, 158, 191, 192
Medellín, 4, 37, 51, 54–56, 59, 61
mestizaje, vii–viii
Míguez Bonino, José, 52
Milward, Peter, 27
mimesis, 13, 69
monism, 70

Mukarovsky, Jan, viii, 35–37, 118, 158, 164–168, 180–181, 184, 191
mystery, 22–24, 184
Mysticism, 127–128

negative theology, 122, 154
Neoplatonism, 80
nihilism, 63–64, 95, 98
nominalism, 95, 97–98, 106, 126
normative science, 114–115, 118

Oakes, Edward, 82
objective affection, 89
objective idealism, 108
Ockham, William of, 32, 95, 97–100, 104, 108, 161–162
Ockham's razor, 97–99, 126, 150–151
O-collection, 151, 153, 159, 163, 165
onto-theology, 95
Origen, 171–173

Peirce, Charles Sanders, vii–viii, 8, 17, 32, 34–35, 61, 90, 95–98, 102–104, 106, 110, 112–121, 136, 148, 155–158, 160, 165–168, 184, 189
percept, 99, 101, 108
"Pied Beauty," 7, 16, 18–19, 22, 26, 34, 37, 118, 195
pinata, 46
Plato, vii, 26–28, 70–72
poiesis, 17–18
popular religion, 4
potentia Dei absoluta, 157, 161–162
potentia Dei ordinata, 157, 161–162
Potter, Vincent, 117
pragmatic community, 111
pragmatism, vii, 17, 96–97, 108, 110–111, 115, 117, 185
Prague School, 164
praxis, 17
Przywara, Erich, 77–78, 80–81
Pseudo-Dionysius, 10, 25, 80–81, 87–88, 165, 185, 190
pulchritudo, 20
pulchrum, 20

Rahner, Karl, 22, 75–76, 78
real distinction, 79

Realism, 126
Reformation, 4, 19, 49
ressourcement, 75
Riches, John, 79
Royce, Josiah, viii, 8, 34–35, 61, 90, 102, 110, 113–114, 119–154, 156–158, 160, 163, 165, 184, 191

Sahagun, Bernadino de, 32, 47–49, 57
Schreiter, Robert, 59–60
Schrodinger, Erwin, 21
Scotus, Duns, 28–29, 31–32, 94–97, 99–106, 129, 132, 148, 161–162, 191
seeing the form, 8, 35, 65, 69, 89, 107, 145, 155, 190–191
semiosis, 48
semiotic domain, 96
semiotics, 5, 8, 17, 36, 48, 60, 119, 173
semiotics of culture, 48
semiotics of poetry, 164
sign, 5, 25, 30, 32–33, 35, 47, 61, 65, 90, 96, 106–108, 110, 123, 133–134, 136, 137–138
signification, 108
signified, 33, 106
signifier, 33, 106
Snow, C. P., 93
Socrates, 73
Soustelle, Jacques, 45
spiritual senses, 158, 170–171, 172, 175
Sullivan, Lawrence, 24, 182–184
symbol, 5, 25, 33, 57, 59, 80
system Sigma, 145, 150

Talmud, 176–177
techne, 18
theology of Beauty, 10, 20
theoria, 17
Tillich, Paul, 15
to kalon, 20
transcendental, 63–64, 94, 102, 113, 121–122
triadic relation, 13, 96

universal, 92–94, 96, 101–102, 105, 111, 129

Vatican II, 4, 37, 51, 75

Will to Interpret, 123, 142
Wisdom, 4, 88, 193
Wittgenstein, Ludwig, 23
Wood, Robert E., 175

Xenophon, 72

yetzer, 118, 158, 170, 175–184